Living at Zero
The New Wealth Hack for Millennials

Jordan Tampien
Community Economic Development Regional Specialist,
Washington State University

WASHINGTON STATE
UNIVERSITY
EXTENSION

ACKNOWLEDGEMENTS

This book would not have been possible without the support of Washington State University, which allowed me to try to address a need in our communities: to engage the Millennial generation and empower them to understand personal finance and make it work for them.

I especially want to thank Whitney, my wife, for helping me edit and think through the concepts in this book. You truly inspire me each day! I want to thank all of the others who contributed insight, comments, and editing for the book. This took a lot of work and I know that I couldn't have done it without you!

TABLE OF CONTENTS

CALL TO ACTION

In my work at Washington State University, I focus on assisting entrepreneurs in rural communities. They have significant barriers to overcome and I realized that we were missing the most crucial step: personal finances. We were talking about projections, marketing, strategic planning, etc., but they really needed a most basic understanding of how to manage their personal finances. This is even truer for the Millennial generation that is lost in the wreckage of the Great Recession, trying to understand how to build a business and grow. This book was written based on research of best practices, financial principles and personal anecdotal experiences, and working with entrepreneurs to show how it works in practice through the Extension model. Extension needs to be aware of changing influences and modify teaching methods to ensure accurate content readability, utility, and evaluation components as they pertain to the end user (Coleman et al. 2011). This book examines a reader-friendly way to introduce financial topics to the Millennial generation.

This book is part of a project to make personal finance education mainstream and provide options for Millennials to live the life they have always dreamed of. To further this goal, for every book that I sell, I will donate one book to a high school library. One hundred percent of the remaining proceeds from the sale of this book will be reinvested in personal finance and entrepreneur education and programs through WSU. The goal of this book is to educate and encourage readers to expand their horizons and live uncomfortably now in order to be comfortable later.

1
INTRODUCTION

"How are we going to pay our bills this month?"

I had just returned from working a long shift at one of my three part-time jobs. Having each received our bachelor's degrees in 2006, my wife and I were ready to change the world. But the world had changed on its own before we had our chance. Instead of endless opportunities, we found a lack of jobs, plummeting housing values, older generations working longer, and the thought of retirement a distant fantasy (McCormick 2009).

Our financial situation was daunting, but it was the stress on her face that cut deeper than any bill. We owned a house worth less than what we paid for it and a car that was almost as old as we were, yet we worked tirelessly to hold onto these possessions as the market took a turn for the worst.

I swear, it was just like the opening scene from the movie *Cinderella Man* where the prosperous living of the Roaring Twenties, exemplified by fancy possessions and a clip full of money on the dresser, turns into a faded gray scene of the Great Depression where the same money clip was empty and most of the possessions on the dresser were gone. The once vibrant face of a successful man, played by Russell Crowe, was now worn from the stress and turmoil he was experiencing as his wife, Renée Zellweger, showed him the past due notices and lack of food and milk for their family to survive. How could things change so quickly?

While our situation was not quite as dramatic, the parallels were uncanny.

1

I couldn't help but think back to when I was a freshman in college with the whole world in front of me. This crazy idea was fueled by the notion that if I worked hard and did well in school, I could have my piece of the American Dream (e.g., white house with a picket fence) (Green and White 1997). Boy, was I wrong.

My name is Jordan. My wife, Whitney, and I are 30 years old with graduate degrees. Hers is a master's in teaching, and mine is a law degree and a master's in business administration. For six years, we worked hard and paid dearly to make that accomplished walk across the stage to get our diplomas and truly start our careers. No, to start our lives. The current reality is that Whitney's not a teacher and I'm not an attorney. Hindsight is a funny thing. Honestly, I never had a job for more than two years; I simply got bored. The thought of being at a job for 30 to 40 years terrified me, and my wife shared this sentiment. So instead of focusing on what career would define our lives, we were determined to define our lives ourselves.

> *I did everything right. I worked hard and got good grades... Why is this happening? Why can I only get part-time retail jobs when I have a $200,000 education?*

The fork in the road came as I had finished college in 2006 and was headed for law school. If I was honest with myself, the real reason I wanted to be a lawyer was that it paid well, and new lawyers were getting hired right out of school. There was *safety* in that profession. I knew we could be comfortable. But in my three years at law school, the market crashed and I graduated into an economy short on jobs, money, and opportunity. The promise that hard work, good grades, and a diploma would earn you a job served only to remind me how much the world had changed. I picked up work where I could, struggling to keep our bank account above $100 at any given time. Our monthly payments were all strategically timed, and the thought of automatic bill pay was laughable.

I constantly laid awake at night thinking, "I did everything right. I worked hard and got good grades… Why is this happening? Why can I only get part-time retail jobs when I have a $200,000 education?" It just didn't make sense and, quite honestly, didn't seem fair.

Does any of this sound familiar?

I had a real gut check moment. I could either spend the next 30 years blaming the economy and feeling sorry for myself or I could work harder—no, *smarter*—to create opportunities for my family.

I wasn't the first person to be dealt a tough hand, and I certainly wouldn't be the last. But despite the down economy, I paused and reflected on the fact that *more millionaires were created during the Great Depression than any other time in American history (Dent 2009)*.

How is it that during one of the most tumultuous economic times, when people were literally jumping from buildings and when soup lines rounded city blocks, more people created wealth than in any other time in our history? Was it possible to look past the unemployment statistics, the foreclosures, and the bankruptcies?

Our story is similar to millions of people today: we had student loan debt, a mortgage, a car loan, and difficulty finding jobs that we pictured staying in for more than a year. Some of these things haven't changed in our life, but the difference is that we changed our lifestyle and never looked back. If you would have asked me five years ago where we would be now, I never would've guessed we'd be living our current lifestyle.

Who Am I?

Millennial. Thirty years old. Husband. Father. Traveler. College graduate. Real estate investor. Associate professor. Attorney. Realtor. Entrepreneur.

As you can see, I still don't know what I want to do when I grow up. My lifestyle change happened because I wanted more out of life. I struggled with the idea of working a job for 30 years only to find my pension and retirement was gone when I needed it and the company outsourced all of the work overseas. I struggled with working at something I didn't care about. I felt like I had so much to give back to society, but no one was giving me a chance. What I soon realized was that before I could change the world, I had to make some serious changes in myself.

This is my story. This book explores my personal finance research explained through the lessons I've learned along the way, most of which were learned the hard way. I challenge you to question what you read in this book, as this approach is not a one-size-fits-all way of life. It must be custom fit to *your* life. My goal is to have you think through the research and the concepts, not just the results.

Start by Changing Your Perspective

It was 2008 and things were not looking good. As I sat in the car pondering my fate, I started writing down all of the things I currently had: a loving wife, family, a part-time job, an education, various skills, the ability to walk…the list went on and on. I set the pen down and began thinking of how lucky I was. Despite the fact that I was drowning in student loan debt, working part-time jobs to survive, and struggling monthly to hang on to my house, what I realized was that I had all the tools necessary to make something of my life. So even though no employer would give me a chance, I was determined to make something happen. In this time of the Great Recession, I had more than most could ever dream of. All I needed was a plan and a shift in perspective.

Whether you think you can or you think you can't, you're right!

Like the saying goes, "Whether you think you can or you think you can't, you're are right!" It's all based on perspective. Take the following story as a great example of perspective:

One day a father and his rich family took his son on a trip to the country with the firm purpose to show him how poor people can be. They spent a day and a night on the farm of a very poor family.

When they got back from their trip, the father asked his son, "How was the trip?"

"Very good Dad!"

"Did you see how poor people can be?" the father asked.

"Yeah!"

"And what did you learn?"

The son answered, "I saw that we have a dog at home, and they have four. We have a pool that reaches to the middle of the garden; they have a creek that has no end. We have imported lamps in the garden; they have the stars. Our patio reaches to the front yard; they have a whole horizon."

When the little boy was finished, his father was speechless. His son added,

"Thanks, Dad, for showing me how 'poor' we are!"

Author Unknown

Once I adjusted my perspective about my current situation, I was not so caught up in the negativity surrounding me. Rather, I was grateful for what we had and hungry for getting more. Now, I'm not saying the money started rolling in and we were paying our bills on time all of a sudden, but I now had hope and the ability to see the forest through the trees.

With this renewed hope and determination, I started searching out opportunities to apply my skills, education, and experience to generate income. The traditional mechanisms just wouldn't work. I had realized I couldn't merely rely on traditional employment and retirement anymore. The recession showed that both of those could go at a moment's notice. If I wanted to have money and retire before I was 70, I would need to find a new way to make it happen.

I talked with friends and family about how to plan and save for the future, and how to work toward the elusive idea of financial freedom where I didn't have to rely on someone else to make money. I began to research every financial topic and the deeper I got, the more frustrated I became. The personal finance books and "gurus" on the topic were advising readers like me based on a system that no longer worked. Times had changed. The American Dream our parents have been chasing no longer exists; it is riddled with consumer debt and false appearances. Even retirement, the way our parents and grandparents viewed it, was no longer a right but an achievement as pensions and Social Security have gone by the wayside. I soon realized our way of thinking about personal finance had to change if I, or our generation for that matter, was ever going to succeed.

What to Expect from This Book

The concepts in this book are not revolutionary. They cover the topic of personal finances for Millennials: those born between the early 1980s and early 2000s—almost 4.7 million people (National Chamber Foundation 2012) So few Millennials have been taught how to deal with money, myself included. High schools and colleges rarely have classes about it, and it is hardly talked about at home. Yet, we are expected to handle our money responsibly as adults.

I have worked with hundreds of clients with financial issues and struggled with teaching them the "recommended" way to save and prepare for retirement. Most people lack the financial education, mindset, and discretionary income to change their financing and build wealth for the future. In fact, many were so far behind, they could not even see how to pay their bills at the end of each month. Here I was teaching them about saving, and all they would ask was, "Save what? We need to eat, pay rent, our kids need shoes," and on and on it went.

There had to be another way than to simply teach people how to save what little they have by putting it in a tax-deferred retirement account, and then tell them to hope and pray the market does well so the money is there for them when they actually need it. Millennials face the even tougher challenge of being able to retire one day. They are saddled with student debt, there are fewer jobs, and the jobs that are available don't pay living wages. There has to be another way!

Millennials are unique. Creative. Educated. Talented. But having experienced the Great Recession, we are hesitant to have our money work *for* us. We fail to understand exactly what it means, and what it takes, to be financially free because our parents' American Dream, the one we were raised to believe in, doesn't align with our current economy or our value system. We no longer trust the process of giving our money to someone 2,000 miles away to invest 10,000 miles away. But I want to let you know there is a way to have an even better American Dream. I wrote this book because there are few books that speak directly to Millennials (and written by a Millennial) with a step-by-step plan to work smarter, to get everything you want out of life, and to explore a new way to follow your passion and retire young—while you can enjoy it.

Don't get me wrong: this path will require hard work, a lot of learning, and, probably, your 9-to-5 job, at least for now. But if you can commit yourself to understanding the principles outlined in this book and applying them to your life, you can be financially free. Free to do what you want, when you want.

This book introduces an unconventional path to a new American Dream created by and for Millennials. The new American Dream is so much more than just the things you have, it encompasses the things you experience, the places you go, the relationships you develop, and the causes you passionately support. People are more willing to make sacrifices pertaining to their career, education, and work in order to have more quality time with friends and family. This is changing the way we think and make decisions about what we do for a living (Galinsky and Friedman 1993). We want quality over quantity.

This is all achievable through the Millennial retirement plan: financial freedom. Essentially, your assets bring in enough income to cover your monthly expenses now, not 30 years in the future. No longer can you just rely on Social Security and tax-deferred retirement accounts; you must take control of your future and start investing in assets that generate income for you now!

This book offers practical tips and advice from other Millennials on how to get your finances in order and acquire income-producing assets that will help you far into the future. The overall concepts and ideas will, if nothing else, give you hope that, despite everything around you, you can still go out there and change the world like you initially set out to do.

Lastly, this book will introduce new technology that will work for you in a relevant, meaningful way. There are so many apps, programs, websites, and handouts that it can be overwhelming to find the information that can actually help you and save you time and money. I will break down key personal finance topics, such as budgeting, saving, credit, investment, and retirement, and provide info on relevant apps, websites, podcasts, and products that can make these processes more convenient for and adaptable to the way you live.

My wife and I are not geniuses; we were not raised in wealthy families. In fact, growing up we used to get the cereal with Japanese writing sold exclusively at Grocery Outlet. But we committed to work hard. More importantly, we committed to have our money work harder for us. We envisioned living a life that didn't have to wait until retirement to begin.

The techniques in this book have worked for countless individuals. Are you ready to become financially free and live a balanced life?

(Cue the music...)

Sit back, buckle up, and enjoy the ride.

Living at Zero

2
FLIPPING THE SYSTEM

The most important thing in science is not so much to obtain new facts as to discover new ways of thinking about them.

Sir William Bragg

Innovation is taking two things that already exist and putting them together in a new way.

Tom Freston

Today's globally connected economy allows for better access to technology, investment, and knowledge to make the world a better place (Abasov 2014). But it doesn't take too many Google searches to see that our economy is in desperate need of repair. From the roller coaster ride on Wall Street to the financial woes in Greece, this global economy is as volatile as ever. With all of this financial chaos, it is hard to know where to begin to fix it. Do you start with unemployment? What about the income and wealth gap? Maybe retirement?

The truth is that the old way of doing things is not working. The idea that Millennials can get a high paying job, put some money in a pension, and retire at 60 is gone. Retirement itself is a novel relic from our parents' generation. Do we really have to wait 40 more years to start living our lives? I don't think so! So how do we change this?

It's Time to Flip the System

The horrors of the Great Recession are fresh in our memories. We have mounting personal and national debt, overburdened Medicare and Social Security programs expecting an influx of Baby Boomers leaving the workforce, and a potential workforce that is being shut out of jobs (US Census Bureau 2006).

The only question one can ask is: are we insane? And yes, I do mean this literally. An often-quoted definition of insanity is "doing something over and over again expecting a different result".

I know posing insanity is a little extreme, but aren't some of the current trends reminiscent of 2006–2007? Are we heading back down the same rabbit hole simply because we don't know any better?

It is time we look at our current condition and find a different way. The issue is that human beings are creatures of habit and like to do things the way they have always been done (Westbrook and Lifer 1976). There is comfort in ritual and tradition. My friend told me a story that really drives this point home.

Two girls were in the kitchen preparing a Thanksgiving meal. One girl was in charge of the 20-pound turkey while the other was preparing the mashed potatoes. The girl preparing the turkey had basted and seasoned it and was preparing to place it in a pan for cooking in the oven.

Before she put the turkey in the oven, she took a knife and chopped both ends off the turkey, placed it in the pan (with plenty of room to spare), and tossed it in the oven. The other girl turned to her and asked, "Why did you cut the ends off the turkey? Was there something wrong with them?"

The girl responded, "No, this is how my mom does it and it always tastes delicious."

"Why does she do it that way?"

The girl shrugged displaying a contemplating "I don't know."

She proceeded to call her mother who explained that was how her mother did it, and she just continued to cook it the same way.

Well they finally decided to call Grandma to figure out her family secret of

10

cutting the ends off the turkey.

Ring. Ring. Ring. *Grandma answered the phone.*

"Hi, Grandma. Why did you cut the ends off the turkey before cooking it? Is it what makes the turkey taste so good?"

Grandma laughed and responded, "No, dear. I had to cut the ends off the turkey because it would not fit in my oven" (Brunvard 1989).

This story illustrates how we, as humans, get so used to doing something "the way it has always been done" that we fail to understand *why* it was done that way in the first place.

From this point forward, start thinking about *why* you are doing something. Your 9-to-5 job? Buying the new car? Keeping up with the Joneses?

I challenge you to intentionally start asking the question: *Why?*

"Why" is a powerful word that triggers the mind to understand the reasoning for doing something a certain way. (Kids are really good at doing this, often at the expense of their parents' patience.)

Are you successful now? Do you have all of the money you need? Are you working your dream job?

Why? Or why not?

> ## Millennial Insight
>
> *Why changed my life. I started asking why. Why was I working at a job I hate? Why was I not pursuing my passion working for the environment? I started to remember why I got my degree again and stopped listening to the excuses anymore.*
>
> Kate, 27

The reality is that there are thousands of books and articles about how to become rich, yet only 2.9% of couples in the US are making over $250,000 per year (Leo 2012). Why is there a disconnect? If we have the instruction manuals to become rich in the palms of our hands, why don't more people use them? Instead, our culture has trapped us into spending and working more and feeling like we're underachieving if we don't.

If you want a different result, you are going to have to stray from doing things the way you've always done them and try a different method. "If you do what you've always done, you'll get what you've always gotten," as Tony Robbins so eloquently put it.

Flip the System

Flipping the system requires a new way of thinking. It forces you to think outside the box and imagine things the way they could be rather than how they are. A study conducted by University of Missouri Extension found that when dealing with change we need to think outside the box, challenge the status quo, and find new ways of conducting business (Leuci 2012). One study participant went on to say, "We can't be the way we used to be. We can't think the way we used to think. We can't perform the way we used to perform and succeed (Leuci 2012)." Remember, we don't have to reinvent the wheel; we just need to figure out how to make it roll better.

> *If you do what you've always done, you'll get what you've always gotten.*
>
> Tony Robbins

Let's start by examining the traditional 9-to-5 job. You are out of bed by 6:00 am. You shower, pick out your work uniform for the day, grab some coffee, and you are out the door to battle your way through traffic until you get to the office. You are then stuck behind your desk for the next 8 to 10 hours taking orders, answering phone calls and emails, and trying to complete never-ending to-do lists, all the while wondering if that expensive college education is really helping you with these tasks. Besides the joy of your 30-minute lunch break and the dentist-office feel of the break room, you could not be more excited when you see that clock strike 5 o'clock so you can pack up and leave. With whatever energy you have left, you fight through rush hour traffic until you get home to have some quality family or friend time for a couple of hours before you have to go to sleep and do it all over again.

I know this isn't the case for everyone, but many often wonder why this pattern (or whatever your pattern is) beats us down. This is certainly not what we pictured as college graduates leaving home in an attempt to conquer the world.

In the last ten years, I can recall many late night conversations with friends over countless bottles of wine as we all complained about and pondered these questions: Why do we have to work a 9-to-5 schedule? Is there another way? Does a job with a better schedule exist? Can we be more productive with our time if we worked 6 hours a day or 4 days a week? Are we really even efficient sitting in an office for 8 hours a day?

I became curious, so I did a little research and found that the 40-hour workweek was started in the 1920s. The issue arose during the Industrial Revolution when it was normal for employees to work between 10 to 16 hour days since factories had to operate around the clock to keep up with demand. It was during this same time period that Henry Ford, founder of Ford Motor Company, established the 5-day, 40-hour workweek that we still have today (History.com 2009).

Ford's logic seemed counterproductive to me until I dug a little deeper. Ford didn't decrease work hours for scientific reasons or for happier employees. Instead, he came up with the idea of the 40-hour workweek primarily so his employees would have enough free time to become consumers, specifically consumers of Ford vehicles (History.com 2009).

In an interview published in World's Work magazine in 1926, Ford explained why he switched his workers from a 6-day, 48-hour workweek to a 5-day, 40-hour workweek but still paid employees the same wages:

Leisure is an indispensable ingredient in a growing consumer market because working people need to have enough free time to find uses for consumer products, including automobiles.

Henry Ford (Brinkley 2003)

Thus, our spending culture was born, a conjoined twin of the 40-hour workweek. We have been following this model for almost 100 years, clear evidence that we are slow to change. Americans don't have to look too far into history to understand that many of our traditions and "ways of doing things" were generated during the Industrial Revolution, a far cry from where we are now.

But, things *are* changing.

Recently, Mexican billionaire Carlos Slim suggested that workers shift to a three-day workweek. He cited that working fewer days would cut down on commute time, increase quality of life, and lead to a more well-rounded employment base (Taube 2014).

Even with traditional employment, things are changing. Freelancing and self-employment are on the rise. According to the Bureau of Labor Statistics, nearly 15 million workers identified as self-employed in April 2014 (Vilorio 2014). That's over 10% of the overall workforce (Vilorio 2014). Websites such as www.flexjobs.com provide telecommuting and freelance opportunities for individuals looking for a more flexible work schedule and location. Employers are starting to embrace this "working smarter rather than harder" model and allowing companies to streamline and grow. They are realizing that it is a win-win proposition.

Change Your Thinking, Change the World!

Changing your thinking is essential. Former Dean and Director of Oregon State University Extension Service, Lyla Houglum said, "We have to be willing to change. No, we have to enjoy change—and be ready to change again and again" (2011).

But how do we change? Let's start with a simple exercise. This exercise may seem trivial or irrelevant, but trust me, it gets your brain thinking differently. I usually do this exercise for 30 minutes everyday.

Think of a traditional industry (e.g., real estate, groceries and food, car sales, etc.) and brainstorm ideas of how you would operate it differently than the norm. Just a side note before we go any further: rule number one of brainstorming is that there are no bad ideas and this exercise is meant to stimulate ideas (Jones and Jost 1993).

For example, let's look at grocery stores. Traditionally, you walk in, pick out your groceries for the week (or month if you are at Costco), and stand in the checkout line to pay for the goods. Now let's flip that on its head... What if you had all of your groceries delivered, saving time and money? Or what if you had meals sent directly to you with the exact ingredients and portions? Or what if you ordered your groceries online and picked them up at a drive-thru window?

One great example of reinventing an industry is the beloved Play-Doh. Most everyone knows or has played with Play-Doh and loves its use for different games or simply fun morphing and creating whatever your heart desires. But what if I told you that it was never created for that purpose. In fact, it was originally used for cleaning. Before World War II, the most common way to heat a home was coal. It was dirty and left soot stains on walls. Noah and Joseph McVicker of Kutol Products, a Cincinnati-based soap manufacturer, created the doughy material to rub the soot off of wallpaper (Walsh 2005). But, after the war, natural gas became a more common heat source. Subsequently coal was used less and less so few people needed Kutol's cleaning product. The company faced bankruptcy. In the early 1950s, Joseph McVicker learned that his sister, a schoolteacher, used the material in her classroom as modeling dough (Walsh 2005). And thus, Play-Doh was born. The McVickers decided to market their nontoxic creation as a children's toy. In 1955, they tested their product at nurseries and schools. A year later, they created the company Rainbow Crafts. The "Play-Doh smell" came from the McVickers trying to hide the original cleaning aroma. Many ingredients of Play-Doh are not publicly known, but it is said that the McVickers added an artificial almond scent to the recipe (Walsh 2005).

A great, recent example of thinking outside the box happened when Amazon CEO, Jeff Bezos, announced that Amazon anticipated using drones to deliver their orders (Gross 2013). People laughed and most said this couldn't be done because of FAA restrictions and other limitations, but it is in creatively thinking of ideas that you may find your new business or passion.

More modern examples would include the effect Zillow has had on the real estate market and the ability to shop for houses from the comfort of your couch instead of driving around from house to house until you find one you like, or how LegalZoom changed the way entrepreneurs establish businesses and families write wills. Again, change your thinking, change the world.

Some ideas are so simple, and all it takes is identifying a trend (or even just a small inconvenience) within an industry and capitalizing on it. I stumbled upon one such example on a recent trip my wife and I took to Eastern Europe. I was sweating under the hot sun on top of the old city walls of Dubrovnik, Croatia, I had my arm outstretched as far as it would go trying to take a selfie of Whitney and I. Failing miserably to capture our image and the beautiful city below us, another tourist walked by with an extended tripod handle connected to her iPhone and snapped a picture of herself. I awkwardly followed her for a minute to see how this contraption worked. Basically, it took the idea of a selfie and made it much easier to accomplish. It was definitely one of those "why didn't I think of that?" moments.

It is difficult to come up with truly original inventions these days, so reinventing or reimagining products, processes, and industries is the way to go. As an angel investor commented, "everyone is working on the same thing" (Yoskovitz 2011). He observes different companies pitching the same ideas. He went on to say, "If no one else is already working on the idea you have, there's a good chance it's a bad one" (Yoskovitz 2011).

Even so, start looking at the routine processes or activities in your life and see if there is an opportunity. It may not turn into a million-dollar idea like Play-Doh, but it could be that secondary income or creative outlet you need. If nothing else, training your brain to think this way will get your creative juices flowing and eventually move your thoughts outside the box.

Thinking Outside the Box

"Thinking outside the box" is an overused phrase in our society, yet we struggle to actually do it. Here is an exercise to kick it off (Figure 1). Try to connect all of the dots with three straight lines, and do not let your pen leave the page (Danesi 2009).

If you were able to do this, congrats; you are well on your way to flipping the system (or you've seen this illustration before.) For those of you who

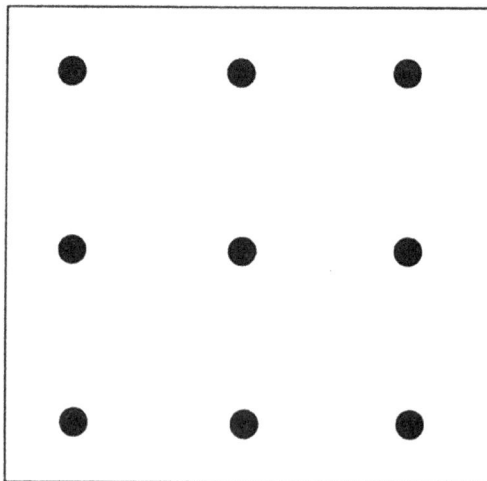

Figure 1. Think outside the box exercise.

weren't, what was the first thing you saw when you looked at the task? The box around the dots?

We are trained to think inside the box from an early age because it is predictable and safe. But what if everyone started to view things in a different light? What if 2 plus 2 does not equal 4? Or a box is not just a box?

We do not ask these questions because we fear the answers or what others will think of us if we even pose the questions in the first place. It is uncomfortable to be outside of the box and expose yourself to ridicule if your idea or path doesn't work. Perhaps thinking outside of the box and stepping outside of your comfort zone are parallel concepts. But thinking outside the box requires you to: 1) follow your passion and 2) be unafraid to fail.

Follow Your Passion

Too often, society forces us into lives we might not have chosen for ourselves. For example, if you go to school to be an architect, society would have you believe that you need to be an architect whether you like it or not. Or if you go to school to be a teacher, then a teacher is what you will be. Sometimes flipping the system simply starts by letting yourself decide your path, regardless of what your college diploma says. Just because you have a teaching degree doesn't mean that all you can do is teach or that teaching is your only talent. Some teachers I know make the greatest investors.

My story is not different. I had to search deep within my soul in considering what I should do with my life after graduating from

> ## Millennial Insight
>
> *I finally got my teaching degree and first teaching job after 5 long years of school. On my first day of class, a 12-year-old student threatened to kill another student, the next day a fight broke out in the cafeteria. I began to realize that I had made a mistake. Teaching wasn't for me, but I didn't know what else to do. I had invested 5 years and tens of thousands of dollars into a degree I didn't want. Despite what everyone told me I quit at the end of the semester and have never been happier.*
>
> James, 29

law school. As I completed the Washington State Bar Exam and celebrated briefly with my classmates for surviving the longest three days of our lives, my thoughts immediately drifted to: what's next? Societal pressure and looming student loans would dictate that I take some attorney position (*any* attorney position) because my blood, sweat, and tears had been spent working towards being a lawyer for the last three years. Friends and family all bantered about what legal expertise I would pursue and my wife was finally going to realize the benefit of marrying a lawyer, not just the long hours I spent studying and the high tuition bills. (We now jokingly refer to this as the "bait and switch" of our marriage.)

As much as I tried to convince myself otherwise, I simply was not passionate about law. I just didn't see myself struggling through a 30-year career as an attorney. So despite the hundreds of thousands of dollars in student loans, three long years of classes and studying, and potentially dashing the hopes of so many friends and family, I decided not to pursue the traditional route as an attorney... and I have never looked back.

Entrepreneur Michael Dell once said, "You've got to be passionate about it…I think people that look for great ideas to make money aren't nearly as successful as those who say, 'Okay, what do I really love to do? What am I excited about?'" (Dell 2008).

So I stepped back and asked these exact questions posed by Dell. My answers weren't very specific at first, but I started thinking outside of the box I had created by going to law school. I kept coming back to the fact that I knew I wanted to help people. Plain and simple.

I wish I could say that was it and I found the job that completely fulfilled me, but it was not that easy. Actually, asking those hard questions was easy. Finding and acting on the answer was the hard part.

There were a lot of naysayers and doubters telling me I had made a mistake by leaving law behind. I promise if you decide to do something outside the ordinary, people are going to question you and comment on the absurdity of your plan. But, you must realize that *you* are the one waking up each day and living your life, not your parents and friends. They don't have to go to your job every day and face your terrible boss; *you* do. Like I mentioned before, you must define your life or others will do it for you.

Coming back to Dell's quote, take a few minutes and really search your soul while pondering the following questions. (No, really, make yourself stop and think before you just read on.)

1. *What is it that you love to do?*

2. *Are you doing what you love to do?*

Flipping the system requires that you are passionate about the change. And, obviously, you must define your passion, even if it's a somewhat loose definition, before you can begin to make changes towards it. You will face challenges and naysayers, so without the passion to fuel you, it is easy to forget why you started in the first place and revert back to your comfort zone.

Fail Early, Fail Often

Why are people afraid to try and fail? Is it humiliating? Scary? I found a quote by Gary Heavin, CEO of Curves, where he said, "You have to be willing to put security at risk in order to have the potential for wealth... People cling to security (Hendricks 2014)."

Failure is the most underrated teaching tool of all time. Failure is seldom discussed, but by understanding why we failed, we can learn from it and avoid it in the future (Decker 1990). Like most of the world, I used to live my life scared to fail, to disappoint others, so I simply wouldn't try if there was a chance of failure.

Coincidentally, that leads me to our first business venture. In 2010, Whitney and I started a photo booth company. (It is worth mentioning that if you would have told either of us five years prior we would be the owners of a photo booth company; we would have laughed in your face.) We deliver a portable photo booth to events and it prints the pictures people take in the

> *You have to be willing to put security at risk in order to have the potential for wealth ... People cling to security.*
>
> Gary Heavin

booth on the spot, just like the old school photo booths but with much better equipment. You find them at almost every wedding and event these days, but when we started there was only one other photo booth company in town. Friends and family laughed at the idea and wished us the best of luck on our venture with a subtle sarcasm.

Photo booths barely worked in the shopping malls so why could they work now, and at weddings of all places? Normally, the chance of failure would have paralyzed me from ever starting, but, with little to lose, we decided to take the risk. Now, almost five years later, our business operates with two photo booths and an Instagram booth, and we've done over 450 events.

We didn't know it at the time, but this business was the catapult for every other venture we undertook. If I would have let failure or the doubts of other people stop us, who knows where we would be today. Perhaps the most important lesson I've learned from our photo booth is: do not let fear of failure stand in the way of your success.

I realize this is easier said than done, especially when the person saying it just described taking a risk that has resulted in success. Yet, it is important to understand that part of the reason we are afraid to take risks is that we are trained from an early age that failure is unacceptable (L'Abate 1975). I have not seen many trophies for last place or rewards for a failing grade in the classroom. We are trained to simply find the right answer instead of exploring new answers. I was an "A" student all through high school, and even though I was deemed "smart" at the time, I realize now I lost out on the opportunity to truly *learn*, not just memorize, the content. I did well in class and aced a lot of tests, but today I couldn't tell you the names of all the US Presidents… And my dad is a history teacher! (Sorry, dad.)

Failure is tough. Nobody is ever laughing and joking when they fail. True, you could go bankrupt, lose your job, lose friends, or maybe, just maybe, you could succeed beyond your wildest dreams. By embracing failure and allowing yourself to learn from your mistakes, you can grow and accomplish things you never thought possible. By getting rid of the negative connotation of failure, you will allow yourself the opportunity to try new things, experience life and create a lifestyle of learning on your terms.

Flipping Personal Finances

Personal finance education teaches you every possible way to save money and cut costs to make your life more comfortable and safe. Obviously, the idea is to preserve the income coming in to make it last and store it away safely in a bank account in case you need it.

What if, instead of focusing on *saving*, we started focusing on *earning more* and making your money work for you? Too many financial advisors focus on "saving for the long term" rather than finding ways to make more money now. It is no wonder that we have three-fourths of American families that say they are living paycheck to paycheck, just trying to get by (Johnson 2013). What if we focused on developing our talents and passions, empowering us to earn more rather than training us to stretch our paycheck?

> ## Millennial Insight
>
> *I was never taught how to handle money at home or in school. By the time I was done with college, I had over $10,000 in credit card debt. Through using the Living at Zero system, I have now paid off all of that debt and finally understand how to make my money work for me.*
>
> Tristan, 29

The truth is Millennials are falling behind financially. A Recent FINRA Investor Education Foundation study reveals that Millennials display low levels of financial literacy, engage in problematic financial behaviors and express concerns about their debt. Low levels of financial literacy hamper most Millennials, with only 24 percent of Millennials able to answer four or five questions on a five-question financial literacy quiz correctly (Smaragdis 2014). The study also found that 43 percent of Millennials engaged in costly non-bank forms of borrowing in the last five years, like using pawnshops and payday lenders. By contrast, 21 percent of boomers and 8 percent of the silent generation used non-bank forms of borrowing (Smaragdis 2014). This can be traced to a lack of financial education. Let's test your current knowledge of financial terms.

Worksheet 1 lists financial terms: Please put a check mark by each one you know and understand in depth.

Worksheet 1. Financial literacy assessment.

1.	Net Worth	_____	6.	Compounding Interest	_____
2.	Inflation	_____	7.	Coupons	_____
3.	Bull Market	_____	8.	Budget	_____
4.	Bear Market	_____	9.	NOI	_____
5.	Track Spending	_____	10.	DTI	_____

So, how many did you get?

My guess is that you got all of the terms that relate to savings, but struggled with those that pertain to growing money.

This is not your fault. How would you know that DTI means Debt-to-Income ratio or that LTV is Loan-to-Value ratio for real estate purchases? You would only know these terms if you've purchased a house or business or happen to be in the lending industry. Yet, understanding these terms (and eventually being able to apply them) is critical for growing wealth.

We only know what we were taught or what we've experienced. Did you ever have a garage sale or lemonade stand as a kid? Did your parents own small businesses and talk about finances with you? This idea of creating value and income are not taught as required curriculum in our public schools and colleges (and they are rarely talked about in the home). Why? Why is the most important education you will need not addressed in school? We may never know the answer to that question, but being aware of our lack of financial education is the first step to changing.

We are taught to spend so much energy holding onto what we have instead of taking a chance and potentially making it into so much more. Even the concept of retirement is mind blowing to me. The gist is that you will work your entire adult life, through your prime years, to stop working one day, and live on what you hope is enough to last. In the meantime, you have forgone travel, experiences, and life to make it happen. What if you could have early retirement and experience life? What if you could have your cake and eat it too? What if instead of relying only on your paycheck to cover bills and get you to retirement over the course of a few decades, you had additional streams of income for another $1,000, $2,000, or $10,000 per month? Or even better, streams of income that sustained you through retirement?

This simple flip in mentality can mean the difference of being poor or being rich, the difference of being financially free or a slave to your employer or dwindling retirement account. By shifting the focus to earning more, you engage your brain to think, find opportunities, be resourceful, and tap into the limitless abilities you have right now. *You* are your greatest resource.

It's time to get to work.

Are You Ready?

Are you ready to flip your life with me? We are going to talk about your finances and passions, your dreams and your goals. But every time you find fear or doubt creeping in, turn back to this page and read through these amazing examples:

Steve Jobs: Live Each Day as If It Was Your Last

When I was 17, I read a quote that went something like: "If you live each day as if it was your last, someday you'll most certainly be right." It made an impression on me, and since then, for the past 33 years, I have looked in the mirror every morning and asked myself: "If today were the last day of my life, would I want to do what I am about to do today?" And whenever the answer has been "no" for too many days in a row, I know I need to change something (Jobs 2005).

JK Rowling: Failure Can Be the Foundation of Success

So why do I talk about the benefits of failure? Simply because failure meant a stripping away of the inessential, I stopped pretending to myself that I was anything other than what I was, and began to direct all my energy into finishing the only work that mattered to me. Had I really succeeded at anything else, I might never have found the determination to succeed in the one arena I believed I truly belonged. I was set free, because my greatest fear had been realized, and I was still alive, and I still had a daughter whom I adored, and I had an old typewriter and a big idea. And so rock bottom became the solid foundation on which I rebuilt my life (Rowling 2008).

Steve Ballmer: Don't Have Passion, Have Tenacity

Passion is the ability to get excited about something. Irrepressibility and tenacity is about the ability to stay with it. If you take a look at all of the companies that have been started in our business, most of them fail. If you take even a look at the companies that have succeeded, Microsoft, Apple, Google, Facebook, you name it, all of these companies went through times of hardship. You get some success. You run into some walls. You try a formula for a new idea, a new innovation, it doesn't work. And it's how tenacious you are, how irrepressible, how ultimately optimistic and tenacious you are about it that will determine your success (Ballmer 2011).

I refer to these examples when I start doubting myself when the fear of failure and embarrassment begin to skew what I know I should be doing: following my passion. If these quotes don't work for you, then start your own list. You are about to embark on a journey few people travel. But if you can make these changes in your life, then you will have what few people ever achieve: financial freedom.

3
LIVING AT ZERO

Twenty years from now you will be more disappointed by the things that you didn't do than by the ones you did do.

Mark Twain

Be willing to be uncomfortable. Be comfortable being uncomfortable. It may get tough, but it's a small price to pay for living a dream.

Peter McWilliams

It was a crisp, cool morning as we boarded the plane in rural England just miles from the London city center. I was nervous and excited all at the same time. I never thought I would do something like this. We sat in our seats as Whitney gave me a sly smile, the same smile she gets every time she convinces me to do something I definitely did not want to do. It was her birthday and she asked me to go with her, so I couldn't say no. I stretched nervously and attempted some small talk with the passenger right next to me as the plane roared down the runway and took flight.

We climbed into the clear blue sky and the airport quickly became a distant dot below us as I peered through the tiny window, trying to pace my breathing patterns.

Five minutes later, a man shouted in my direction, "Ready, mate?! You are up!"

I remember thinking, "No, how could anybody be ready? This is crazy!"

Then the man got out of his seat and swung the side door of the plane wide open, exposing the view of the now tiny earth below us. It was all happening so fast, which, looking back on it now, I'm convinced is part of their plan so people can't back out. My tandem partner edged us towards the open door, and in an instant I was dangling outside the plane, 12,000 feet above the ground.

3. 2. 1…The countdown to my demise.

We jumped and the rush of cold wind stung my cheekbones, and our clothes and skin flapped against the turbulence of the free fall.

It felt like forever, but I was told later it was only 30 seconds of a free fall. My partner pulled the parachute and we catapulted upwards, beginning our controlled descent to the landing zone below.

"What did you think, Yank?" My tandem partner kept referring to me as The Big Yank, and his well-timed question left me speechless. I had just paid a lot of money to jump out of a plane from 12,000 feet. The Jordan five years prior would have shaken in his boots at the thought of skydiving, but this was a new me and I had never been more excited for the new lifestyle Whitney and I had embraced. We touched down on the runway and I raced over to my wife.

"Happy Birthday!" I shouted.

She couldn't quit laughing and we hugged, thankful to be on the ground in one piece.

The skydiving adventure highlighted the change in our approach to life. I wanted to experience life now, not just sit on the sidelines until I retire. I wanted to eat lobster in Maine, ride a motorcycle in South America, ski in the Alps, ride an elephant in Thailand, and climb a glacier. But this would not have been possible on my monthly salary alone. We could barely make ends meet up to this point. It's hard to plan for the future when you are trying to survive each day.

Since deciding to make a lifestyle change in our lives, we have lived in London, cheered on Manchester United at Old Trafford Stadium, explored ancient ruins in Athens, sipped wine in Paris, navigated the streets of Rome, hiked along the Cliffs of Moher in Ireland, golfed St. Andrews Old

Course, seen the Northern Lights in Iceland, and even jumped out of a plane from 12,000 feet...just to name a few. Here is the best part: we didn't get new jobs or an inheritance to do it; we just shifted our priorities and lifestyle. It has made all the difference in the world.

What is an LAZ Lifestyle?

So now to the question I know you have been asking yourself since you picked up this book. What exactly is a Living at Zero (or LAZ, as I ironically call it) lifestyle and, more importantly, how will it help me reach financial freedom and the life I have been dreaming of now not having to wait until I retire?

Personal finances in general are an interesting topic. Most experts teach you to save money in order to be secure and comfortable, rarely challenging you to do more and envision more for your life. So when I followed this approach, I clung to each dollar and couldn't envision my slowly growing savings account allowing me to quit my job and follow my passions. Instead, I was forced to be content with what little we had, even if it was only $100. The idea of retirement was but a distant fantasy of a far off land, never quite in view.

Quite honestly, I stumbled into the LAZ Lifestyle. In my case, I was tired of being the person who lived vicariously through other people's adventures and Facebook posts, laughing mockingly when they would tell me anyone could do it. I was tired of plowing through life, living only for the weekend, and constantly shoving my "change the world" dreams onto the back burner of my life.

The film *Secret Life of Walter Mitty* is a great example of this. He spent his entire life living through someone else's lens, and only started to truly live when he cast aside fear and doubt. You could see the freedom on his face as he traversed down the mountainside on his long board. It's a great movie, but an even greater message: to find what drives you and go live it yourself. But, in order to do this, you must start by overcoming fears and getting outside of your comfort zone. You must take that leap out of the airplane.

The reality is that I had been living my life by this LAZ concept and didn't even know it. Let me explain. I love *things*. Small things, shiny things, fast things. I just love the feeling I get when I buy *stuff*. When I have money in my wallet or bank account, I will always find a way to spend it quickly and usually impulsively. I tried budgeting our money, but somehow I would always find ways to justify why I "needed" something. I've kept emergency funds, but soon everything was an "emergency." I tried making small adjustments, such as cutting back on things like candy and soda (I know, both seem like such a childish vice, but who can say no to Swedish fish?), but this fad only lasted three weeks and I would always give in to my old habits. Basically, any time I knew there was a way out, I took it.

> *We decided to live paycheck to paycheck, but in a completely different way. It made all the difference.*

About two years into our marriage, with roughly $1,000 to our name, Whitney and I decided to try something else. Whatever we had been doing up to that point was not working! We loved travelling, hanging out with friends, barbecuing on a hot summer day, but could rarely afford to do any of it. We were strapped with student loans, car loans, and a mortgage, which eventually left us wondering whether we should just move in with one of our parents to save money. We decided to live paycheck to paycheck, but in a completely different way.

I know you are thinking that you already live paycheck to paycheck, so how is our approach any different? But I'm not talking about relying on each paycheck to live. I am talking about harnessing the survival and resourceful instinct that comes with consciously living with only enough money to support your lifestyle and putting the rest of it into Income-Producing Assets (IPAs, not the beer by the way). Again, this idea definitely goes against the grain and flips the norm of purchasing *things* and shifts the focus to purchasing IPAs. So you can feed your need to buy things and build wealth at the same time.

As the name suggests, an IPA is an investment that produces income. The difference is that Whitney and I had our traditional savings and spending accounts, much like most of you do, but we introduced an IPA-only purchasing account that was funded automatically each month from our savings. We would pay ourselves through our savings accounts, pay our bills, and the remaining funds would go into our IPA purchasing account. So each month our checking account would go back to zero and we would start the process again. This forced us to be resourceful and find new ways to generate income as we were literally Living at Zero.

The concept prevents splurging whether you make $30,000 a year or $300,000 per year. For example, if you know you only have $1,000 to spend in your checking account, you are not going to splurge and buy a 60-inch big screen TV, as you simply do not have the funds to do so. In reality, even though you only have $1,000 in your checking account, your IPA account has $50,000. But that money is strictly to be used on IPAs (investments that make you money.) This is the paycheck-to-paycheck living I am talking about.

The LAZ Lifestyle is not just a structured savings plan, it is a lifestyle that forces you to live a balanced life filled with passion and fueled by the ultimate goal of retiring financially free through passive income. Most financial books teach you various methods to be secure and comfortable with your life and your finances. That is why they pitch long-term retirement accounts that you put money into until you are 65. It's safe, they say. They say you need emergency savings, house savings, investment savings, and just-in-case savings in order to have financial security and to be comfortable. I agree to a point, but what I propose is a different way to look at saving, spending, and investing money to truly make it work for you and move you towards financial freedom before you are too old to take advantage of it.

The LAZ Lifestyle encourages you to live life UNCOMFORTABLY now so you can be comfortable later. It encourages you to push yourself to do more, earn more, learn more, and buy more of the right kind of things.

In an interview with advertising entrepreneur and founder of ad agency MODCo Sara Rotman, she was quoted as saying,

> **Millennial Insight**
>
> *Living at Zero was not easy. In fact, it took me several months to actually do it. But once I started to see my IPA account grow, there was a change that happened. I started looking to cut expenses and get more income to buy more IPAs.*
>
> Tiffany, 34

The best advice I ever received was from my first accountant when I was discussing the launch of my company. We were speaking about my business plan and how much money to borrow to launch. She wisely said, 'Only have enough cash on hand to barely survive; never so much that you are comfortable. It's important to stay scared in the beginning.' While I prefer to describe that feeling as staying hungry rather than scared, I thought it was indeed great advice. I have found this hunger to be an incredibly important motivator during my entire career. Being comfortable is the enemy. Staying hungry forces you to push yourself to continue to survive, grow, and evolve (Nisen 2013).

The LAZ Lifestyle promotes the uncomfortable as a challenge and forces you to keep improving and staying hungry so you can truly experience life. Do you feel that way now? If not, when was the last time you did something outside of your norm or challenged yourself to meet a tough goal?

How is the LAZ Lifestyle Different?

Please note that I do not refer to this at the LAZ Financial Plan or the LAZ Get Rich Quick Scheme; this is definitely an LAZ Lifestyle. LAZ addresses not just your finances, but your life as a whole. It addresses your money mindset and increases your financial knowledge as it leverages modern technology and principles that you can apply in your life. It challenges you to always expand your comfort zone, personally and financially.

For example, public speaking is among the top fears for people (Ingraham 2014). Why? I see the people that won't shut up with their friends, but you put them in front of a group and for some reason their knees start shaking, heart races wildly, and beads of sweat pour down their face. The reason is they have moved outside of their comfort zone of speaking to a small, intimate group. Rather than practice to make this fear part of their comfort zone, most people just avoid it altogether. Many people live their life the same way, becoming too scared of the unknown to experience it. They tell themselves that it can't be done rather than challenge themselves to find a way to get it done.

By constantly pushing the limits of this imaginary line (or whatever your imaginary line is), we remove the greatest threat to your success: YOU!

A Balanced Approach

Too often financial books only focus on finances, which seems like a no-brainer, but hear me out. I liken it to watching the hit HGTV show *Property Brothers* where they help a family purchase a fixer house within their budget and renovate it to create their "dream home." In reality, they usually only fix up two rooms, and I always end the show wondering what they did with the rest of house that looked so horrible in the initial walk-through. This is similar to many financial recommendations. You are advised on plans to save money, spend money, and invest money, but rarely are all of the other parts of your life connected to this plan. You are only fixing up the kitchen and bathroom when all the bedrooms need remodeled as well. Basically, you are creating a financial plan rather than creating a lifestyle that you experience every day.

At its core, LAZ is NOT about making money; it's about creating a lifestyle. A 2010 study for National Academy of Science found that once income exceeds $75,000 per year, it has no variance on a person's moment-to-moment happiness (Kahneman and Deaton 2010). The reality is that when someone focuses on money, they have a mindset focused on making more money (Liu and Aaker 2008). So accordingly, this person would spend more time on work (Mogliner 2010). But, similar to *Property Brothers*, you can't have it all and in the end something has to give. For example, if you are making a lot of money, maybe your relationships with family or friends suffer. You only have 24 hours in a day, so start thinking about where you want that time to go!

No matter how many times you've heard it, the following analogy helps put the importance of lifestyle into perspective and should help you begin thinking about what is truly important in your life.

A professor stood before his philosophy class and had some items in front of him. When the class began, he wordlessly picked up a very large and empty mayonnaise jar and proceeded to fill it with golf balls. He then asked the students if the jar was full. They agreed that it was.

The professor then picked up a box of pebbles and poured them into the jar. He shook the jar lightly. The pebbles rolled into the open areas between the golf balls. He then asked the students again if the jar was full. They agreed it was.

The professor next picked up a box of sand and poured it into the jar. Of course, the sand filled up everything else. He asked once more if the jar was full. The students responded with a unanimous "yes."

The professor then produced two beers from under the table and poured the entire contents into the jar effectively filling the empty space between the sand. The students laughed.

"Now," said the professor as the laughter subsided, "I want you to recognize that this jar represents your life. The golf balls are the important things—your family, your children, your health, your friends, and your favorite passions—and if everything else was lost and only they remained, your life would still be full. The pebbles are the other things that matter like your job, your house, and your car. The sand is everything else—the small stuff."

"If you put the sand into the jar first," he continued, "there is no room for the pebbles or the golf balls. The same goes for life.

If you spend all your time and energy on the small stuff, you will never have room for the things that are important to you. Pay attention to the things that are critical to your happiness.

Spend time with your children. Spend time with your parents. Visit with grandparents. Take your spouse out to dinner. Play another 18. There will always be time to clean the house and mow the lawn.

Take care of the golf balls first—the things that really matter. Set your priorities. The rest is just sand."

One of the students raised her hand and inquired what the beer represented. The professor smiled and said, "I'm glad you asked. The beer just shows you that no matter how full your life may seem, there's always room for a couple of beers with a friend."

Unknown

Take a few minutes to fill out Worksheet 2. Write down your three "golf balls" (i.e., the most important things in your life).

Worksheet 2. Personal assessment of most important factors in your life.

1._____

2._____

3._____

Now keep these in mind as we start creating a lifestyle plan for you.

LAZ Lifestyle Must-Haves

The LAZ Lifestyle utilizes information from personal experiences, research, and other experts to create a system to buy and grow IPAs. But before we begin talking about the LAZ system, we need to look at a few key areas of your life in relation to some basic concepts in order to create a baseline.

Money Mentality

Before we can go any further, I need you to ask yourself, "How do I view money?" Is it a means to an end, the key to happiness, or the bane of your existence? Do you control your money, or do you find that more often it is your money controlling you and what you do? Your thoughts and beliefs about money will determine your ability to have more of it.

Here is a simple exercise: Close your eyes and picture a man or woman in a tailored, blue-striped suit, driving a Mercedes Benz CLS550. He or she pulls up to a 15,000-square-foot mansion, slowly gets out of the car and tosses the keys to the butler as they disappear through the front door.

Can you picture it?

Now, what thoughts immediately came to your mind about this person? Greedy, trust fund baby, hard worker, kind, giving? What if I told you that he was homeless just five years ago and gives $20 million a year to help homeless youth while housing 30 kids in his large house? And that the butler was actually his brother whom he borrowed the car from? Does it make a difference in what you think of him?

> *Your thoughts and beliefs about money will determine your ability to have more of it.*

Again, how you think of money and the "rich" determines whether you will ever have it or not. We are bombarded by societal pressure telling us that, in many ways, being rich is bad. Church-goers may say that money is the root of all evil, picketers rally against the injustice of the top 1%, parents talk to kids about how greedy and stingy rich people are, or the prevalent stigma that rich people only care about themselves. If this is the way you think of people with money, why would you ever want to have it?

In his book *How Rich People Think*, Steve Siebold touches on a key element to finding success in life. "No wonder everyone is broke because they think so negatively about money," Siebold says. "Why would we ever try to acquire something we have such disdain for? Look at your beliefs and look at the beliefs of the wealthy and how they think about money. They see it as a game. They're just playing a game, and they're having fun. They're moving things and they're creating value for society and they're getting richer all the time" (Siebold 2014).

> ## Millennial Insight
>
> *I never liked rich people. People are starving all around them and they are sitting in their mansions counting their money. They are greedy. They take advantage of the working class to make their money! I realized this was my mindset about being rich and prevented myself from being rich because of it. I guess I just didn't like the term "rich". But I needed the money to help people and that is what drives me to make money.*
>
> Kara, 31

Do you view money as a game? Or is money a painful subject in your life?

Ultimately, the rich define what their money does for them, while the poor let their lack of money define their life.

Siebold goes on to say, "I told my friends years ago I wanted to be rich…. They said money isn't going to make you happy. 'Why do you want to be rich? Rich people are greedy. Rich people are narcissists.' If I didn't have anyone coming in and teaching me differently, I probably would be like most people and repeat the same things and I wouldn't take action to pursue wealth. I would struggle with money my entire life (Siebold 2014)."

You need to start now by changing your general concept of money and the "rich". Later in the book, we will discuss your money mentality more in depth, but for now the rich I am talking about doesn't equate to *having* things it means that you have freedom and time to *do* things. Big difference.

So money needs to become just a tool that helps you experience life. The reality is that money is neither good nor evil. It has no character or feelings; it is simply a currency of exchange. You are the one who gives it a personality and a priority.

"I can't afford it."

"I have too much debt."

"I never catch any breaks."

The poor constantly use these excuses to justify their lack of money. As a broke, highly in-debt college graduate, I used these excuses time and time again. I was employed to help other people gain control of their personal finances, yet I struggled with the concept of money, always seeing it in a negative light. My money mentality kept me from moving forward. Is your money mentality helping or hurting you?

Vision for Your Future

The next required element is creating a vision for your future. You need to understand what you want the money for. You need to develop your Why! It becomes the drive when your motivation fades or the naysayers tell you it can't be done. It keeps you on the path when you start making a lot of money.

This is the most important step in the journey. When Whitney and I sat down to discuss how we were going to change our lives, we started with these four questions:

What would we do if we could retire today?

We would travel, volunteer at local non-profits, coach a Little League team, learn to waterski, and try every restaurant in the state. (We are foodies to our core).

How much money do we need to do that?

This calculation is more of an estimate, but it gives you a target to shoot for. By taking our monthly expenses and adding in travelling and fun expenses, we found that $10,000 per month would get us there. Again, this number can be defined further, but it is good to have a start. Too often people think their "retirement" number is so much more than it really is, by discussing it and quantifying it, the number becomes manageable and achievable.

What would be (or is) on our bucket list?

We wrote down pretty specific things, such as: ride an elephant in Thailand, see the pyramids in Egypt, go on a safari in Africa, own 50 rental units, skydive, and many more. Each year we cross more and more off the list and add more and more to it. This question allows you to think not using your current income and situation, but what you would ideally be doing.

What do I consider important or high priorities in my life?

For us, this is family and friends. Relationships. So any decision we make will be weighted with the effect it has on my family and friends. For some, this might be kids, travel, work, or fishing. We have found that your priorities will determine what you make happen in your life. If you are currently not doing it, it's not a priority.

By understanding your major priorities, you can craft a vision that focuses your life and allows you to reach financial freedom. Once you understand and define your vision, we can create a realistic plan to get there. If you need $100,000 per month, we are going to have to ramp up your investments and other income vehicles to make this happen, which will take a little longer but that's okay. Once you know where you are heading, it makes it much easier and more feasible to get there; all we have to do is give you the tools and get out of the way.

Mental Shift from Saving to Earning

The next requirement is making a mental shift to focusing on *earning* more money rather than simply *saving* more money. Everything I taught in my personal finance classes was about how to save money; rarely did we explore ways to make money.

How many times have you heard that if you cut your cable, you can save almost $1,000 per year or more? Or if you don't buy that latte every day you can save over $100 per month? The common thought in American financial literacy is that it is better to teach a person to fish than to simply give them fish, but what we are in fact doing is teaching people to hang on to what little fish they have rather than showing them ways to catch more. Not enabling, but empowering.

The rule to having more money is simple: either spend less or make more. I want to push you to look at the latter and find ways to stimulate your current income. Of course, saving money is important, but we have shifted too much focus on saving that we forget to identify ways to make more money and leverage the education and experiences we have paid so dearly for up to this point in our lives.

Most financial literacy books start with countless ways you can save money and limit your lifestyle just so you can eek another $3,000 a year out of your budget. This cold turkey or crash approach doesn't work for dieting and it won't work for your finances either.

What LAZ starts with are all of the ways that you can utilize your talents, networks, and education to make money. When I started LAZ years ago, I had my law degree, MBA, BA, experience with rental properties, real estate flipping experience, a full-time job at a non-profit organization, and a lot of great friends and networks throughout our city. Taking all of these things into consideration, I deduced that I could fit into something in real estate with a flexible schedule without much training or need for certifications. My wife suggested I become a realtor, and a month later I applied, took the test, and was awarded my Washington State realtor's license. I could now legally sell real estate and start making extra income on the side while still working my full-time job. I was able to share my personal experiences and unique educational niches with my clients during their home search, and they were able to work with my schedule since it was usually similar to their own. Rinse and repeat.

Once I was comfortable with the situation, I again looked to see what else I could be doing with my talents in my spare time. Some general examples I came up with were: freelance with writing or photography, starting a blog, selling artwork or items on eBay and Etsy…the list is as endless as the ingredients you've got in your cupboard.

This is the mentality shift I want you to consider. Start looking at your skills, life experiences, and connections as tools you can use to build a career or a part-time, supplementary income. Added income is invaluable as we work towards financial freedom. Our goal is to create multiple streams of income. Believe me, you'll be amazed what you can do with just $10,000. Not only are you making additional income, but you are learning another skill or experience that can benefit your entire life.

LAZ Lifestyle Plan

Once you understand or have an idea of what you want to do with your life, you can work to create an LAZ Lifestyle plan to get you there. Having a plan is very important. When you start to wander or doubt your direction, it points you back to the trail and can be the motivation you need to keep pushing on.

Like Jim Rohn said, "If you don't design your own life plan, chances are you'll fall into someone else's plan. And guess what they have planned for you? Not much" (Dasal 2014).

Yet, I would look at the plan as just that…a plan. Plans are meant to be a guide, but just as life changes constantly, your plan needs to be able to adjust and adapt with it. Though I won't quote him often, Mike Tyson hit it on the head when he said; "Everyone has a plan 'till they get punched in the mouth" (Berardino 2012).

As you walk through the LAZ Lifestyle approach, you will find there are many options for growing your net worth. You don't have to have a genius-level IQ or even graduate from college to become financially free; like most things in life, you just have to want it and have a realistic plan to get there.

Siebold sums up his thoughts about growing wealth, "You don't have to be a genius. Most of these millionaires that I've interviewed are normal people like you, me, and everybody else. They're not Rhodes Scholars. They're average people who changed their mindset and went to work… Most are not living in giant mansions. They're living quietly. They're our neighbors, but they have millions of dollars in the bank. They never worry about money and never have to worry about it again (Siebold 2014)."

This is where I want you to be. Don't just work for money, let it work for you and fund a passion that drives you. The next time you see the flashy car drive by or wander past a 10,000 square foot mansion, understand that the true value of money is not in the things it allows you to buy, but in the freedom that it can provide.

Now that you have an idea of where you want to go and have begun thinking of a plan to get there, it is time to dive head first, or swan dive if you prefer, into the 10 steps to an LAZ Lifestyle.

The LAZ Lifestyle System

The LAZ concept is not revolutionary, but it can definitely revolutionize your life. What LAZ does is make change easy to understand and apply to your life through real life examples, technology, and advice from others.

We introduce innovative technology and principles, but if you don't apply them, this book is worth little more than a paperweight or doorstop (but at least it's got a flashy cover!). Without further ado, here are the 10 steps to the LAZ Lifestyle:

1. Understand Your Money Mentality
2. Take Control of Your Financial Life
3. Understand the Credit Game
4. Get Rid of BAD Debt
5. Develop Your Potential to Earn More
6. Grow Your Social Capital
7. Buy IPAs
8. Protect Your Assets
9. Live Your Passion
10. Give Back

I will discuss each of these briefly, and we will examine them more in depth later on. Much like a syllabus you receive on the first day of class, this is the order of the training for this book. This approach allows you to get a holistic view of your finances and recommends ways to change and build wealth.

If it sounds like you have heard it before, you probably have. The same theories of "if you save money, you will have it later" and "if you spend less, you will have more" still apply, but I want to provide an automated, twenty-first century way to leverage new apps and utilize the techniques of innovative companies that are flipping the system and introducing new ways to look at your finances and your life.

This is not your parents' approach. LAZ understands that you don't do cold turkey very well and you really do like to travel and drive a car that wasn't built before Y2K. It understands you want to follow your passion now, not when you're 65.

Step 1: Understand Your Money Mentality

What you think about money will determine whether you have it or not. Before we even mention the word "finances", we need to understand how you think of money and retrain your brain to think rich. This can be the hardest part, but it is the most crucial. By understanding your money mentality, you can be aware of the self-destructive behaviors that have prevented you from growing your money to this point.

Step 2: Take Control of Your Financial Life

We need to know where you are now financially. You will track your spending for one month. This is usually eye opening when you see that your latte-a-day fix is costing you $150 per month. For Whitney and I, our habit of eating out is the most notable, as we usually set that part of our budget at $400, but we end up spending over $1,200 per month. By knowing where your money is going, we can reallocate it into IPAs without much effect on your bottom line.

Most importantly, we will teach you to automate EVERYTHING! We will utilize the concept of Pay Yourself First, a concept popularized by David Bach (2004) in his book *The Automatic Millionaire*. This means that you, not your bills, are the first to get paid each month, which immediately forces you to think creatively of how you are going to pay your bills and budget accordingly...all the while letting your money grow for you.

Next, we will craft a budget that allocates your income in to expenses, savings, and investment accounts allowing you the ability to begin investing in IPAs. We advocate finding savings where you can but not foregoing that latte or the pedicure if that gets you through the day. The LAZ Lifestyle is not about foregoing fun now like many financial plans out there. It realizes that you will never be younger than you are *right now* and need to experience each day to the fullest. So go ahead and buy that five-dollar latte from Starbucks. You have my permission.

Step 3: Understand the Credit Game

Credit is the key to growing IPAs quickly so you can live the life that you want sooner. You will learn how to clean up your credit and increase your credit score and better understand how credit will help you purchase IPAs.

This concept is easier when thought of as game, so we will give you the tools you need to win at this game—from removing charges from your credit report to understanding what you need to qualify for a mortgage.

I get asked the most about how to qualify for a loan. For most, this is a daunting process, but I will show you what you should be looking for and how to get the best rates and the lowest fees.

When was the last time you checked your credit report? Never. There are websites and apps that can help you prevent identity theft and monitor your progress towards a perfect credit score!

Step 4: Get Rid of BAD Debt

Robert Kiyosaki (2000) talks about good debt and bad debt in his amazing book *Rich Dad, Poor Dad*. Until I read this book, I did not understand the impact of debt on my ability to grow wealth. I now use the simple standard that a debt is bad if it does not produce income or lead to you producing more income.

You will learn to understand what is good debt and what is bad debt in your own life. The goal is to get rid of all of your bad debt as soon as possible by paying off the smallest balances first, as recommend by Kiyosaki and Ramsey. By getting rid of these debts, you can now use the money you are no longer paying to the bank and have it start making money for you. Then we will teach you how to leverage good debt to purchase IPAs and grow your wealth responsibly.

Step 5: Develop Your Potential to Earn More

The key element of an LAZ Lifestyle is developing your skills and talents to make them work for you to earn more money. We will look at where your income is currently coming from, whether it is full-time employment, self-employment, freelance, public benefits, or whatever. Then we will walk through creative ways to possibly add a secondary income that doesn't require another four-year education to increase your buying power of IPAs. With the unique economic circumstances our generation has experienced, it is nice to know there are multiple streams of income coming in just in case another bubble bursts.

We will also examine ways to increase income while keeping a work-life balance at a sustainable level. By adding multiple streams of income, you can move to financial freedom more quickly, but I don't want you to go insane doing it. We will introduce sites and online trainings that can help you find and qualify for a variety of part-time, flexible schedule jobs that fit your full-time gig.

Step 6: Grow Your Social Capital

In our over-connected world of Facebook, Instagram, and Twitter, many opportunities can easily be found through social connections. You will learn to develop productive relationships in your life and how to drop toxic ones. By expanding your network, you are able to find new job opportunities, investors, or partnerships for businesses that you may never have had access to. You will learn how to work a crowd and move from small talk to closing a deal.

Step 7: Buy IPAs

Do you want to work for the rest of your life? I didn't think so. But with pensions and Social Security in jeopardy, what are your options? I will show you the Millennial retirement plan of building multiple streams of income that you can use now. Why wait until you are 65 to start living life? By investing in IPAs you get the long-term benefit of equity with the present value of monthly income. Sweet deal! Best part, you have the control, not some broker or "family friend."

We will discuss the benefits of real estate ownership, how to find a good deal, how to finance the deal, and how to do this all while keeping a full-time job. Owning real estate works nicely with the "work from the beach" investment strategy that we will discuss later on.

We will discuss the benefits of owning a business on your income and tax bill. We will walk through the startup process, what to look for in a good business model, and how to find funding for your business. This venture is daunting and scary for most, but it can pay off big in the long run.

No passive income strategy is complete without IRA or 401k retirement vehicles. I will give you apps that can help you put money into a savings account by simply rounding up to the nearest dollar on every purchase and other apps that allow you to track your investments on a daily basis.

Step 8: Protect Your Assets

Fire. Mother nature. A terrible renter. There are so many forces that can take away the IPAs that you have worked so hard to collect. We will discuss different insurance options, the best fit for your portfolio, how to negotiate your rates, and steps you can take to minimize these costs. We will hear from experts about the pros and cons of different insurance options. The right insurance can give you peace of mind in a world that is completely unpredictable.

Step 9: Live Your Passion

This is the foundational element and the driving force for each tenant of the LAZ Lifestyle. None of this will last if you are not passionate about what you do and maintain a good work-life balance. I will show you ways to not just identify your passion, but actually live a balanced life each day and find ways to challenge yourself and grow through travel, education, and simple life experiences. Too often we are forced to plan and live in the future and we forget to enjoy the present.

Step 10: Give Back

You can't take any of your possessions with you to the grave. I read an article where a woman left her $13 million fortune to her cat (Dolak 2011). Not that I have anything against cats, but I'm hoping we can collectively agree to think beyond ourselves (and our pets) with our money.

It is important that before you gain your wealth you develop a habit of giving back. There is always another deal to be had and another reason why you need that $1,000, but trust me, giving back is part of living a balanced life. I will give you a list of apps and websites that can make giving back easy!

LAZ Lifestyle Moves
- Stay hungry to grow and develop. You want to live uncomfortably now so you can be comfortable later.
- Craft a vision for your future that you can turn to as we move through the 10 steps in the LAZ Lifestyle system.
- Understand your money mentality to prevent self-destructive behaviors.
- Shift your focus from saving to earning more.

Wrap Up

I encourage you to question everything while still keeping an open mind. I am speaking from my research illustrated through my life experiences and how these concepts have changed me personally. These ideas may ring true in a different form for you, so feel free to make personal adaptations to make my concepts work better for you when applicable. Before we get immersed into the content, I want you to take a second to think about and answer the four questions I previously introduced and start thinking about your vision. Write your responses in Worksheet 3.

Worksheet 3. Questionnaire to assess and document personal vision.

What would I do if I could retire today?

How much money do I need to do that?

What would be on my bucket list?

What do I consider important or priority in my life?

4
MONEY MINDSET

"A good financial plan is a road map that shows us exactly how the choices we make today will affect our future."

Alexa Von Tobel

"Every financial worry you want to banish and financial dream you want to achieve comes from taking tiny steps today that put you on a path toward your goals."

Suze Orman

What would you do if you won a $200 million lottery today? Would you buy a new car? House? Give to charity? Did you know that on average 90 percent of lottery winners go through their winnings in five years or less? (Richards 2012). The reality is financial responsibility is not about how much money you have; it is about your money mindset. At the end of the day, finances are a mental game.

Our money mindset is formed at a young age, when we are taught lessons about life from our parents, family, friends, experiences, and culture (Jorgensen and Savla 2010). Studies indicate that children need financial knowledge to be financially stable in the future (Beverly and Burkhalter 2005) in order to avoid the financial pitfalls of bankruptcy, debt, financial crisis, and divorce (Conger et al. 1990). The reality is that parents talking about money can shape children's long-term beliefs about finances (Petronio 2002). If your parents fought about money or constantly said they could not afford things, you are going to have a much different mindset about money than that of a person growing up in a rich family. The problem is that financial education is rarely taught in schools and is non-existent in discussions at home (Mandell 2008). Thus, if we are never properly taught to handle money, we are going to emulate the people and influential figures around us.

The lessons you learned about money growing up have undoubtedly directed your current relationship with money. They have either helped you or hindered you in one way or another. Take this example of the Elephant Rope Mindset:

As a man was passing the elephant, he suddenly stopped, confused by the fact that these huge creatures were being held by only a small thin length of rope tied to their front leg. No chains, no cages. It was obvious that the elephants could, at any time, break away from their bonds and become free, but for some reason, they did not.

He saw a trainer nearby and asked why the animals just stood there and made no attempt to get away. "Well," the trainer said, "when they are very young and much smaller we use the same size rope to tie them, but at that age it's strong enough to hold them. By the time they have grown up, their minds have become conditioned to believe that no matter how much they try, they will never break the rope. They still believe the rope can hold them, so they never try to break themselves free."

The man was amazed. These animals could, in an instant, break free from their bonds but because they believed they could not, they were stuck right where they were (Morton-Ross 2014).

Are you still stuck in the lessons learned about money as a child? In this chapter, we will explore the way you look at money and how to develop a positive money mindset.

How Your Mind Works

Our brain is trained to think a certain way and act accordingly in a given situation. Please read the following paragraph:

"Aoccdrnig to rscheearch at Cmabridge Uinvervtisy, it deosn't mttaer in waht oredr the litteers in a wrod are, the olny iprmoetnt tihng is taht the frist and lsat ltteer be at the rghit pclae. The rset can be a ttoal mses and you can sitll raed it wouthit a porbelm. Tihs is besauae ocne we laren how to raed we bgien to aargnre the lteerts in our mnid to see waht we epxcet to see. The huamn mnid deos not raed ervey lteter by istlef, but preecsievs the wrod as a wlohe. We do tihs ucnsoniuscoly wuithot tuhoght." (Rawlinson 1976).

Even though few words were spelled correctly, you were able to read this. Why?

You have trained your brain to recognize words and phrases so all you need to see is the first and last letter. Similarly, you have trained your brain to think a certain way regarding your money and finances.

An embarrassing example for me is with snacks. Without fail, I would buy candy and a soda whenever I went on a road trip of any kind. I started looking forward to it each time I hopped in the car heading out on the open road. Well, I had just started dating Whitney and she wanted to introduce me to her grandma. We were at her parents' house and when we got in the car I asked, "Can we stop and grab a few snacks?"

Incredulously, Whitney looked and me and didn't say a word; she just started driving as if she didn't hear me.

Feeling unheard, I asked again, "Can we grab a few sn..."

Before I could finish she had turned into another driveway that was a block away. It was her grandma's house.

This road trip snack issue was a tough one to kick but I began to realize that even if I didn't want candy, I still bought some just because I was going on a road trip. I had trained my brain to associate a road trip with needing a snack. I had this similar effect with going to the movies; I always felt the need to buy a soda or snack.

We make these same associations with money. We look at someone with a nice house and car as being rich when in reality they can be in debt up to their eyeballs. Our associations with money can be shaped at an early age.

How to Change Your Money Mentality

Let's look at your concept of money. We can practice all of the budgeting and investing tricks in the world, but if your money mentality is negative, it will do us no good. The LAZ Lifestyle is a mentality shift and relies on the person who knows you best: YOU!

Let's start with some word association. Please take 15 seconds on each line in Worksheet 4 and write the words that immediately come to mind. Don't take too much time to think; just the first words that pop into your brain!

Worksheet 4. Assessment of money mentality related to wealth and money.

Money is _____

Wealth is _____

Rich people are _____

Poor people are_____

Any surprising answers? Try to think of where these thoughts and beliefs come from. Experiences? Family? Television? By understanding the origin of this mindset, you can begin to change it.

Have you ever heard the saying "control your money or it will control you"? Well, it's true. Money affects every part of your life. If you didn't need money, would you be working where you are? If you had unlimited cash, would you be living where you are?

In one way or another, money has an impact on your life. Like Zig Ziglar (2016) said, "Money isn't everything... but it ranks right up there with oxygen." No matter what your thoughts are on money, you must learn to control it.

Repeat after me:
I will control my money and not let it control me.

I can afford it.
I deserve to be wealthy.
I will be financially free.

You must learn to shift the focus from this scarcity view (trying to save every penny) to the abundance view (to expand your skills and talents to earn more income.) Don't get me wrong, we will still discuss saving money, but only as it relates to buying more IPAs and moving you to financial freedom.

If you're beating yourself up about your current money mentality, don't. It's not your fault. At a young age you were taught ideas about money that probably limit your understanding of it. How many people know what a piggy bank is used for? Are you sure it is not a coffee mug or a vase?

Chances are that this was an easy question for you. Why? Because you were taught at a young age to save your pennies in a piggy bank. As a child, you are reliant on your only source of income: your parents. Without an increase in your allowance or holes in your parents' pockets, the number of pennies never grows.

Instead, why weren't we taught different ways to make money and increase the sources we get our pennies from? Much like our allowance, most people rely on their job as their sole source of income. Why are we not being more creative about how we make money? Millennials are the most educated generation EVER in a society where opportunity is all around us. But if you were never trained to recognize an opportunity, it is difficult to see and take advantage of. You just have to train your brain and change your money mentality to see it.

Rich vs. Poor Mindset

As you begin to understand the role of your money mindset, what you will find is that it is one of the greatest differences between the rich and poor. Harv T. Eker (2005), author of *Secrets of Millionaire Mind: Mastering the Inner Game of Wealth*, wrote a book about the importance of your mindset (Table 1). He made the following observations about the difference between the rich and poor mindset:

Table 1. Analysis by Harv T. Eker to evaluate differences in a rich vs poor mindset.

Rich Mindset	Poor Mindset
Believe: "I create my life"	Believe: "Life happens to me"
Play the money game to win	Play money game to not lose
Committed to being rich	Want to be rich
Think big	Think small
Focus on opportunities	Focus on obstacles
Admire rich/successful people	Resent rich people
Around successful people	Around unsuccessful people
Promote themselve	Think promotion is negative
Bigger than their problems	Smaller than their problems
Excellent receivers	Poor receivers
Paid based on results	Paid based on time
Think "both"	Think "either/or"
Focus on their net worth	Focus on working income
Manage their money well	Mismanage their money
Money works hard for them	Work hard for their money
Act in spite of fear	Let fear stop them
Constantly learn and grow	Think they already know

Source: Eker 2005

Eker (2005) makes it very clear that mentality is the major separating feature of the rich and poor. As you read through those lists, which side did you associate with more: rich or poor? Think about these differences as we work through this section. Start consciously thinking about how you deal with money or think of this with or without money. We want to move you to the rich mindset if you are not there already!

Your Money Mindset

Throughout your life, you have subconsciously developed a money mindset whether you like it or not. What we want to do is to make sure that your mindset is moving you towards financial freedom. This mindset alone can cause you to be poor.

For example, one of my clients struggled with his relationship to money. He had a good paying job but, for some reason, he still could not save money. Initially, we talked about what he spent it on and how to budget better, but I soon realized it was deeper than that. I asked him who was the wealthiest person he knew. Immediately, his face hardened and he told me it was a relative who had treated his family poorly in the past. I asked if others in his family were rich. He shook his head. What we started to uncover was that he would spend most of his money so that he purposely didn't have money in his account. He didn't want his family to think he was rich, and if they did ask him for money, he could tell them honestly that he didn't have any to give.

His view of being rich prevented him from having wealth as he sabotaged every advance towards financial freedom. His decisions were based on the bias imposed by his family. Once we discovered this, we were able to set up different retirement accounts that he could start contributing to so he could not pull the money out without penalties, yet save for the future.

Let's have you try the same exercise. Think of the richest people you know. What are your immediate thoughts? Write them down in Worksheet 5.

Worksheet 5. List of wealthiest people in your life.

_____

_____

_____

_____

These thoughts are either helping or hurting your chances of ever having money, and they most likely need to be addressed before going forward. The truth is, why would you ever want to be rich when it was attached to so many negative connotations?

Scarcity Mentality

Many poor people live with what is called a scarcity mentality. Basically, this means they believe that everything in the world is limited, or as author Stephen F. Covey says, it's based around the idea that there's not enough of the pie to go around (Dailyworth 2012).

This scarcity mentality never allows you to think and plan for the future because you are so concerned with surviving each day. In an article by Tina Rosenberg (2013) called _Escaping the Cycle of Scarcity_, she explains that poor people have more self-destructive habits than middle class people. They tend to not plan as well for the future and are more prone to turning to instant gratification than middle class people.

She cites the book *Scarcity*, in which the authors conducted a study in New Jersey where random people were asked about their income and then classified (without their knowledge) as either poor or rich. They were then given the question: *Your car needs a repair that will cost you $150. You can take a loan, pay in full, or postpone service. How do you go about making this decision?* After they answered, the subjects took tests that measured fluid intelligence and cognitive control (Rosenberg 2013).

> ## Millennial Insight
>
> *I never have enough. I always try to hang on to every dollar and lived a very reactive life. By thinking bigger I have started finding ways to get more income. I am relieved to start planning ahead.*
>
> Jane, 36

The result was that both poor and rich people did equally well on the test.

The researchers then added one caveat when they altered the question and instead of participants needing $150 for the repair, they needed $1500. The rich participants had similar results as the test before, but the poor group did not. In fact, their scores dropped the equivalent of losing 13 or 14 IQ points (Rosenberg 2013).

What the researchers concluded was that this phenomenon was caused by scarcity, not from lack of money but the actual capacity to think and make decisions (Rosenberg 2013). When faced with scarcity, people get tunnel vision and focus on only solving the emergency at the moment rather than looking to its ultimate impact. Thus, poor people will borrow payday or title loans at insane interest rates to pay a bill due today and have their car repossessed when the vehicle loan payment is due next week (Rosenberg 2013). Their mentality never lets them think of the future.

Are you caught in this rut of robbing Peter to pay Paul, or hoping your check comes in on time to pay most of the bills? If you are, how often are you even thinking about saving for the future?

By understanding and simply being aware of this scarcity mentality, we can create ways around it and get you moving forward no matter where you are right now. A simple exercise to start with is to take a piece of paper and write down a list of the things you *do* have. Be thorough. I want you to read it every night before you go to bed. You will begin to shift your focus towards what you do have rather than what you don't. You can start to see that things are not as bad as they seem.

Think Big!

For years, I had a scarcity mentality and limited myself by the way my mind worked. I could never dream of buying a 50-unit apartment building because I didn't think it was possible; I didn't know where I would get the money, expertise, or opportunity. I was so focused on what I couldn't do that I never looked at what was possible. But when I changed my money mindset and understood the role that money played in the transaction, I started to see the bigger picture. No longer could I not afford things, instead I was challenged to find a way to get them.

A key element of an LAZ Lifestyle is to think big! I recently watched some fascinating videos of humans skydiving, base jumping, flipping through the air, breaking speed records, and some feats I didn't even know humans could accomplish. But we do. It just goes to show that human beings continually push the boundary of what is possible.

So why can't it be you? Why can't you challenge the limits of life, pushing and striving for more?

Harv T. Eker (2005) said it best: "The biggest obstacle to wealth is fear. People are afraid to think big, but if you think small, you'll only achieve small things."

For far too long, I was so stressed and couldn't see the forest through the trees. As my financial advisor put it, I was being penny wise and pound foolish. I was struggling to hold onto the little I had, rather than ask why I couldn't have more.

Success requires you to think big, as wealth is simply a state of mind.

Think Big!

By Walter D Wintle
If you think you are beaten, you are.
If you think you dare not, you won't.
If you like to win, but don't think you can,
It's almost a cinch that you won't.

Living at Zero

If you think you'll lose, you've lost,
For out in the world you'll find
Success begins with a person's will;
It's all in the state of mind.

For many a game is lost
Before even a step is run
And many a coward fails
Before his work is begun.

Think big and your deed will grow;
Think small and you will fall behind.
Think that you can and you will;
It's all in the state of mind.

If you think that you are out-classed, you are;
You've got to think high to rise.
You've got to be sure of yourself
Before you can win the prize.
Life's battles don't always go
To the strongest or fastest man
But sooner or later the person who wins
Is the person who thinks she can (Wintle 2008).

How often do you convince yourself that you can't do it? If I asked you to save $100,000 in a year, what would your response be? Did your first thought go to all of the reasons why it couldn't be done?

A key element to achieving an LAZ Lifestyle is thinking big and believing in yourself. In *Four Hour Workweek*, Tim Ferriss states "think big and don't listen to people who tell you it can't be done. Life's too short to think small." (Ferriss 2007; And to add to his quote, those people telling you it can't be done are likely too scared to do it themselves. Think about it the next time someone volunteers advice: would they even do it and what have they done that allows them to give the advice?

I heard on the radio awhile back an interview of self-made millionaires and they were asked whether they hired a financial advisor or not. Some did, some didn't, but it was one millionaire's response that stuck out to me. The man's net worth was about $10 million and when asked why he doesn't use a financial advisor, he responded with the question, "Why would I trust a person who makes $50,000 a year to watch over my $10 million?" Good point!

I have learned to take advice with a grain of salt. Most people haven't done what you are now setting out to do. The average salary in the US is $51,100 (as of 2013) with less than 20% of American households making more than $100,000 (Guillot 2015).

> *Those who are successful just want it more and understand how to get there.*

So rather than think about and listen to all of the reasons why it can't be done, start finding ways to get it done! Believe in yourself, think big, and achieve big results.

You Must Believe in Yourself

Stop listening to other people! People will always have a suggestion for how to live your life, how you messed up, how you could be different, but rarely do they ever look in the mirror. Just remember you are the one who has to live with your decisions, not them. It all starts with believing in yourself!

Did you know that Albert Einstein did not speak one word until he was four years old? Many people thought he was not smart growing up. In fact, his teachers thought he was lazy and wouldn't make anything of himself. He scored well on tests but could never focus on lessons in class. Well, as we all know, he developed the Theory of Relativity and is known as one of the smartest people to ever live.

We are all different, unique, creative people. By blocking out the negativity and finding *your* passion, you can live an inspired life determined by you. You can do what other people only dream of. How many times does an idea come to you and you convince yourself that it is not possible?

It will take too much time. You are not qualified. Someone else is already doing it. It's too risky.

These excuses keep you from following your dreams and achieving personal success. I always thought celebrities and the wealthy had a secret to success that escaped the reach of the rest of us. But this is simply not true; those who are successful just want it more and understand how to get there.

Socrates, the ancient philosopher, once told a story of how to find the secret to success that is applicable here:

A young man asked Socrates the secret to success. Socrates told the young man to meet him near the river the next morning. They met. Socrates asked the young man to walk with him toward the river. When the water got up to their neck, Socrates took the young man by surprise and dunked him into the water. The boy struggled to get out but Socrates was strong and kept him there until the boy started turning blue.

Socrates pulled his head out of the water and the first thing the young man did was to gasp and take a deep breath of air. Socrates asked: "What did you want the most when you were there?" The boy replied: "Air." Socrates said: "That is the secret to success. When you want success as badly as you wanted the air, then you will get it. There is no other secret."

Do you want success or financial freedom that badly? It doesn't matter what is in your way, if you want the LAZ Lifestyle as much or more than you want air, you WILL achieve it. How badly do you want it?

Let's Create a Plan!

It's January 1st. You are ready to start the year and make some major changes. You set your yearly goals: learn a new language, lose weight, read more, exercise daily, (fill in the blank). How many of those changes lasted until June 30th of the same year? Or even January 30th? Why is that? Why can starting a regular workout plan seem so important one day and a broken promise to yourself the next?

This process of creating random, societally influenced goals has got to stop. You rarely have commitment towards these goals and your motivation lasts only as long as you see results, or until the next keg party your friend throws.

What I am proposing is a quality over quantity approach. It's being so invested in the goal that it can't fail and making it totally manageable that it doesn't feel so overwhelming. Goal setting works and is a successful strategy to change behavior and focus your energy on accomplishing the goal (Locke 2002).

For some odd reason, I was up early one Saturday morning sitting in the park watching runners and bikers pass by one after another. I couldn't help but initially judge them, thinking to myself, "What overachievers," as I sipped on my venti iced coffee.

But I started to notice that there was something more, something different about these people. They looked committed to the task at hand whether it was a steep hill or just pushing that extra mile. They were committed to their passion for running or cycling or the results achieved by participating in this activity. It was a commitment that continued, that got them out of bed when their entire body was demanding more sleep. And more importantly, it looked like they actually enjoyed it and were having fun. Who would have thought?

Running is just not my thing. But I talk to my brother, who was not a runner growing up, and he actually *misses* it when he can't go for a run. He has become so committed to it that he actually *misses* running.

This is how I want you to feel about your goals.

> ## Millennial Insight
>
> *I never used goals. I kinda just picked something I wanted to do and went for it. Goals always seemed so official and hard. The Micro-goals have helped break down what I want to do into easy steps to follow. I feel like I learn so much.*
>
> Brian, 33

But, just as I would not start by competing in an Ironman competition if I did decide to pursue running, you need to start with smaller, achievable goals. I don't want you to just create normal goals; I want you to create *micro-goals*.

A micro-goal is like a "to do" list to reach a specific objective. The downside of a *normal* goal is that you are constantly failing until you actually achieve the goal you set. For example, if I set a goal to lose 10 pounds, I have failed until I actually lose 10 pounds. And, if, heaven forbid, I could not lose that 10 pounds of holiday weight, I would never have reached my goal and therefore reinforced my inability to achieve anything.

This subconscious feeling of failure prevents many people from setting or attaining goals as they become overwhelmed, blame themselves, or develop excuses for why they could never reach a goal. With a micro-goal, I never set a goal to lose 10 pounds; instead the micro-goal consists of small, achievable action steps that lead to the end objective of losing 10 pounds.

Early on I tried to set long-term, five-year goals, as if I could actually predict the next five years. I would achieve some and fail dramatically at others. The problem I continually faced was how overwhelming the journey of achieving a goal seemed. Even before I started, the sheer number of steps and obstacles made reaching that goal difficult to fathom.

However, what I realized was that I was great at checking things off a to-do list. In fact, I even downloaded the Do! app that made the sound effect of a pencil drawing a line across the to-do list item when the task was completed. Actually, some people believe that the act of checking an item off your list releases endorphins that are linked to happiness (Wessel 2014). It's science!

So, what if we completely changed the way we did goals to have them commit and motivate us towards the end result, rather than overwhelm and disappoint us? And we started to focus on enjoying the journey towards our goals rather than just the destination?

Micro-goals are a behavior shift to make reaching and maintaining your end objective manageable and more achievable. Here is a good analogy I once heard:

A farmer bet a friend $1,000 that he could lift a full-grown cow over a fence. The friend laughed, "I'll take that bet." The farmer walked over to the cow and lifted it over the four-foot fence. In disbelief the friend ran over and looked for a hidden lift but with no machine in sight, he asked, "How did you do that?" The farmer smirked and replied, "Just strong I guess."

Shocked, the friend paid the farmer and walked away in disbelief. The secret is that the farmer had to lift the cow over the fence every day since it was a calf to get it into the pasture to eat. The moral of the story is that even the most daunting tasks, when tackled one day at a time, can be achievable.

Life is too short to simply wait for a goal to be achieved, but it is long enough that we need to be working towards something. Micro-goals allow for this flexibility and allow you to celebrate victories daily and adjust as needed because life has a tricky way of changing over time.

How to Create Micro-goals

There are five steps to creating achievable micro-goals.

1. Create a vision for your life (refer to Chapter 2)
2. Create strategic objectives
3. Research, research, research
4. Create micro-goals
5. Re-evaluate

We have spent some time in the previous chapter talking about your vision for your life. Your vision is the guiding light for your LAZ Lifestyle. The key is to make sure that your micro-goals align with this vision. Your vision can definitely change over time, so make sure that your micro-goals change with it.

Once you have a vision in mind and written out, the next step is creating your strategic objectives. A strategic objective is similar to a goal, but requires that it align with your vision. Some examples are buying a house, buying a car, losing weight, and getting to a positive net worth, becoming financially free. It is important to write these down and hang them on your refrigerator or create picture boards. For example, when I wanted a house, I took a picture of the exact house I wanted down to the colors and large front porch. I kept the picture on our refrigerator so I could see it every day. Use whatever method you prefer but make sure it is more than just a verbal objective.

The next step is research, research, research. I find it very difficult to make a goal to lose 10 pounds when you are not sure how to even do it. I have been an athlete and worked out all of my life, but it wasn't until recently when I hired a trainer that I felt like I was finally working out properly. I was doing workouts that complimented each other and gave my body the right amount of rest. If I had just tried to lose 10 pounds on my own, I would have gone right to the bench press, doing 3 sets of 10 and drinking my protein shakes, all the while wondering why I wasn't losing weight.

Or I would have tried the starvation approach, ending up binging two weeks later, gaining back any weight I had lost, and feeling more miserable than when I started. So we need to ensure that you understand and have a pretty good knowledge about the strategic objective you are about to undertake. You don't necessarily have to become an expert, but you need to be informed.

The research stage is also your chance to broaden your understanding and knowledge of different topics. By being educated in one area of your life, other parts are affected as well. For example, if you are trying to lose weight by working out, most research will suggest having a diet as well to maximize results. It is a fun domino effect of learning that will benefit you the rest of your life. Who knows, you may love it so much that you start helping others with their nutrition and fitness to make additional income.

The next step is creating micro-goals. These micro-goals will be informed by your research and should not be created until you have researched your strategic objective thoroughly. It is important to set micro-goals that are SMART. SMART stands for Specific, Measurable, Attainable, Realistic, and Timely (Haughey 2015). Again, it is better to think of these goals like to-do lists.

> ## Millennial Insight
>
> *I never realized how much I would learn in the process. Creating micro-goals helped me narrow my focus and really make an achievable plan to get to financial freedom.*
>
> Jasmine, 28

Lastly, you need to re-evaluate your micro-goals if they aren't achieved or as your life changes. Sometimes it is difficult to assign a timeline to a task so just evaluate and adjust as needed, never losing sight of your overall vision and strategic objectives.

Micro-goal Example

Let's walk through an example of what this whole thing looks like. Whitney and I have a vision of becoming financially free with about $10,000 per month coming in from our investments. As a goal, this can be overwhelming. Where do I start? It's so much money.

We know our vision and now we need to complete the first step of determining a strategic objective that moves us towards our vision. We will use the example of buying real estate to generate income, starting with our first home. The first thing you need to do is answer this question: why do I need a house? Is it so you don't have to rent, a long-term investment, you're starting a family, etc.?

Once you develop your answer to *Why* and it aligns with your vision, then we can move on to the next step. For example, we decided that owning a home will help reduce our costs in retirement, which will allow Whitney and I to travel more. Or, a house can become rental income down the road. You must make sure that the strategic objectives fall in line with where you ultimately want to be. This is why the book started with determining where you want to end up and working backwards. Take a second and flip back to your list. Does your strategic objective fit?

As a realtor, I hear many clients wanting to buy a home so they don't have to renew their lease or because all of their friends are buying houses. The most recent crash in our economy should be a strong indication that homeownership isn't always the solid investment it is advertised to be. For many, the reasons to buy a house are not sustainable and when financial obstacles arise, the goal is easily abandoned and thought of as too difficult. (We will discuss this more later whether your home is in fact an investment.)

Thus, make sure when creating these strategic objectives, you ask, "How does purchasing a home get me closer to where I want to be, closer to my vision?"

Once your strategic objectives are established, you are ready to move on to step two: research, research, research. By educating yourself on what it is going to take to achieve your objective, you become more and more committed to achieving it. I often use Google as a search reference to help me find out what is needed to accomplish my objective.

For my example, there are several checklists online for the process of buying a house. These checklists now inform our creation of our micro-goals. The to-do list breaks down in front of you like an organized list of mini tasks that help you achieve your strategic objective.

Here is an example home-buying checklist:

1. Pull your free credit report on www.annualcreditreport.com
2. Talk to a loan officer to determine how much money you qualify for or use the Zillow app
3. Determine the location in which you want to buy a house
4. Determine the number of bedrooms, bathrooms, and amenities you want
5. Contact a realtor
6. Begin searching online databases

This to-do list can begin to guide our adventure in an ever-evolving list that leads us to achieving our strategic objective. Like I mentioned before, I use a free to-do list app called *Do!* that allows me to cross off each task as it is completed. There is a mental change that happens as you cross more and more things off the list. It shows you that you can do it and creates momentum towards your strategic objective.

Now you want to create micro-goals. We can use the to-do lists to advise us. Once the micro-goals are completed, more micro-goals will arise. For instance, once I talk to the lender, he will require documents to get pre-approved. Just remember to break them down and put a reasonable timeline on getting them completed. Once each one is completed, take a large black marker and cross it off the list or click the checkbox on your app. Ahh…such a good feeling!

We can now set a timeline of when you want to achieve each task. It would be pointless to say from the get-go that you want to buy a house in six months when your credit won't allow you to purchase a home for two years. You would have failed before you even began and may never revisit this objective.

Some examples of micro-goals would be:

1. Contact a lender by Wednesday.
2. Contact a realtor by Friday.
3. Find five houses for sale on Zillow that I like before talking with the realtor.

You can have multiple strategic objectives, but make sure they are achievable and tied into the overall vision for where you want your life to

---

Wealth Hack Tools

GoalsonTrack

Cost: FREE to download, but requires a paid subscription.

GoalsonTrack allows you to set goals and track your progress on achieving these goals. You can manage tasks, track time, work towards building habits, and even record your progress through a tracking journal. The app allows you to create SMART goals like we discussed. You can monitor your progress in real time and create real-time tracking of habit changes. For example, if you wanted to start waking up before 7:00 am, the app allows you to track each day on the calendar that you woke up before 7:00 am.

Balanced

Cost: FREE
This is just a fun goal app. It allows you to set goals and track your life improvement. It focuses on setting micro-goals (objectives) as simple as taking a great photo or writing a blog entry. The app provides up to 50 suggested activities, so you will never run out of things to do. Simply choose the best fit for you.

Urge

Cost: FREE

How much would you save each month if you didn't buy that latte each day or that pack of cigarettes? Do you ever think of how much you can save? Well, Urge helps with that. Each time you decide *not* to make that purchase, Urge can transfer the amount you would have spent into a savings account (to have it go towards a more productive asset.) It also keeps a running tally of how many times you have "urged" and what the total dollar amount is that you saved. Good concept but it needs some ironing out to be an effective app.

---

go. The beauty of this process is that you become educated along the way and can be more informed when making decisions, even if you do not ever end up purchasing a home. By establishing a direction and steps to achieve each strategic objective, your chances of success increase dramatically.

Like Zig Ziglar said, "You can't hit a target you cannot see, and you cannot see a target you do not have."

LAZ Lifestyle Moves

- Write down what being rich means to you.

- Create one strategic objective complete with micro-goals to accomplish it. It should align with your vision. Remember the five steps to creating achievable micro-goals.
  1. Create a vision for your life (refer to Chapter 2)
  2. Create strategic objectives
  3. Research, research, research
  4. Create micro-goals
  5. Re-evaluate

- Download a to-do list app. (The free ones work great!)

Wrap Up

Your money mentality will predict whether you have money or not. Take a minute to think about your current mentality, your history, experiences, and see if you notice any patterns. You will find some good and some bad. We want to start reshaping your current view on money and the rich. You will be able to use micro-goals to change your behaviors and accomplish your vision. Bring on financial freedom. But imagine the headline: Joe Gives Up Latte and Gets an Investment Property.

5

TAKE CONTROL OF
YOUR FINANCIAL LIFE

Look at our society. Everyone wants to be thin, but nobody wants to diet. Everyone wants to live long, but few will exercise. Everybody wants money, yet seldom will anyone budget or control their spending.

John C. Maxwell

The way to build your savings is by spending less each month.

Suze Orman

"The car needs a new transmission!"

I can still hear the words reverberating in my head. We were living paycheck to paycheck (not the LAZ way) with no room for a sudden $1,000 repair to the car. We were struggling to pay our bills each month. The thought of "just-in-case" money was comical. No matter what we did, unavoidable expenses surfaced each month. We were caught between asking family for money and using expensive payday lenders with high interest rates. The hardest part to stomach was that we both had jobs and were working...a lot. We just never seemed to have enough money at the end of the month.

"Where did it all go?"

This question is asked by thousands of households across the country, regardless of their income. A 2013 Bankrate.com survey showed that 75% of Americans are living paycheck to paycheck (Bankrate 2013). The report went on to show that fewer than one in four Americans have enough money in their savings account to cover at least six months of expenses, or to cover the emergency expenses that might come up or stem the tide in case of job loss or medical emergency (Bankrate 2013).

In another survey, the Corporation for Enterprise Development (CFED) found that 44% of Americans are living with less than $5,887 in savings for a family of four (Lawton 2013). This statistic doesn't just refer to the poor. In fact, one in four middle class households (those earning $56,113 to $91,356 annually) have less than three months of savings (Lawton 2013). Even worse, 56% of Americans have sub-prime credit (Lawton 2013). This financial concoction means that if emergencies arise, many Americans are forced to resort to high-interest debt from credit cards or payday loans as they lack the savings necessary to keep them afloat. They are one crisis away from financial ruin.

So, no matter where you are with your finances, just know that you are not alone. Millions of people are living paycheck to paycheck across all income levels. Something is not working in this country. Let's examine your finances and find out why.

What Do You Know About Money?

In general, studies indicate that Americans lack necessary personal finance knowledge (Chen and Volpe 1998). How did it end up like this? Think back to high school. How many classes did you have on money? Were you taught how money works and how to make it work for you? Most people answer *no* to both questions. School was great for teaching us how to work for money. Just look at the standard of success: if you followed rules and did what you were told, you were considered an "A" student. If you didn't, you were the troubled child. (Talk about needing a system flipped.)

Most people don't get an introduction to money until they are in their late teens, others even later. So, in case you haven't been properly introduced, I am going to introduce you to money. Money meet Reader. Reader meet Money. Money is a form of currency used to exchange value for something you want. For instance, you want a soda and the societal (market) value in terms of US money is $1.00. Instead of trading your shirt or your first-born child, you give the owner of the soda a crisp dollar bill and he gives you the soda. Wouldn't it be funny if we were paid in chickens or cows? Money is a lot easier to pack around.

When you work for money it is considered *active* income. What I want to teach you is how to make money without having to work for it each day. It is called passive income, and it will change your life.

Financial Life Bucket Analogy

In an LAZ Lifestyle, there are four key areas that comprise your financial life: income (cash flow), expenses and liabilities, savings, and IPAs. I like to think of these in a little different, more visual way. Your financial life consists of several buckets:

The 1st bucket is your monthly income. This includes your paycheck, investments, alimony, child support... Basically, any money you have coming into your account.

The 2nd bucket is your monthly expenses and liabilities. This gets larger or smaller depending on your monthly expenses, such as rent or a mortgage, car payment, cell phone bill, utility bill, food, etc.

The 3rd bucket is your savings account. It includes emergency savings and retirement accounts.

The 4th bucket is your IPA account. The average person does not include this bucket while rich people find ways to make this bucket larger and larger. This account can only be used to purchase IPAs, such as real estate, notes, and businesses.

Once your monthly income hits your bank account, it fills up the Income bucket. The average person then fills the Expense bucket until it is full and anything left over goes into the Savings bucket or they simply increase the size of their Expense bucket. Very little, if any, ever gets put into the IPA bucket (Figure 2). More often than not, there is not enough

Figure 2. Depiction of typical savings categories.

in the Income bucket to even fill the Expense bucket, so nothing goes to savings let alone IPAs. It is often at this point that you start borrowing from future income to cover expenses.

At this rate, if your expenses are larger than your income or you spend more than you make, there will be nothing left for emergencies, savings, or IPAs. I know you want that new car, but you have a finite amount of money. So we need to make the Income bucket larger or make the Expense bucket smaller. Simple equation (Figure 3).

Remember, just as the Income, Savings, and IPA buckets can grow and shrink, so can the Expense budget. The goal is to grow the other three buckets while shrinking the Expense bucket. This is how the buckets need to work for you to reach financial freedom

The first step is to start with a minimum fixed amount (10% of net income) to contribute to the Savings bucket. Next, we fill up the Expenses bucket, and whatever is remaining gets dumped into the IPA bucket. The fixed savings amount grows at a steady pace, the Expenses bucket gets paid each month, and any remaining money goes towards IPAs.

Figure 3. Depiction of LAZ savings categories.

For an easy math example, let's say I make $5,000 after taxes per month and my expenses are $2,000 per month. I would put $500 in my Savings bucket the first of the month, then I would pay my $2,000 in expenses, and the remaining $2,500 would go into my IPA bucket. My goal is to ramp up asset spending. (There are a couple variations to this process and we will be discussing them in detail later in the chapter.) By decreasing the Expenses bucket and increasing the Income bucket, you can see how the IPA bucket would continue to grow.

Now you might be asking, what money do I have left over if something comes up? Basically, each month you start over. By all accounts, you are Living at Zero. You are living paycheck to paycheck, but your Savings and IPA buckets are growing. As you develop more IPAs, your Income bucket gets larger and larger, but your goal is to keep your Expenses bucket the same, meaning more and more money goes into your Savings and IPA buckets.

It becomes very motivating as you see the IPA bucket grow and you start actually purchasing IPAs. Soon you will find yourself wanting to decrease your Expenses bucket as much as possible and trying to find ways to grow your Income bucket. It becomes addicting. You'll start comparing every purchase

Millennial Insight

Once I saved enough in the IPA account to buy my first rental, I just had to have another one. I have 3 rentals now and I try to cut my expenses any way I can so I can get the 4th. The bucket analogy made sense. The smaller the expenses, the bigger the income, the more money I will have. My expense bucket was always bigger than every other bucket in my life.

Sara, 36

to the rental property you could buy if you just put more in your IPA bucket.

By starting over each month, you are Living at Zero, staying hungry, and continually working to improve your lifestyle to generate more income and find ways to cut expenses. You will be amazed at how many things you put back on the shelf because you don't have the money in your "spending" account to make the purchase.

This is the general philosophy for how your money should move through your life. Next, we need to examine the five steps that allow you to accumulate more IPAs to reach financial freedom and start experiencing the LAZ Lifestyle.

Step 1: Where Are You Now?

It is very difficult to plan for something if you don't know where you are now. If I want to travel to Italy, it makes a difference if I am already in Europe or in Moses Lake, WA. Like Lewis Carroll once said, "If you don't know where you are going, any road will get you there."

In order to begin, we are going to take a 40,000-foot view of your financial life. We need to start by understanding the big picture before getting too much closer. The first stop is determining your net worth.

Your net worth is basically all of the things of value that you own minus the debt that you owe.

To determine your net worth, we need to look at your assets and liabilities. To put it simply, assets are good, liabilities are bad. We are part of a society that lives in the gray area, but the reality is that the more black and white you can make your finances, the more successful you will be. Later on in this book, we will discuss good debt vs. bad debt as a vehicle for growing wealth, but *no debt* is always the best vehicle.

If you're still unsure, assets refer to the things that add value, such as equity in your home, rental properties, stocks, bonds, etc., and liabilities refer to your outstanding obligations, such as your mortgage, car payment, credit card debt, student loans, etc. To calculate your net worth, you subtract your liabilities from your assets. The end goal is to make sure the value of your assets is higher than your liabilities (Table 2).

If you do not know the value of your home, just use the tax assessed value for the property that can be found at your local tax assessor site.

Table 2. Example of assets vs liabilities.

Assets	Value	Liabilities	Amount
Residence	$150,000	Mortgage	$130,000
Rental Property	$105,000	Mortgage	$70,000
401K	$5,000	Credit Card	$15,000
Silver Coins	$1,500		
Total	$291,500	Total	$315,000
Net worth –$23,500			

In this case, our example has a net worth of –$23,500. Never fun! This was our family just three years ago and now we are over six figures in the positive. So don't worry if you do this exercise and your net worth number is zero or negative. You can start today to build up the asset column and pay down the liabilities.

I never wanted to do this calculation because, in my head, I knew what the outcome was. But, by putting it down on paper, I could now see my whole financial picture and make a plan to change it.

Your first step is to get to a net zero. That means that your asset column minus your liability column equals zero or greater, not negative. Start by looking at your liability column and see where you can start chipping away at debt. You need to create a monthly payment amount (that would be included in your Expenses bucket) as you start paying down the debt. We will discuss later how to prioritize which debt to pay off first, but the goal should be to get to net zero. If you already have a positive net worth, it is time to build the asset column.

You should update and reference this tool often to get a quick picture of your financial growth and track your success. Now that you know where you are at in terms of net worth, we can develop a plan to move you forward.

Step 2: Where Does Your Money Come From?

Now that you have a grasp on the current overview of your financial life, the next step is to really understand how much money you have coming in each month. This could be in the form of a paycheck, benefits, retirement accounts, investment properties; basically, any money that comes into your bank account. This is also referred to as cash flow. This amount will be after taxes are already taken out of your checks, or the net income. Use Worksheet 6 for help.

Worksheet 6. List of income sources for each individual.

Sources of Income	Amount
Paycheck:	$
Retirement Accounts/Pensions:	$
Investment Income:	$
Public Benefits:	$
Child Support/Alimony:	$
Other Income:	$
Total Income:	$

As we discussed earlier, there are two types of income: active and passive. Active income refers to income where you work and get paid for the work. This includes wages, tips, salaries, commissions, and income from businesses where you are involved and directly participate in the work. Passive income is money generated without you having to be directly involved, such as a rental property, limited partnership, or another entity where you are not actively involved.

The formula for an LAZ Lifestyle is to use active income to help generate passive income. I don't want you to think you never have to work again. The fastest way to financial freedom is to generate income from working and invest it properly in IPAs to convert it to passive income. For example, if you have ever played Robert Kiyosaki's cashflow game, you will understand that it is far easier to exit the "rat race" if you start with a doctor's salary rather than a janitor's salary because you are able to fill your IPA bucket up more quickly. Having a consistent active income makes it easier to generate savings for the 30% down payment and provides the source of verifiable income needed to purchase a rental property. (I have a few suggestions on how to bypass the large down-payment requirement in the real estate chapter.) Yes, creating passive income outlets does take more work upfront, but it has a sweet payoff.

I am living proof of that. Right now, I have active income from my salaried position that I have to be HIGHLY involved with to generate income. But I have rental properties, stocks, bonds, and long-term real estate notes, which make up my current passive income. It is important to note that I could not have purchased any of these IPAs without my active income sources.

The key to the LAZ Lifestyle is to focus on generating passive income. Again, active income is only seen as a means to an end for generating passive income. Now, if you really love your job, great! Stay at your job and be happy, but you will still have the option to do something else if you want.

Be honest with yourself and go ahead and add up your income and get a total for your monthly income. Write it below.

Total Monthly Income: _____

For those of you who are freelance or contract workers, planning and budgeting are very important so you can stem the low tides. So, if you get sporadic or fluctuating income payments, write down an average over a one-year period so we can have a number to work with.

Step 3: Where Does the Money Go?

The next step is to figure out where your money is going on a monthly basis. (This is what Worksheet 7 is for.) For some reason, there never seems to be enough money in your bank account at the end of each month. Even though you got a raise, you are still living paycheck to paycheck. It seems like the expenses just keep rising with your income with no end in sight. Instead of a five-year-old Honda, you bought a new Jeep Grand Cherokee when your car broke down. Not a bad purchase in and of itself, but now

Worksheet 7. Expense tracker for daily spending.

Daily Spending Tracker		
Description	**Category**	**Amount**
Starbucks Coffee	Eating Out	$3.24
		$
		$
		$
		$
		$
		$
		$
		$
		$
		$
		$
		$
		$
Total		$

your insurance is higher, gas bills are higher, and you are paying more each month just to own the Jeep. Sound familiar?

What I have found is that it is usually the incidental costs that get us. They seem to be in stealth mode within the budget. I plan every month for our mortgage and car payment and utility bills, but I don't plan for the lattes or the golf rounds each month. What we need to do is track where *every* dollar goes, not just the bigger line items. Case and point: when we started tracking our spending, we found that we were spending $2,000 per month on eating out. More than our mortgage, car payment, utility payments, gas bill, and cable bill combined! (Remember, we live in Spokane where the cost of living is extremely low.)

I want you to start by tracking your spending for one month. This includes large payments such as your mortgage or rent, car, insurance, etc., all the way to the small outlays of cash, such as coffee, cigarettes, Redbox rentals, etc. We need to get a better idea of how much you are spending each month.

I have included a manual sheet above or you can use sites like www.Mint. com and the LevelMoney app to track where your money is going in the palm of your hand.

This can be an eye-opening exercise filled with awe, humility, and frustration. Too often, we forget about the holes in our budgets. David Bach talks about the latte factor in his book *The Automatic Millionaire* when he highlights the overall impact that saving on one latte and reinvesting the money can have towards your retirement goals (Bach 2004). He states, "All you need to do to finish rich is to look at the small things you spend your money on every day and see whether you could redirect that spending to yourself. Putting aside as little as a few dollars a day for your future rather than spending it on little purchases such as lattes, bottled water, fast food, cigarettes, magazines, and so on, can really make a difference between accumulating wealth and living paycheck to paycheck" (Bach 2004). By focusing on plugging holes in your budget, you can start to use the saved money on IPAs that will help you generate more income.

If you had the choice between one venti latte a day for one year or owning a rental property, what would you choose?

I know this sounds like a crazy question, but one latte a day at $4.00 adds up to $1,460 per year. If you put that $1,460 into a market account that returned 10% for 30 years, you would have $25,476.13. *That's enough for a down payment on a property*. You can do this same equation with any seemingly small expense in your life.

Again, I use Mint.com to track expenses, and many banks and credit unions now offer similar features. It allows you to track your income and expenses and categorize your spending so you know where your money is going. It does not track cash purchases so I tend to charge to credit or debit cards more than I used to (and pay the balance at the end of each month) just so I can have an accurate look at what I spent that month.

Step 4: To Budget or Not to Budget

Now that you have tracked your expenses for one month and we know your income, let's create a budget for your expenses. You probably just cringed upon reading the word "budget," but you knew at some point this topic would have to be discussed. A budget helps you plan for where your money goes. The less money that goes into your Expenses bucket, the more that goes into your IPA bucket.

We have examined your total income coming in and where your money is going each month. I have used my budget and a friend's budget as an example (Table 3). Take a look.

Table 3. Example comparison of two individual budgets.

Jordan's Budget		Tim's Budget	
Income	$5000	Income	$5000
Expenses		Expenses	
Mortgage/Utilities	1000	Rent/Utilities	1500
Insurance/Gas	350	Car/Insurance/Gas	700
Food/Ent./Other	1150	Entertainment	1000
Savings	1000	Savings	500
IPA Account	1500	Food/Other	1000
Total Expenses	5000	Total Expenses	4600
Net	*$0*	*Net Profit*	*$300*

As you can see, we are both living paycheck-to-paycheck, just in different ways. I have tried to minimize my expenses so I can fill up the IPA bucket as much as possible. My friend has a newer car, larger rent payment, and other increased expenses, leaving little left over for IPAs. (At least he is trying to save though.)

Notice how many things my friend has that will not increase his income or decrease his expenses, whereas my expenses are lower and more money is being deposited into my Savings and IPA bucket each month.

There are several different mediums in which to create a budget, but it is naïve of me to assume you would work better with an Excel spreadsheet budget and show that example when you might despise Excel. So here are a few ways to create a budget:

Excel Spreadsheet

Similar to above, list your expenses in one column and the amount you budget for each category. Then have a column for your income. The more

IPAs you have, the more it will fill up.

Envelope Method

Here you create an envelope for each category, including discretionary spending. When you get your paycheck, you get it turned into cash and put the budgeted amount into each envelope. So you are only allowed to spend the money in each envelope on that particular expense. It removes the option of overspending, but does require discipline to work effectively.

Accountability

Here you have a friend or family member design and go through a budget together with you, and at the end of each month or even twice a month, you compare the budget to your actual expenditures. This information is then shared with your accountability partner. The accountability is a strong motivator to stay on budget. Ultimately, once the habit is developed, you would move away from this option...or maybe not.

Online/Apps

Here you can use sites or apps like Mint.com or your bank to track spending and income. It works really well for all debit and credit purchases and you just have to manually enter any cash purchases and income. This is a great way to have your budget with you at all times and know where your numbers are at any point in the month.

> **Millennial Insight**
>
> *I think it's all about having a monthly budget. You know you are going to put this much in savings, this much to giving and this much to spend.*
>
> Natalie, 32

It is imperative to remember that a budget is not the end all be all. It changes and adapts with your life, but it ultimately allows you to make a conscious choice to spend or not spend money on something. I referred to the David Bach's latte factor above, but it is very difficult to give up my venti iced coffee (with no sweetener and light nonfat milk, in case you were wondering). So rather than feel guilty about buying it every single day, I just need to account for it.

Basically, an effective budget needs to represent your life, simply ensuring that you are spending less than you make. If you know you are going to buy a coffee, put it in the budget. If you know you are going to shop for clothes, put it in the budget. If you know you are going to go to Vegas four times a year, that's another issue, but put it in the budget. Budgeting is not designed to scare you or prohibit you from doing something. It just needs to accurately track your funds so you know where your money is going. A friend of mine works for a multi-millionaire and constantly remarks how he knows where every dollar is being spent. So if he can do that with millions of dollars, we should be able to do it with far less. You are building habits that apply whether you have $1,000 or $1,000,000 in your bank account.

As we move through this book and I show you the power of IPAs, you will want to stop spending frivolously and start investing. All of a sudden you will think of money and spending in terms of rental units or number of widgets. But without a clear picture of your cash flow, investing is difficult and can be risky.

Go ahead and plug in your expenses in Worksheet 8 or on one of the apps or websites provided. You can use Mint to set up budgets and spending alerts, and you'll have your budget with you everywhere.

Step 5: Pay Yourself First, Pay Yourself Last!

One line item that is noticeably absent from most budgets is Savings. You pay every bill on there and whatever is left over is deemed worthy enough to be savings. Why don't you pay yourself first?

Scary I know. I have heard people tell me that they would have nothing left for bills and all of the stuff they needed each month, but this is simply not true.

J.D. Roth, in his blog *Get Rich Slowly*, states, "To pay yourself first means simply this: Before you pay your bills, before you buy groceries, before you do anything else, set aside a portion of your income to save. Put the money into your 401(k), your Roth IRA, or your savings account. The first bill you pay each month should be to yourself. This habit, developed early, can help you build tremendous wealth" (Roth 2013).

Pay yourself first is not a new concept and has been proven to work time

Worksheet 8. Expense tracker for all monthly expenses.

Expenses	Amount
Housing (mortgage or rent)	$
Utilities	$
Food (at home and away)	$
Transportation (including car loan)	$
Car insurance	$
Cable	$
Phone	$
Debt repayment (student loans and credit cards	$
Memberships (gym, magazines, etc.)	$
Personal Care	$
Savings	$
Clothing	$
Entertainment	$
Other	$
Other	$
Other	$
Total	$

and time again, yet most people don't do it. I highly recommend trying to deposit at least 10% of your net income in savings and retirement accounts each year (we will discuss these accounts in a later chapter). This 10% should come right off the top at the beginning of each month and thought of more like a bill that needs to be paid.

The 10% is first used to fund your emergency savings account to ensure that you have at least three months of expenses saved specifically in a separate account (that you have to physically go down to the bank to withdraw from.) This account is for emergencies *only* and should be set up as a savings account. Once you have three months of emergency savings, then the 10% goes towards retirement accounts. Trust me, you do not want to incur penalties for accessing your retirement accounts early. So in the case that you have to use any funds from your emergency account, then that 10% gets reallocated to fully fund the emergency account again before funding the retirement accounts.

Once you've paid yourself, now you pay your expenses. If you want to save for a vacation, new car, kids sports, or another one-time expense, then account for it in your budget so you can apportion money to it when you pay your expenses. This is where budgeting can really help you.

Once the expenses are paid, you pay yourself again at the end of the month by depositing into your IPA account. To determine how much to put in your IPA account, you need to take 50% of the remaining amount of income (after depositing into savings and paying your expenses) and deposit it into your IPA account (if it is too uncomfortable to put the entire remaining amount in your account). I do recommend keeping a buffer for operating unknowns. You will have your emergency account available if there are any larger, unexpected emergencies.

That might sound confusing but let's look at the numbers:

Step 1: Receive net income: $5,000.

Step 2: Transfer 10% ($500) to the Savings account.

Step 3: Pay Expenses that total $2,500 this month.

Step 4: Assess remaining income in account at $2000.

Step 5: Take 50% of the remaining income ($1,000) and deposit in the IPA account.

Step 6: You have $1,000 in your account, just in case.

Step 7: At the end of the month, deposit the remaining balance into your IPA or Savings account.

At the end of the month, you can decide to keep the $1,000 in your retirement account, add to savings for a specific goal, add to your IPA account, or increase your emergency savings. This allows you to cover unknown expenses that may arise so you do not have to dip into your IPA or retirement accounts, but does not allow you to spend frivolously.

See, not too hard. For some, living so close to zero is uncomfortable, but it is a vital part of the LAZ Lifestyle.

You are essentially forcing yourself to live paycheck to paycheck, but in a productive way. By keeping just a small portion of your income in your operating account, you remain motivated to keep pushing and never get complacent. You keep that hunger alive, all while your retirement and IPA accounts continue to grow exponentially and your lifestyle and expenses remain the same.

For example, as soon as we get $10,000 in our IPA account, I start looking to purchase an IPA, such as real estate, notes, or a business that fits my passive income criteria. By having the IPA funds in a separate account and only using it to buy IPAs, I don't get tricked into buying the newest car, television, or whatever is being advertised on QVC at 2:00 am.

Then, each month you reset to zero and repeat this cycle as you continue to grow your IPA account. Before long, you won't even know that the money going to your IPA account is gone. You will stop looking at clothes, toys, and electronics and start looking at how every dollar affects your bottom line and gets you more IPAs (that will ultimately grow your passive income and make you less reliant on active income).

Don't Just Buy Things, Buy Assets!

Now that you have saved up and grown your IPA account, let's start looking to buy IPAs. This is what all of that money in your IPA bucket is for. It's time to spend it. *Note: I will go into more depth later in the book on each asset listed below.*

It is very difficult to be financially free without passive income. I know savings are important to financial success, but Whitney and I were not able to get ahead and build wealth with savings alone. It was just not possible to save that amount of money on our salaries alone. We are not frivolous spenders. The key to our advancement was the purchase of IPAs, not just things.

Millennial Insight

By automating my life, I don't even miss the money I put into my savings and IPA account. It's like it wasn't even there. Now I just watch those accounts grow and I can't wait to buy my first IPA.

Rebecca, 33

The major IPAs to invest in are: retirement accounts (stocks and bonds), real estate, and business ownership. We invested in all three with what little savings we had and our sweat equity. For example, with real estate, we got our start with our primary residence. Normally, this is seen as a liability as it doesn't produce income, but we targeted homes that needed some work and that we could purchase under 50% after repair value (ARV). We would fix up our home and then sell it after two years to avoid capital gains tax, or we'd keep it as a rental property. (According to today's tax laws, if you live in your home for two of the last five years, you are exempt from paying capital gains tax when you sell the home—up to $250,000 for a single person or $500,000 for married couples.)

The money we made from each sale (as well as the commission I made from being our realtor) was deposited into our IPA bucket, and we would find another investment to purchase. Our commitment to purchasing IPAs and increasing passive income has allowed us to invest in a broad spectrum of business and real estate IPAs in the last five years.

There are some guiding principles for investing in IPAs. I will discuss this in further detail later in the book, but all of our IPA purchases must fit our "work from the beach" investment strategy. What I mean is that an IPA must be able to be operated or managed from a beach with only an internet connection and laptop. So it is pure passive income, or able to be in a short amount of time. Another requirement is that you need to understand what you are investing in. The only times I have lost money on an investment were when I did not have enough knowledge about what I was investing in. For instance, when I was in college I invested in a multi-level marketing scheme for downloadable music that promised me instant riches for doing nothing. I bought it hook, line, and sinker. I have since stayed away from those and developed criteria for which we invest, the first of which is: if it sounds too good to be true, it probably is.

I recommend having a narrow focus on what IPAs to purchase when you start. In order for Whitney and I to purchase an asset, for example, it must meet the following criteria:

1. Potential appreciation over time
2. Generate passive income
3. Operate with third party management
4. Be in our knowledge base, area of interest, or passion

By focusing on these areas, we are able to weed out opportunities that might not fit. For example, we generate income from our photo booth business that increases in value as we do more business, operates with employees, and is in an industry that we understand. But, it *does* require active management. For this reason, we consider this active income rather than passive. But our real estate properties fit every category listed above, as we have a property management company that operates each property. By narrowing our focus, it has allowed us to operate our ventures from anywhere. (I actually checked on our properties while on a beach in Greece!)

As for our budget, we try to allocate at least 30% of our total income to an IPA account and when there is enough money in the account, we purchase an IPA that fits our criteria.

For example, we recently purchased the commercial real estate and business assets for a local restaurant that we renovated and rebranded. Now, on its face, it looks like an active income investment, but we structured the deal so that we were a limited partner in the business. This allows us to generate income each month without the responsibilities of management, which fits well within our "work from the beach" investment strategy. We also happen to love food and the community-building impact that a restaurant can bring to a neighborhood.

So as I mentioned before, we have used the following overriding question that aligns with our vision before making any IPA purchase decisions: *Can we run this investment from a beach?* This weeds out those investments that require us to be present in order for them to operate effectively and is in line with the vision we created for financial freedom, which was to have enough passive income to travel with our family and eventually not have to work. Otherwise, we are just trading one active income source for another.

Don't worry, this was meant to just be an overview of investment criteria for your IPA purchases. We will discuss these options in much more detail later in the book, but we have found real estate and business ownership with management to be the vehicles that give us the greatest returns and flexibility.

Automate Your Life

The idea of having to physically go to the bank and make deposits to your savings and IPA accounts can seem daunting. Since everything these days is automated, why aren't your finances? How many times have you just forgotten to pay a bill or justified a reason why you shouldn't? By automating your payments, you take yourself out of the equation and are allowed the chance to focus on increasing your income.

Automating payments can help you avoid late fees, forcibly save for retirement and IPA purchases, and have your financial picture in the palm of your hand. It frees up your mind to focus on more important things and simply relax about your finances.

The LAZ Lifestyle is one of convenience and harnessing new technology to make your life easier. The idea is to automate payments to savings, IPAs, and other wealth-building tools so you don't give yourself the option to spend it frivolously. My life is completely automated as far as bills and savings go. This is what it looks like:

1. 10% of net monthly income is transferred to savings and retirement accounts.

2. Every bill is ACH deposited and paid by the 10th of each month (or a different date based on your pay schedule).

3. At the end of each month, I transfer money to our IPA account, reducing my operating accounts for the next month.

You need to get in the habit of automating your bills. Be honest, do you still send in checks for your payments each month? This is a waste of your time and money. Most banks and credit unions offer bill-pay services and most companies accept automatic payments; in fact, you can even get discounts for doing it. Ask your bank to help you get this set up or call their online customer service number. It is easier than you think. Plus, you don't have to physically see the check for your student loan payment each month. Just another added bonus.

LAZ Lifestyle Moves

1. Get to zero (income greater than expenses and net worth)
2. Put one month of expenses in emergency savings
3. Get $1,000 in a retirement savings account
4. Get $5,000 in your IPA account
5. Find ways to add $500 per month to your Income bucket

Wealth Hack Tools

Mint

Cost: FREE

Mint.com allows you to track, budget, and manage your money all in one place so that you can see where the money is coming from and where it is going. It has bill pay alerts and offers advice on ways to save money. It is very simple to upload your bank, credit, loan, and retirement accounts and let Mint do the rest as it automatically tracks and categorizes your transactions.

I was worried about security and having my accounts all in one spot, but Mint is safe and secure and is a view-only site, so you can't actually move money. You also have a four-digit pin that will prevent unauthorized use if your phone is lost or stolen.

Simple

Cost: FREE

Simple is exactly what the name implies. It offers budgeting and helps you track your spending in real time. This is actually a bank, so unlike Mint and Level Money, you can transfer funds as needed, set goals, track your spending, and have support when needed. Many banks have started using mobile apps, and for the new generation of clientele that does not need a brick and mortar location, this may be a good alternative. Are you ready to replace your bank?

Xpenser

Cost: FREE

Xpenser allows you to record your expenses, receipts, time, and mileage. This is perfect for small business owners who are tired of hanging on to every receipt and forgetting to record the mileage from their last trip. This app allows you to record from your phone, then review, print, export, create an invoice, or simply submit for reimbursement online. Xpenser integrates with Quickbooks for easy transition to your expense reports.

Cashish

Cost: $0.99

Cashish is the ultimate spending tracker app. Unlike Mint and Level

Money, Cashish only focuses on tracking your spending and allows you to enter transactions manually when you spend with cash. If used correctly, it should work like a check register and you should know how much cash is in your wallet based on what the app reflects. I recommend this for those who spend with cash more frequently. Personally, cash just burns a hole in my pocket, so this app makes it easier to track.

Level Money

Cost: FREE

Level Money is a simple way to track your daily cash flow and take control of your money. Similar to Mint, it links to your accounts and updates in real time. This prevents you from having to enter the transactions manually. Level Money is a great way to see what you are spending and help you meet your financial goals. The interface is more trendy than Mint, but both are very user-friendly.

BudgetBoss

Cost: $0.99

Budget Boss is for the uber budgeter. It automatically predicts your future balance based on your budget and saving and spending habits. It provides insight into the effect that your current budget will have up to two years out. This app allows you to visualize the savings and have a graphical reminder of what your budgeting and savings now will lead to in the future. I would not recommend this for the daily tracker of your finances, but in coordination, it can be an effective tool.

HelloWallet

Cost: FREE

HelloWallet allows you to track your spending, budget more effectively, and have a personal financial snapshot anywhere you are. It is similar to Mint, just not as popular and not as easy to use. It has the same syncing features and a clean interface with a crafty wellness score that analyzes your finances and spending and gives you a score out of 100.

> **Manilla—Bill and Account Manager**
>
> Cost: FREE
>
> Did you ever want a professional organizer to take over your life? Wait no longer. Manilla offers an easy-to-use system to manage your daily finances, household bills, travel rewards, magazine subscriptions, and healthcare accounts. You get automatic reminders and easy-to-access statements. You can even add your smaller monthly bills to the account in order to better track those monthly outflows of cash.

Wrap Up

Wow, that was a lot! Now you know how to go through your finances with a fine-tooth comb. Start the habit now of knowing your net worth and adjusting it at least monthly. You need to have a snapshot of your finances to know whether you are growing or not. Next, know where your money is going. You work so hard to get it, let's try not to give it away unless it is used to purchase IPAs. You are well on your way to make the changes and get your financial house in order. We will revisit the concept of the "work from the beach" investment strategy and how to apply it to your life to start generating significant passive income.

Advice from Millennials

Name: Jose
Age: 28
Occupation/Job Title: United States Military Officer/Senior Logistician
Annual Income: $73,010 (before taxes)/$4,686 (after taxes)
Family Size: 5
Where do you live? Fort Campbell, KY
Do you own your home or rent? Rent (own rentals in WA)

One a scale of 1 to 10, how comfortable are you with your finances? Why?

That is a tricky question. I am very comfortable **managing** the finances I have been given/earned, not as comfortable with the amount I earn. Overall, I would say I am at a comfort level of 8.

Do you use a budget? Why or Why not?

Yes!! It is absolutely imperative to understand where your money goes if you have the desire of "financial freedom" in your future. As an Army officer, there are multiple demand signals that require my attention and immediate action on a daily basis. If I do not deliberately account for where I am spending money, it is very easy for life to run away with it.

Does Budgeting work for you? Why or why not?

Yes. The methodology of accounting for every dollar spent has proven to be more work and deliberate thinking upfront but less stressful for the family in the long (over the course of a month/year) run.

What is the most difficult thing about using a budget?

Sticking with it!!! There will be times where you will want to "rob Peter to pay Paul", when in reality you should administer a little self-discipline and practice delayed gratification in order to stick with your game plan (budget). In order to stick with a budget, whether you are single or married, ALL PARTIES MUST BE ON THE SAME PAGE; IN AGREEMENT!

What do you use to track your finances?

I use an Excel spreadsheet (who doesn't?). This spreadsheet has simple formulas built in to where we input expenditures within their given lines of accounting and ultimately tells me where we stand for the remainder of the month. Keep all receipts!!! Manual input has proven to work best for us.

How much do you set aside for savings each month? Why?

Currently, I am the sole provider for the family so our savings is not as robust as families where both parents work. That being said, we are able to take a percentage out of my check every month without us seeing it. Right now, 6% of my base pay has seemed to be the magic number. I would recommend first finding your baseline in requirement for basic amenities for a month and then establish how much you will be able to set aside for savings.

Do you have an emergency savings account? Why?

With tight times, we have set our tax return aside every year as emergency savings. It is very important to have an emergency account. Your personal priorities are going to drive your ability to make this a robust account.

What single piece of financial advice has made the largest impact in your life?

I would not attribute my drive for financial clarity and financial freedom to any one piece of advice, rather to my upbringing and lessons learned along the way. However, there is one quote that I will always remember: *If you will live like no one else, later you can live like no one else.* Dave Ramsey

What advice do you have for people trying to save?

1. Assess your income against your requirements (get a baseline of what you're working with.)
2. Set feasible priorities/goals for yourself (if single) or **with** your spouse (a sustainable budget.)
3. Create a game plan (where you want to be in 1yr, 2yrs, etc.)
4. Stick with your game plan!!
5. Constantly review and revise as necessary.

NOTE: Understand that this is a fluid document. It is **NOT** the end of the world if you have to reallocate monies where you did not originally plan to.

Living at Zero

6

DEBT: YOUR FRIEND OR YOUR ENEMY?

Debt... An ingenious substitute for the chain and whip of the slave-driver.

Ambrose Bierce

Debt is like a crazy aunt we keep down in the basement. All the neighbors know she's there, but nobody wants to talk about her.

Unknown

"Can I borrow a dollar?" my brother yelled, while clutching a bag full of candy. "I'll pay you back later." Even as kids, we grew up learning to borrow and pay back, most of the time. When you didn't pay back in my family you just got punched and usually didn't get lent anything for a while. We didn't worry about interest, terms, amortization schedules, and points. We just knew we wanted something *now* and if borrowing was the only way to make it happen then so be it!

Debt is a socially acceptable epidemic in this country. Personal debt continues to rise (Bennett 2006). *At its most basic form, debt allows you to get something today that you can't afford until tomorrow.* This sense of debt or being indebted to someone has an impact on your life and most of us have accessed debt in some way, whether it be student loans, credit cards, payday loans, or a home mortgage. But is debt a good thing? I have to be honest, without debt financing, the LAZ Lifestyle will be difficult to accomplish. Whitney and I would not have been able to accomplish what we have because, for instance, no matter how hard we work, $150,000 would be a lot of money to pay in cash for a rental. The key is learning to use debt responsibly but also learning how to make debt work in your favor.

Keeping Up with the Joneses

The Great Recession has taught me two major lessons. First, *do not live beyond your means.* Too often we use debt to buy what we can't afford and justify it by saying we will earn it later. Just because they have a 0% interest offer for 1,000 years doesn't mean the item is worth purchasing. Second, *just because you can qualify to borrow money doesn't mean you should.* You need to have a plan when looking to borrow money. During the Recession, many people were pulling all of the equity out of their homes and buying vacations, new cars, etc. rather than investing in IPAs. (I never recommend pulling equity out of your home unless it is to buy an IPA.)

Trying to keep up with the latest fashion and toys that your friends have will drive you crazy and take a toll on your budget. This has been the most important lesson for us to learn, and I wasn't quite sure where to include this in the book. In fact, I would have put it in every chapter if I could have, just to drive home the point.

I am not saying you can't have toys or a big house, but make sure doing so is within your means. In 2012, the average American household (with at least one credit card) had nearly $15,950 in credit card debt, according to CreditCards.com, with the average interest rate running in the mid-to-high teens at any given time (Bortz 2012). *Almost $16,000 in credit card debt alone!* Think of the IPAs you could buy with that.

What you will find when you look inside most of the opulent homes and new Maseratis is that they are leveraged to the hilt and the owner has become a slave to that possession. Now they must work that much harder to pay for and support their lifestyle. That's not the LAZ Lifestyle way. We want to invest in IPAs so we can increase our experiences and passions in life.

Strive to be true to yourself and resist the need to impress or keep up with your friends. Most people do not experience the concept of being financially free and can never live the LAZ Lifestyle simply because they are a slave to their jobs, possessions, or financial situation. What looks perfect on the outside is almost always empty on the inside.

Again, I must stress the importance of finding your identity. The reality is despite your efforts to keep up with the Joneses, they might be trying to keep up with you! The grass always seems greener on the other side.

Instead, lead the way and they will follow you. As Ralph Waldo Emerson stated, "Do not go where the path may lead, go instead where there is no path and leave a trail."

The Debt Raincloud

In college, I did not understand money, debt, or credit. I abused all three and constantly wondered how I had dug a hole so deep. I felt like Eeyore in the Winnie the Pooh cartoons with a raincloud that just hovered around me, not really raining but definitely blocking the light and disrupting just about everything in my life. This is no way to live, and when I sought help, I was simply told that I had another 25 years of this until my student loans and consumer debt were paid off.

So there I was, $200,000+ in debt with little to show for it. I sat in my office staring at the three small pieces of paper on the wall, wondering how they could have cost so much. In front of me, in $10 black, plastic frames was over $300,000 worth of education in the form of diplomas, and on my desk, I had the deeds to over $600,000 worth of rental properties. Sure, people tell me I wouldn't be where I am now without that education, but when I just look at the numbers, the rentals generate $6,500 per month in gross rents while my diplomas are just collecting dust. I didn't need a piece of paper telling me that I could reach financial freedom.

> *Things are the best distraction from where you want to go.*

Rich Dad, Poor Dad author Robert Kiyosaki goes into great detail about the difference between good and bad debt; I highly recommend reading his book. (I read it twice a year and still pull things out of it.) To sum it up, good debt helps generate income while bad debt is simply a liability (Kiyosaki 2000).

For example, a triplex that has a $100,000 mortgage but generates $6,000 per year after paying all expenses would be considered good debt. It allows your money (your debt) to make money. On the contrary, bad debt is referred to as a liability that only costs you money. So according to this definition, your primary residence is considered to be bad debt, as it does not generate income. Sorry, I know you did not want to hear that.

Another interesting example is your vehicle. Your vehicle is worth less and less each day, it needs continuous upkeep, and costs you interest every month on the vehicle loan payment. They literally tell you a car loses 20% of its value the day you drive it off the lot. Is this a good debt or a bad debt? It depends. This one is arguable because, in a roundabout way, it can help me generate income, but generally is seen as a bad debt. On its face, it is a debt that does not by itself generate income since I do not rent it out. But without it, I am unable to generate income as a Realtor or by commuting to work, so it definitely falls in the gray area.

The reason we need to determine the difference between good debt and bad debt is that we want to get rid of all bad debt and want to learn how to leverage good debt to purchase more IPAs and grow our passive income stream.

Now that you have a basic idea of debt, let's look at good debt, bad debt, and the ever-growing student debt. Gurus such as Dave Ramsey teach people to live debt free. I think some people need this as a necessary first step. So in theory this is great, but it discounts how smart we as humans can be. The no debt theory is based on this understanding that most people abuse debt through store credit cards, over-priced cars, and any other frivolous purchase not made with cash. We get too greedy with other people's money that we overextend and start living outside of our means. But, I struggle with this concept. I think the debt free method would be great if I wanted to retire when I was 65. It puts the pressure on generating enough active income to pay off debt and fund your retirement. It would take a long time to reach financial freedom without utilizing the power of good debt. So I want to teach you how to use good debt to get ahead and avoid bad debt altogether.

Good Debt

"Good debt" sounds like an oxymoron. Yet, without good debt, I could never have purchased the real estate and businesses that I have been able to up to this point. Good debt basically leverages debt to help you purchase an IPA. Leverage can be a powerful tool for building wealth.

The question I always ask when deciding to take on debt is: Will this generate more income than I will pay to cover it including the interest owed?

For example, if I buy a car, will the income that I can produce or the fuel savings I can realize by having a different vehicle more than cover the $400 per month payment?

The motor vehicle advertisers definitely know what they are doing. I cannot drive by a Jeep lot and not want the 4-door Jeep Wrangler with custom tires, winch, hardtop, and every other feature available. But what will that Jeep do for me? Nothing. I realize this would only be a debt and the Jeep, though awesome, would only decrease in value and cost me hard-earned money I could be investing in IPAs.

This is where most people get in trouble with debt. They find ways to justify the purchase and the insane 0% interest for three years at $700 per month. But, before you ever purchase something without cash, ask whether it will generate income for you. If it won't, then wait until you have cash to buy it. It will save you a lot of grief down the road. You really don't *need* that Jeep Wrangler...and besides, I found out they are actually really loud when driving on the freeway.

So, what exactly is good debt? Good debt is debt used to invest in IPAs. This includes mortgages on rental properties, student loans (sometimes), business loans, and lower interest loan options to help you generate income. Again, in some cases, a vehicle would fit in this category as well. For example, if I am a contractor, a truck will make far more sense than a hybrid Prius. But be reasonable; ask yourself if you really need the new, fully-loaded Chevy Silverado Crew Cab or if a 3–5 year old version would serve your purpose just as well. Again, it is avoiding the shiny object syndrome so you can ultimately achieve your vision. "Things" are the best distraction from where you want to go.

Let's apply this to your life by looking at your current debt, which means ANY money you owe to someone else, and figure out how much of that is good debt according to our definition. I have provided an example below. Now let's put your debt in Worksheet 9. (Remember, this includes if you owe your brother $500 from 10 years ago.)

Total Debt/Good Debt = Good Debt ratio.

Remember, good debt must produce cash flow or help you produce significantly more cash flow.

Worksheet 9. Debt tracker to document total debt obligations.

Debts	Amount Owed	Good	Bad
1. *Chase Credit Card*	*$7,600.00*		X
2.			
3.			
4.			
5.			
6.			
7.			
8.			
9.			
10.			

Ideally, the amount of good debt would be near 100% but that is not always realistic. Honestly, when I did this exercise, I was hovering around 63%. Yes, I had mortgages on rental properties and student loans (again this is more of a gray area asset), but I also had high consumer debt like credit cards and car payments.

The last piece of advice: do not borrow more good debt than you can afford. This is the point where you become over-leveraged. I know it becomes tempting to borrow as much as a bank or investor will lend, but understand that the IPA may cover the debt now but what if it is vacant. Always consider the worst-case scenario to make sure you are covered. Rome wasn't built in a day and neither will your IPA empire. There will always be good deals out there. The moral of the story... Grow your IPAs slowly.

Bad Debt

Cue the Star Wars theme music when Darth Vader walks into a scene, and you immediately know that he is a bad guy. Bad Debt has a very similar theme song. Every time you get a pre-approval credit card letter in the mail, this theme song should start playing in your head.

So, what exactly is bad debt? It is most easily thought of as everything outside of what we just defined as good debt. Essentially, any debt that does not generate income or assist in helping you generate more income is bad debt. Common examples include credit cards, car loans, possibly mortgages, in-store credit cards, etc.

Robert Kiyosaki defines bad debt as, "Debt that makes you poorer." He goes even further saying, "I count the mortgage on my home as bad debt, because I'm the one paying on it. Other forms of bad debt are car payments, credit card balances, or other consumer loans" (Kiyosaki 2000).

The American spending culture is fueled by bad debt. Americans like to use their plastic. Like I mentioned above, the average American household with at least one credit card has nearly $15,950 in credit-card debt (in 2012), according to CreditCards.com (Bortz 2012). These interest rates vary but the average hovers near 17% interest.

It always begins with the justification that you will just pay off the balance at the end of the month, but more often than not, the time arrives and there is not enough cash to make the payment. Bad debt rears its ugly head in my life and I struggle to refrain from using it to get the $10 off my next plane flight.

I recommend having 1–2 credit cards that can be used only if your emergency savings is not enough. I would rather you use the credit card than incur the fees and outrageously high interest of payday loan lenders.

Eliminate Bad Debt

Your mission, if you choose to accept it, is to eliminate bad debt in your life. It costs you money every month, money that you could be putting towards productive assets. Similar to Dave Ramsey's *Debt Snowball* teachings, let's start with your smallest bad debt balance and work from there (Ramsey 2009).

How much can you afford to pay each month? Look at your discretionary income or the amount remaining after you fund your IPA account.

For a while, I could only afford the minimum payments each month. Be realistic with where you're at and set aside a fixed amount each month that just goes towards bad debt. Don't make double payments or additional principal payments on your good debt; just focus on bad debt for now. In Worksheet 10, list your bad debt below, starting with the lowest balance debt first, so we know what we are working with. (Add lines if you need to. I know I did.)

Worksheet 10. Debt analysis with minimum monthly payments.

Creditor	Balance	Minimum Monthly Payment
1. *Chase Credit Card*	*$3,500.00*	*$100.00*
2.		
3.		
4.		
5.		
6.		
7.		
8.		

Now I want you to log in to your online banking program and set up automatic payments to the lowest balance debt first. You are going to allocate the fixed amount you decided on above to come out of your bank account on the 5th of each month until the balance is paid off. This way it will be paid at the same time you are paying your monthly expenses.

You are then going to set up automatic minimum monthly payments for the other bad debt balances to be deducted on the same day. This will ensure that your payments are made on time and we can tackle your bad debt, one balance at a time.

Next, you are going to use a fixed amount (you decide on the number) of the remaining money after funding your IPA account to make an additional payment on the bad debt with the smallest balance. We want to focus on getting each debt paid down as soon as possible to move on to the next one.

The normal logic is to pay down the highest interest debt first, but finances are so much more mental than that. Let's say your highest interest debt balance is $15,000 at 15% interest and you can afford to pay $200 per month. It would take you 224 months and you would pay $29,638 in interest on top of the $15,000 in principal.

If you take 224 months (which is 18.6 years) to pay off your debt, I can guarantee you'll lose momentum and motivation to pay off this debt. Instead, by paying off the smaller balances, you create a behavior shift, instilling the confidence and the motivation to continue paying off the other debts as you see the positive effects of the debt paydown.

Remember, this is a marathon, not a sprint. Try to find ways to carve out an extra $100–$200 per month. The small steps you take today will benefit you in the long run and the more bad debts you get rid of, the more IPAs you can acquire. Credit Karma has a great calculator that can estimate your payoff period depending on monthly payments.

How to Deal with Student Loans

Then there are student loans, the proverbial elephant in the room. This form of debt definitely falls in the gray area between good and bad debt.

With the average student debt near $26,600, graduates are leaving college with a dark cloud that constantly hovers over them, rarely letting in light (Institute for College Access 2012). Millennials, though the most educated generation, are trying to make their way with a ball and chain hindering their advancement.

This debt can force you into a particular job or strip away any discretionary income that you could potentially invest. Though society has done away with debtor prisons, one can't help but feel shackled by this debt.

> ### Millennial Insight
>
> *I had $26,391 in student loan debt. It might as well have been $100,000. I wasn't sure how I was ever going to repay it. But, I started looking into forgiveness programs and found my employer offered a program. I now will have it paid off in less than 5 years!*
>
> Carolyn, 27

The topic of student loans is near and dear to my heart. I am going to preface this by saying that I had no prior education on loans and their impact on my financial life before I incurred my student debt. I attended a private undergraduate college with some scholarships and need-based grants, but mostly used student loans to get me through. I leisurely signed those thick documents, indenturing me to indebted servitude until those loans were paid back. The money almost didn't even seem real in my head at the time. $10,000 here, $20,000 there, and before I knew it, I was six figures in debt.

To add insult to injury, I decided to go to law school at another private institution and simultaneously pursue my MBA at the same institution. Oh yeah, I can't forget to throw in the semester abroad during law school where I studied in London, probably one of the most expensive cities in the world. In their defense, each institution I attended taught me important lessons, but those little paper diplomas I received paled in comparison to the bank notes I was faced with six months after I graduated.

Needless to say, I didn't really understand the concept of money during my college years. I was lucky if I had $100 in my wallet, let alone be able to wrap my brain around what $200,000 was. It might as well have been $1 million.

I have asked people to guess my total student debt and they usually start around the $75,000 range. I laugh and begin to dream what that would be like, gesturing with my index finger, pointing higher.

$100,000?

$150,000?

$200,000?

When I point higher still after that guess, their jaws drop and, in a state of shock, they usually just ask me point blank, "How much do you owe?"

I always try to keep my voice casual when I respond, "$230,000." I literally owe more than most people's mortgage for the education I received…and I'm not even practicing law!

Instead of dwelling on my number, I dealt with the debt and found my dream career, all while keeping the debt manageable and forgiven in less than 10 years. Yes, I said *forgiven*. Zero. Nada. No debt left.

Student loans can be daunting and overwhelming, but creating a manageable plan can make all the difference.

Dischargeable Circumstances

In true form, the first thing my heartless wife asked me upon my law school graduation was, "Do I have to pay your student loans if you die?"

I paused for second. "I actually don't know."

"You better check on that!" in a sarcastic, yet truly concerned, voice.

I did my research and found that unless she cosigned on the loans with me, she was not responsible to pay them if I died. (Though there could potentially be an issue since we live in Washington, a community property state… What's mine is yours, babe.) I found out that death was only one of a few ways to discharge my student loan debt. Since me dying was not really an option, I had to come up with the best way to repay it or have it forgiven.

Below is a list of dischargeable circumstances when you would no longer owe your remaining student loan debt:

1. If the school closes when you are attending or within 90 days of leaving it.
2. Bankruptcy (in rare cases).
3. Fraud from identity theft or false loan certification by the school.
4. Death…lucky me?!
5. Total and permanent disability, certified by a physician.

Since none of those options applied to me, I started by looking at programs and careers that offered loan forgiveness in industries I was interested in.

Forgiveness Programs

As I was sitting through another exit loan counseling workshop conducted by the "Loan Ranger," I realized that programs existed that would allow me to work in a field I would enjoy *and* help pay back my student loans.

My first thought was to join the military as a JAG officer, so I looked into military student loan forgiveness benefits. They have loan repayment for active duty health professionals and high school students now attending college. Then I saw the National Guard Student Loan Repayment option where I could work part-time and get repayment while serving our country.

National Guard Student Loan Repayment

<u>Overview:</u>	Loan forgiveness for enlisting in the National Guard for a minimum of 6 years. You have to meet certain qualifications, but it is a reserve position.
<u>Amount:</u>	$7,500 annually, with a $50,000 maximum forgiveness amount.
<u>Qualifying Loans:</u>	Stafford loans, Consolidation loans, Grad PLUS loans, Perkins loans.

Since I was not ready for a 6-year commitment, I looked into the Navy program, which had different benefits but required me to be active duty at some point.

Navy Loan Repayment Program

<u>Overview:</u>	Open to active duty borrowers who enlist for a minimum of 3 years.
<u>Amount:</u>	33 1/3% of the remaining principal balance or $1,500 (whichever is greater) per year, with a maximum of $65,000.
<u>Qualifying Loans:</u>	Stafford loans, Consolidation loans, Grad PLUS loans, Perkins loans.

Two of my brothers served in the military and I have always respected them for that and continue to value their service to our country, but even if I received that full amount, I would still owe over $150,000. (And my wife was casually mentioning divorce every time I mentioned the military.) I needed something larger or this student debt would never go away. I had always been interested in public interest work that helps build communities and works with the less fortunate, so the next program I looked into was in community services.

Segal AmeriCorps Education Award

<u>Overview:</u>	For service with the AmeriCorps program. For those of you not sure what this is, it is worth a look as you get practical experience in a field of interest to you while giving back to communities. You must sign up for this before you start serving as an AmeriCorps and it will be awarded upon completion.
<u>Amount:</u>	Up to $5,550 a year for 4 years. Your current loans are deferred during your service.
<u>Qualifying Loans:</u>	Stafford loans, Consolidation loans, Parent loans, Grad PLUS loans, Perkins loans, State-funded loans.

Again, with such a large debt amount, I needed to pursue something more lucrative and with better pay. The experience would have been beneficial, but I had to support a family at the same time. The next plan was referred by a friend that was a teacher; he thought I needed more school?!?!

Teacher Loan Forgiveness Program	
Overview:	Open to teachers that teach full-time for 5 consecutive years in a designated elementary or secondary school or educational service agency serving low-income families. There are more requirements if interested, but this is the major eligibility criterion.
Amount:	$5,000 a year or up to $17,500, depending on when the service began and what subject they teach.
Qualifying Loans:	Stafford Loans, Consolidation Loans.

I considered it for a moment, but realistically I could not endure more schooling to get my teaching license. I was not ready for another test. This idea eventually led me down a path towards the program I have committed to: Public Interest Loan Forgiveness.

Public Interest Loan Forgiveness	
Overview:	Eligible to persons that make 120 qualifying payments under the standard, income based, income contingent, or Pay as you Earn Repayment Plan. You must be working full-time (30 hours or more) at a public service or nonprofit organization when these payments are made. Only payments made after October 1, 2007 will qualify and it is not retroactive.
Amount:	*100% of the remaining outstanding balance* after 10 years and 120 eligible payments. These payments do not need to be made consecutively to qualify. But this is all or nothing. If you work 9 years and 11 months and never complete that last month, then you get $0 forgiven.
Qualifying Loans:	Direct Stafford Loans, Direct Parent and Grad PLUS loans, Direct Consolidation loans. You must consolidate into the Direct Loan program to qualify.
More Information:	https://studentaid.ed.gov/repay-loans/forgiveness-

Finally, I found a program that would take care of all of my debt and allow me to work in a field of interest while being able to pay the monthly payment and find some fulfillment in my work. Another financial beauty of this program is that the amount forgiven is not taxable like many other programs, so when you have made your 120th payment, your debt is forgiven from that point forward. The first eligible participants will be debt-free in 2017, so we will be able to see the impact of the program on the government's budget.

Repayment Plans

Next, I had to figure out what type of repayment plan would work best for my student debt. I have listed a description of each payment plan below:

Standard Repayment: Payments are a fixed amount of at least $50, calculated based on paying the loan off in 10 years. These are usually the highest monthly payments but you will incur the least amount of interest.

Graduated Repayment: Payments are lower at first and then increase (usually every two years) but are calculated based on paying the loan off in 10 years.

Extended Repayment: Payments may be fixed or graduated but are based on paying the loan off in 25 years. More interest is accrued but the monthly payments are lower.

Income-Based: Payments are based on a maximum monthly payment of 15% of your discretionary income. Discretionary income is calculated by the difference between your adjusted gross income and 150% of the poverty guideline for your family size and place of residence. Your payments change as your income changes and your debt is forgivable after 25 years. You MUST have a partial financial hardship to qualify. This will give you lower monthly payments until your income increases.

Pay as You Earn:	Payments are based on a maximum monthly payment of 10% of your discretionary income. Discretionary income is calculated by the difference between your adjusted gross income and 150% of the poverty guideline for your family size and place of residence. Your payments change as your income changes and your debt is forgivable after 20 years. You MUST have a partial financial hardship to qualify. This will give you lower monthly payments until your income increases, but it is only for borrowers on or after October 1, 2007.
Income Contingent:	Payments are calculated each year and are based on your adjusted gross income, family size, and the total amount of your Direct Loans. Your payments change as your income changes and your debt is forgivable after 25 years.
Income Sensitive:	Your monthly payment is based on your annual income, and your payment will adjust as your income changes. The term can be up to 10 years.

Since I had committed to the Public Interest Loan Forgiveness program, I decided it would be in my best interest to keep my monthly payment as low as possible. The program only requires that I make the "qualifying payment" for 120 months while working full-time at a public interest or nonprofit organization.

A "qualifying payment" includes the Income-Based Repayment Plan, Pay As You Earn Repayment Plan, Income-Contingent Repayment Plan, 10-Year Standard Repayment Plan, or any other repayment plan where your monthly payment amount equals or exceeds what you would pay under a 10-Year Standard Repayment Plan.

To maximize my forgiveness amount, I wanted to keep my payment as small as possible, especially since my income at my first nonprofit job was not something to write home about. So I opted for the Income Based Repayment plan and I continue to make those payments, counting down the days until that dark cloud no longer hovers over my head.

This is a much-needed program that encourages people to work in the public interest field. With salaries below market value, this program made the difference for me to stay in the public interest arena when all my friends told me to come over to the private sector.

What If I Don't Qualify?

You might be thinking, "This works great if you want to be a social worker or school teacher, but what about the rest of the world?" The short and simple answer is: you must work to repay your student loans. Keep in mind, lenders do offer deferments and forbearances if you are having trouble making your payments.

A deferment is "a period during which repayment of the principal and interest of your loan is temporarily delayed." You do not have to make payments during deferment, but for most loans (unsubsidized) you are responsible for the interest that accrues. Deferment is not automatic and you will need to contact your lender to request one.

If you are struggling to make a payment, forbearance allows "you to stop making payments or reduce your monthly payment for up to 12 months. Interest will continue to accrue on your subsidized and unsubsidized loans." There are both discretionary and mandatory forbearances, so check out this website to see if you qualify for either:

http://studentaid.ed.gov/repay-loans/deferment-forbearance.

If you can manage your payments, I would check with your employer to see if they offer student loan forgiveness programs (as it is not usually advertised.) Your HR representative would be able to tell you right away.

The only real perk to having student debt is that the interest you pay on your student loan may be deductible on your taxes. According to the IRS, "if your modified adjusted gross income (MAGI) is less than $75,000 ($155,000 if filing a joint return), there is a special deduction allowed for paying interest on a student loan (also known as an education loan) used for higher education." I know that may not seem like much, but it could save you some money come tax time.

I know this was a broad coverage of student loans, but the key is to be knowledgeable about programs designed to help alleviate some of your student loan debt. You signed on the dotted line, attended classes (maybe not all of them), and used the financial aid dollars at the college snack shop, so you are responsible for the debt. The key is to not let it define your life.

By understanding the repayment plans and forgiveness options, you don't have to be stuck in that dead-end job just to pay your student loans. Plus, more and more attention is being directed at student loans, and we could still see some reform coming down the line in the future.

Wealth Hack Tools

Student Aid

https://studentaid.ed.gov

This website has tons of information about student loans, forgiveness programs, and any other information you will need. You can fill out your FAFSA and get a better understanding of the student loans available.

StudentLoanHelp.org

Cost: FREE
http://studentloanhelp.org

StudentLoanHelp.org is the preferred nonprofit resource for borrowers challenged with excessive student loan debt to receive comprehensive financial counseling, education, and assistance.

Student Loan Forgiveness

Cost: FREE
http://www.staffordloan.com/repayment/forgiveness.php

This great site has options for different fields complete with information and what is required to qualify. It is very informative and can help you navigate through the available forgiveness programs.

ReadyForZero

Cost: FREE

The ReadyForZero app is a great tool for helping you reach debt-free status. This app helps you create a debt-repayment plan and track your progress as you go. When you sign up, simply add your credit card, student loan, and/or mortgage accounts to get started.

LAZ Lifestyle Moves

- Write down all debt and designate whether it is good debt or bad debt.
- Set up a plan to eliminate all bad debt that you currently have.
- If you have student loans, look into forgiveness programs and check with your employer for any student loan forgiveness programs.

Wrap Up

Debt is a double-edged sword. On one hand it can be the tool that gets you to the LAZ Lifestyle and on the other it can lead to dark time of being crushed under consumer debt. By understanding the difference between good and bad debt, you can work to eliminate the bad debt and use good debt to purchase IPAs. The beauty is that you can always change your circumstances. If you have tens of thousands of dollars of student loan debt or you just spent a lot on those college credit cards, you can start today to eliminate the high interest and take control again.

Advice From Millennials

Name: Ashley
Age: 30
Occupation/Job Title: Physician Assistant
Annual Income: $100,000
Family Size: 2
Where do you live? Seattle, WA
Do you currently own or rent your home? Owns

How many years of school do you have under your belt?

After elementary, junior high, and high school, I have a bachelor's degree and master's degree. That is 19.5 years total.

What did you go to school for? Was it worth it?

Master's in medical science, physician assistant studies. Yes, it was worth it; it's a good career with good compensation and job security.

Do you regret your decision to pursue education? Why?

I think everyone at some point second guesses their career choices and wonders what they are doing with their lives. But truthfully, no, I don't regret it. I get to take care of people and think critically everyday. That is fulfilling.

If you were going to sum up your educational experience in one word, what would it be? Why?

I loved being a student. My experience was great. I was blessed to be able to go to two fantastic universities for my bachelors and master's degrees. I am now riddled with debt, but I am still hopeful that it was all worth it.

Do you have more than $50,000 of school loans? If so, does it seem overwhelming? Why?

Yes, I have twice that much in debt. It is incredibly overwhelming. It feels like it will never get paid off, and despite making a good income, it never feels like I will catch up.

How do you manage your student loans?

At first I just paid my monthly minimum payments to the government banks and when I could I paid more. About a year ago, my grandfather-in-law gave me the money to pay off my loans, and then in return I would pay him back at a lower interest rate. This has worked out well and over the life of the loan I will save money. But many people aren't as lucky as I am and are saddled with ridiculous student loan interest rates.

If given the opportunity, would you go back for further schooling? Why?

Possibly. But at this point I don't know what more that would be.

Living at Zero

7
THE CREDIT GAME

Attempting to succeed without embracing the tools immediately available for your success is no less absurd than trying to row a boat by drawing only your hands through the water or trying to unscrew a screw using nothing more than your fingernail.

Richie Norton

A person's credit report is one of the most important tools consumers can use to maintain their financial security and credit rating, but for so long many did not know how to obtain one, or what to do with the information it provided.

Ruben Hinojosa

$9.81.

I was a sophomore in college and I remember checking my available credit on a card with a $4,500 limit to see only $9.81 left. Where had I spent it all?

Could it have been the groceries? *No.*

What about the books for school? *No.*

Maybe it was the horse I tried to buy with a cash advance (that's another story for another day) or the money I advanced off the card for partying Friday and Saturday night. Or, just maybe, it was all of this.

I treated my credit card like a bank account. I had maxed out every card I ever received. I was a perfect credit card customer.

I struggled to pay the bill each month and the times I wasn't able to cover it, I was greeted with late payment notices. On one particular occasion, my bill was $285 (which was just the minimum monthly payment) and I had a $20 bill left to my name. So, as any prudent 20-year-old boy would do, I doubled down on blackjack at a nearby casino, and you can probably guess what happened. Little did I know, this lifestyle would have a devastating long-term effect on my credit. I have been rebuilding it ever since.

Contrary to the story I just told you, credit, if used correctly, can be an invaluable tool. Without credit, it will be difficult to create the LAZ Lifestyle in a reasonable amount of time, as credit is a very important part of buying IPAs. You need banks, friends, and crowd funders to trust you and your credit score enough to lend you money. If you are like me in my college days, don't despair; the best part about credit is that it has short-term memory.

As we've established, I didn't understand the importance of a credit score on my life and I certainly did not know how to use credit properly. In this chapter, you will learn why you need credit and how to win at the credit game. I don't want you to fall victim to the same traps that I did. Even if you have bad credit or no credit, I can show you how to build your credit and have credit scores in the 700s.

Do You Really Need Credit?

We live in a credit-driven society where delayed gratification and cash has been cast aside for impulsive spending and the simple swipe of a card. In fact, it looks like we won't even need a plastic card pretty soon with the advances in smartphone technology.

The day I graduated from high school, I received three credit card offers in the mail and, of course, I opened all of them. I maxed out each card on rent-to-own furniture, gaming systems, and too many fun weekends to count. I never understood credit or how my irresponsible spending would affect me down the road.

When I think about it now, credit is like Dr. Jekyl and Mr. Hyde. One side offers the ability to leverage your current income and payment history to purchase IPAs and grow your net worth, but the other side traps the impulsive spender who wants toys and to have a good time.

Credit should only be used to grow your net worth!

Credit is not designed to help you take a vacation, buy a new boat, eat out every night, or any other guilty pleasure you succumb to. Credit card companies make billions of dollars on the fact that the vast majority of people will not pay their bill in full and can't control their spending habits. Sound familiar?

We could talk about return on investment all day but when you are paying 20–30% interest on your credit card, a 10% return on your 401k seems irrelevant. With that said, if you would rather have toys and things and are not interested in buying IPAs, you should do the following right now:

1. Dig through your drawers and find a pair of scissors (make sure they are sharp!).

2. Grab each of your credit cards out of your wallet/purse and set them on your dining room table.

3. Cue "Hit the Road Jack" on your Spotify station.

4. Cut up each card into the smallest pieces you can.

5. Throw the bits of plastic into the garbage. No more credit cards.

Simply use your debit card from this point forward. Oh, and you can skip to the next chapter. By getting rid of your credit cards, you will save yourself a lot of blood, sweat, tears, and money because the truth is: without the need for credit, your credit score is of very little importance. If you want to use credit responsibly to build your net worth, continue reading, and as I will show you how to win at the credit game.

Should I Use Credit?

Since you continued reading, I will assume you want to use credit to grow your net worth rather than complete the ritualistic cutting of the cards scenario. But, before diving into how to make credit work for you, you must truly understand the evil side of credit.

Credit can be a double-edged sword if not controlled. It can be your greatest asset and your worst nightmare. It can easily become a "rob Peter to pay Paul" situation with high interest rates that can swallow you whole, throwing whatever is left of you down a path of uncontrollable spending just to cover the minimum payments.

Recent studies found that people will spend more with a credit card compared to cash. Specifically, a Dunn and Bradstreet study found that people spend 12–18% more when using credit cards than when using cash (Hardekopf 2010). Even more impressively, McDonald's found that the average transaction rose from $4.50 to $7 when customers used plastic instead of cash (Polgar and Goldstein 2015).

There is something about handing over cold, hard cash that makes us think twice before making the purchase. After college, I spent two summers commercial salmon fishing in Alaska, and both summers my boat caught over 210,000 pounds of salmon. Every purchase I made when I got home involved me counting how many salmon that purchase had cost me. New shoes = 10 salmon; new car = 1000 salmon. Trust me, I put way more things back on the shelf when I looked at money this way.

Many financial gurus recommend not using credit at all or only in rare circumstances. This advice is usually targeted at people struggling with overspending or living outside of their means. Even if *you* are the person those financial gurus are targeting and your credit score is awful, here's the awesome thing about credit: no matter how bad it is now, you can always make it better. Regardless of whether you have bad credit or no credit, I will show you how to generate an excellent credit score. All it takes is persistence and time.

Credit can be the tool that grows your net worth and allows you to borrow money at ridiculously low rates. Since your credit score means so much, let's take a look at what it is right now and how we can get you the best score possible.

The Cost of Bad Credit

You may be thinking that your credit score doesn't mean much in the grand scheme of things. Well, let's look at how impactful a bad credit score really is (Table 4).

By simply having a better credit score, you can save thousands of dollars per year. That money can then be used to grow your net worth and can

Table 4. Examples of rate and terms for varying asset purchases.

For Credit Cards ...		
Credit Score	Interest Rate	One Year Interest Cost
Excellent	10.9%	$327
Fair	19.8%	$594
Poor	22.99%	$689
For Auto Loans ...		
Credit Score	Interest Rate	One Year Interest Cost
Excellent	2.64%	$437.98
Fair	6.14%	$480.27
Poor	9.42%	$522.08
For Mortgage Loans ...		
Credit Score	Interest Rate	One Year Interest Cost
Excellent	4.134%	$849
Fair	4.533%	$890
Poor	5.723%	$1018

directly impact your IPA bucket. Saving money is the reward for having good credit, a pretty worthwhile reward if you ask me.

You can use calculators like Loan Shark to illustrate the amount a 1% decrease in your interest rate can save you. You would be amazed with how a simple percentage can affect your overall debt payment. Now let's look at the rules to this credit game to see how to play.

Rules for the Credit Game

I am a very contextual person. You let me know the rules and what I need to do to be successful, and I will find a way to make it happen. My credit and credit score are no different.

Do you ever wonder why you even have a credit score or how that score is calculated? Basically, lenders are using an algorithm of historical financial events in your life and assessing whether you would be a good risk today. What is even more bizarre is that your income is not even calculated on your credit report to determine your ability to repay!

So, do you know your credit score? Wait. Let's start with an easier question. When was the last time you checked your credit report? For that matter, have you ever looked at your credit report?

Whitney and I used to apply the "out of sight, out of mind" approach to our credit. We couldn't pay our bills on time every month so we would rack up late payments and overdraft fees. It got so bad that I didn't even want to see my score. We had bounced several checks, over-drafted our accounts, and late payments were the new normal. I even found out that gas stations only ran your card for $1 when at the pump even if you filled the tank, so I would accept the $30 overdraft fee just to get a tank of gas. I am sure they have corrected that glitch by now, but by year's end we had paid over $500 in overdraft fees.

I am going to let you in on a life-changing secret, one I wish someone would have impressed upon me back then: check your credit report! You can't hide from it forever. The first step to building your credit score is to know what is on your credit report. You must actually look at it to know, go figure.

If you have never pulled your credit report, you are able to get it for free at www.annualcreditreport.com. You can get one free report per year from each of the three credit bureaus: Experian, Equifax, and TransUnion. It will not have a score attached but you can at least make sure that your report is accurate, as even the smallest mistake can cost you valuable points. (Of course, you have to pay to actually get your score).

Next, you must understand what kind of debt will be on your credit report. Not every bill you pay will be listed. The creditor must actually report your payments to the credit bureaus for the debt to show up on your report. Consequently, your rent and utility payments will not show up unless you are sent to collections, but your car payment, student loan payments, and credit cards will all be on there.

Fortunately, people have realized this flaw in the system and are currently creating programs to allow you to count your rent and utility payments on your credit report. But for now, we need to focus on the debt that will actually show up on your credit report, for it is important to know when we discuss buying a house or investment property.

Credit Score Parts

Perhaps most important when playing the credit game, you need to understand what makes up your credit score (Figure 4). Your credit score can range from 300–850 and is comprised of the following:

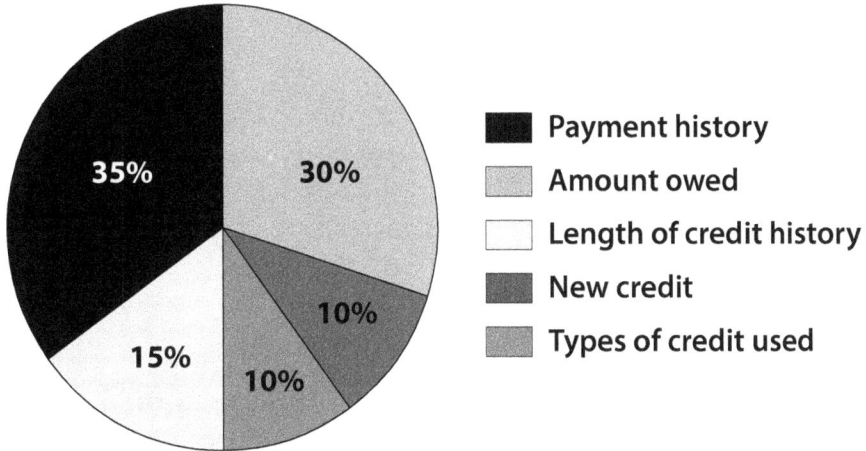

Figure 4. Credit score allocation chart.

Payment History

This is a big one. It equates to 35% of your credit score. Your payment history is composed of every payment reported, whether it was on time, late, or in default. Late payments can be a killer and should be avoided at all costs. Accounts that are sent to collections will remain on your credit report for seven years. The best piece of advice to increase your credit score is to simply start making on-time payments.

Amounts Owed

Better known as credit utilization rate, this is the amount you owe on your credit cards relative to the limits on those cards. It comprises 30% of your credit score, and is important to keep an eye on. Balances over 70% of your total credit limit on any card bring your score down considerably. The blow to your score gets less with balances at 50%, and ideally you should keep your balance under 30% of your limit.

For example, if you have 3 credit cards with limits of $5,000 each and you are carrying balances of $3,000 on each card, you would have a credit utilization rate of 60% ($9,000 ÷ $15,000 = 60%). In order to get maximum points toward your credit score for this category, you must stay below 30%.

Length of Credit History

The amount of time you have had credit makes up 15% of your score. The assumption behind this category is that by having credit longer you have become more responsible. So they are ultimately looking to see how long you have had credit established.

For this reason, it is a good idea to keep your oldest credit card account open even if it is that high interest card that arrived in the mail the day you left for college. Keep the card and call the company to negotiate a lower rate. This will maintain a longer length of credit history and increase your score.

New Credit or Inquiries

Are you always tempted to open those credit cards at Nordstrom or GAP to save 10% on your purchase? Every time you apply for new credit, it is a ding on your credit report. It is a small ding, but small dings can add up if you continue to try and access credit in a short amount of time. New credit only makes up 10% of your score but if you are going for the best score possible, keep an eye on your credit applications.

A small caveat is when you are checking your free credit report or working with a credit counselor, this activity does not hurt your credit score. They call it a soft credit pull.

Types of Credit

The different types of credit you have make up 10% of your score as well. This category is easy to get maximum points.

There are two types of credit: installment and revolving. Installment credit refers to fixed payment loans, such as your mortgage or a car payment. Revolving credit refers to changing payments, such as credit cards. To get all of the points here, you need to make sure you have at least one of each.

For example, a program offered at a local credit union gave a $300 loan with a monthly repayment of $14.97. The $300 was used to get a $300 secured credit card. This instantly provided an installment *and* revolving credit line. By making on-time payments, this little card had the ability to dramatically increase someone's credit score. Clients with no credit score have built their score to over 700 because of this little tool.

Important Credit Caveats

Much like any great game ever invented, there are some interesting caveats within the rules of credit. Here are just a couple quirks to be aware of:

1. Let's say you are shopping for a home. Normally, each time a lender checks your credit report, it would be a hard inquiry and actually hurt your credit score. But, understanding the importance of shopping for the best rate, if you apply at multiple lenders in a short time frame, all of the inquiries are counted as a single inquiry, thus minimizing the effect on your credit.

2. Closing a credit card can actually hurt your score. The reason lies in credit utilization rate, which takes all of your credit balances owed and divides the total by the overall limits. When you get rid of a card, it reduces the limits while keeping the balances the same, thus increasing your credit utilization rate. However, it is only a minor ding and shouldn't prevent you from eliminating credit cards if needed.

3. Paying off your cards will not improve your score! I thought for sure this would be seen as a good thing in the credit world, but unfortunately it has no benefit unless it lowers your credit utilization rate.

4. If you can't pay down your credit cards, the best way to maximize your credit utilization rate is to evenly distribute balances among your different credit cards rather than carry a large balance on one card.

5. Every time you apply for credit it hurts your score. Again, it's not a huge ding, but that new car financing application, credit card application, or Home Depot in-store card all add up and are seen as "hard pulls" on your credit.

6. Seeking assistance from a credit counseling service will not hurt your FICO score. It is seen as a "soft pull" on your credit, similar to accessing your free report online.

How To Improve Your Credit

Now that we know the rules and guidelines, let's look at how to win the credit game. Improving your credit should be a high priority. But remember, it takes time to improve your score, so not everyone will have an immediate change.

Below are six basic steps to better credit:

1. Pull your credit report. Check it for free every four months. (Just pull your free report from a different credit bureau each time.)

2. Negotiate and correct any errors on your credit report.

3. Focus on making your monthly payments on time.

4. Make sure none of your credit card balances are over 30% of the card limit. If they are, follow the debt repayment plan we set up in the previous chapter.

5. Do not apply for more credit or close any accounts.

6. Make sure you have revolving and installment credit. If you do not have a credit score, open a secured credit card with a limit of at least $300 with a local credit union or bank.

Let's look into specifics on the steps above.

Step 1: Pull your credit report.

As mentioned above, by law, you are entitled to one free report from each credit bureau per year. This free report can only be accessed at www.annualcreditreport.com. If you mistype that address by even one letter, it takes you to a pay-for-your-score site. Avoid doing that unless you want to see your score as well.

There are more and more credit monitoring sites that you can use to keep an eye on your score. On Credit Karma, you can get an estimated score for free and it allows you to see anything new that comes on your report and track your progress. When looking at your report you want to make sure that the credit information being reported is correct, as it directly impacts your score.

Step 2: Negotiate any errors on your credit report.

Once you have your report, scan the items listed and search for any errors or fraudulent charges. Believe it or not, most reports contain errors.

Since your credit report has the information lenders will use to calculate your score, one key area to focus on is late payments. Make sure there are no late payments incorrectly listed for any of your accounts and that the amounts owed for each of your open accounts is correct. If you find errors on any of your reports, dispute them immediately with the credit bureau and reporting agency. The only way to fix any errors on your credit report is to contact the credit bureau that is showing erroneous information.

Experian	
Online:	https://www.experian.com/consumer/cac/InvalidateSession.do?code=CDIRESELLER&rid=R004
Equifax	
Online:	https://www.ai.equifax.com/CreditInvestigation/home.action
TransUnion	
Phone:	1.800.916.8800
Mail Address:	TransUnion Disputes 2 Baldwin Place P.O. Box 1000 Chester, PA 19022
Online:	http://www.transunion.com/corporate/personal/creditDisputes.page

Above is the contact information and website for each bureau so you can follow the process of disputing any errors if need be. Make sure to track your activity, as credit bureaus have been known to lose information.

Step 3: Make your monthly payments on time.

It is important to remember that making your monthly payments on time makes up the largest percentage of your score. According to www.myfico.com, "delinquent payments, even if only a few days late, and collections can have a major negative impact on your FICO score. The longer you pay your bills on time after being late, the more your FICO score should increase. Older credit problems count for less, so poor credit performance won't haunt you forever. The impact of past credit problems on your FICO score fades as time passes and as recent good payment patterns show up on your credit report." The sooner you can establish a good payment history the better. Your goal should be to minimize and eventually eliminate late payments in order to maximize your score.

This concept goes back to our discussion about automating everything. If you are paying your bills automatically, it will be difficult to miss a payment, plain and simple. There are several apps you can use to remind you about payment dates for your bills, and if for some reason you can't make a payment, contact your creditor. Silence is never the best option. They may be able to work with you if you just communicate with them. If you do not let your creditor know you aren't making a payment (regardless of the reason), you can be sent to collections, which remains on your credit report for seven years. Not good.

In summary, pay your bills on time and if you can't, call your creditors immediately to work something out. Remember, they want your payment probably as much as you don't want a late payment on your credit report.

Step 4: Reduce your credit utilization rate.

You want to keep your total balances at or below 30% of your total credit limit. When tallying your score, the algorithm will aggregate the total to get this percentage. The best way to improve your credit utilization rate is to pay down balances to below that 30% level. Do not leave one card that is maxed out while the rest of your cards have small balances, as the maxed out card will hurt your score.

For a short-term plan to boost your score, make sure you do not close any credit cards as your overall limit will decrease (which will increase your utilization rate and decrease your score.)

Step 5: Do not close or open new accounts.

This advice is most applicable when you are trying to improve your credit score. If you have time before you plan to make a purchase using credit, then these small dings on your credit report should be of no significance.

Just know that your credit utilization rate might be affected when you close an account.

Step 6: Ensure you have different types of credit.

As previously discussed, you want to have a good mix of revolving and installment credit. According to www.myfico.com, "In general, having credit cards and installment loans (and paying timely payments) will rebuild your credit score. Someone with no credit cards, for example, tends to be a higher risk than someone who has managed credit cards responsibly. Note that closing an account doesn't make it go away. A closed account will still show up on your credit report, and may be considered by the score."

By maintaining this mix of credit, you will watch your credit score grow. Just make sure to be responsible with the credit and don't just open new lines, as it may affect your score.

Dealing with Debt Collectors

In the unfortunate event that you get sent to collections, here are a few tips on how to deal with debt collectors.

First, take a deep breath. You have protection under the Fair Debt Collections Practices Act (FDCPA) and the process will be much easier if you understand your rights.

1. **Get everything in writing.** If you get a call, ask the debt collector to send you the information in writing, either through snail mail or email. Under FDCPA, within five days of initially contacting you, they are required to send you a written notice with the amount you owe, the name of the creditor, and what you should do if you don't owe on that debt. It is important to not admit that you owe the debt on the phone. By admitting to the debt on the phone, you can accidentally restart the statute of limitations (two years), or basically the amount of time the creditor legally has to collect on the debt. Most importantly, make any dispute about the debt in writing. According to FDCPA, if a collection agency doesn't respond within 30 days of stating you do not owe the debt, then they can no longer contact you.

2. **Keep tedious records.** Make sure to start a file and track every step of the process. Print copies of the letters you send, start a log of any phones calls or messages. Try to make brief notes about each conversation, when it was, and who you talked with. Keep any and all letters, faxes, or emails that you receive. *Note: Send everything via certified mail. Collection agencies lose a lot of documents frequently.*

3. **What debt collectors can't do.** The FDCPA restricts what debt collectors can say or do, which include:
    - Using abusive or obscene language.
    - Harassing you with repeated calls.
    - Calling before 8 AM or after 9 PM (local time), unless you agree.
    - Calling you at work if you have asked them to stop.
    - Talking to anyone but you or your attorney about your debt.
    - Misrepresenting the amount of your debt.
    - Falsely claiming to be an attorney or a law enforcement official.
    - Falsely claiming to be a credit bureau representative.
    - Threatening to sue you unless they actually plan to take legal action.
    - Threatening to garnish wages or seize property unless they actually intend to do it (Fair Debt Collection Practices Act 1978).

    (Make notes of any violations of the list above.)

4. **Keep it simple.** You do not need to become friends with the debt collectors. Say only what is needed, and, again, request all information in writing.

5. **Negotiate.** If you do owe the debt, try to negotiate with the debt collector. Likely they bought your debt for pennies on the dollar and are willing to take less just to get some money from you. Gerri Detweiler, co-author of *Debt Collection Answers: How to Use Debt Collection Laws to Protect Your Rights* has a suggestion for you. He suggests you ask the debt collector if they would do what is called a "payment for deletion."(Detweiler and Reed 2015). This means that the past due debt would be removed from your credit report for payment in full. "The debt collector would contact the credit bureaus directly to remove the debt," Detweiler says. "If you're lucky enough to get a debt collector to agree to a pay-for-deletion (deal), get it in writing in advance" (Detweiler and Reed 2015).

Removing a negative account from your report should increase your credit score.

Identity Theft

As of February 6, 2014, identity theft hits a new victim every two seconds (Ellis 2014). That is a record number of people whose identity has been compromised, and the numbers just keep climbing. With more and more consumers shopping online, the convenience opens the door even wider for identity theft. Just recently, Home Depot and Target had their systems hacked exposing millions of consumers' credit card information.

I don't want to scare you from buying online, I just want you to be aware and ready to act if you notice something wrong on your credit report. Bank of America put together a detailed checklist of what to do if you ever suspect you're a victim of identity theft:

- Contact all of your financial institutions immediately so they can protect your existing accounts either by closing them or by adding passwords. Be sure to check every account at every company to see if you do not recognize any of the transactions.

- Contact the three major credit bureaus listed below to place a fraud alert on your credit file. The fraud alert requests creditors to contact you before opening any new accounts. You also can order a credit report to identify any additional fraudulent activity.

  Equifax 1.800.525.6285
  Experian 1.888.397.3742
  Trans Union 1.800.680.7289

- Contact every company that has a fraudulent account in your name (including, if necessary, phone companies and other utilities) and have them freeze the account.

- Keep good records, including copies of every communication with creditors and credit reporting agencies as you try to repair the problem.

- File a police report. Get a copy of the report to submit to your creditors and others that may require proof of the crime.

- File a complaint with the Federal Trade Commission (FTC). The FTC maintains a database of identity theft cases used by law enforcement agencies for investigations. Trained counselors are available to help victims (Bank of America 2016).

There are several sites such as Lifelock that can monitor your credit and insure against fraud for a monthly fee. They estimate it can take you 33 hours to resolve an identity theft issue so the monthly fee may actually be worth it.

By keeping an eye on your credit report you can monitor your credit for free with notification if there are any unusual spending patterns from Mint.com, Credit Karma, or Quizzle.

Common Questions Worth Answering

1. **Why is my score referred to as a FICO score?**

   FICO stands for the Fair Isaac Corporation, which developed the algorithm that generates your score.

2. **I applied for a car loan and they told me I don't have a credit score. Why?**

   You have little or no credit history to generate a score. Simply opening a low limit credit card and making on-time payments should have a drastic effect on your credit and provide you with a great score.

3. **I pay on my cell phone each month. Does my phone bill affect my credit score?**

   Generally not. Your bill is not reported to credit bureaus unless you are sent to collections. Don't let this happen.

4. **Does closing or cancelling a credit card help or hurt my credit score?**

   Too often people think that if you cancel or close a credit card that it will help your score, but remember it decreases your credit utilization rate which affects your score. This is a small ding on your credit, so in the long run it won't hurt unless you have had that credit card for a long time or the credit limit is high which helps your credit utilization rate.

5. **If I pay off a collection account, will it increase my score?**

   Unfortunately, it won't. All collection accounts stay on your report for seven years from the original delinquency date. The only way to get it removed from your report is by negotiating with the collection agency to pay in exchange for a deletion on your credit. Basically, you pay a negotiated amount and, in exchange, the creditor takes it off your credit report as it reflects as paid. (Always get these in writing!)

6. **I just got to college with no credit and no job, how can I build my credit?**

   I would recommend getting a secured credit card from your local credit union or bank. Basically, you give them a set dollar amount that is held in a secure account and the bank or credit union authorizes a credit with that limit. It can be a great way to build credit and learn to use credit responsibly.

7. **If I co-sign on a loan, will it help my credit score?**

   It depends. If you have no credit, you can benefit from positive payments and types of credit on your report. But remember, if the person stops paying, you also can get the negative effect as well. But for those looking for credit, it can be a good way to start building credit.

LAZ Lifestyle Moves

Take the following steps to check and fix your credit:

1. Pull your credit report. Check it for free every 4 months (one report from each credit bureau).

2. Negotiate and correct any errors on your credit report.

3. Focus on making your monthly payments on time.

4. Make sure none of your credit card balances are over 30% of the card limit. If they are, just follow the debt repayment plan we set up in the previous chapter.

5. Do not apply for more credit or close any accounts. We want to build your score.

6. Make sure you have revolving (e.g., credit cards) and installment (e.g., car payment) credit. If you do not have a credit score, open a secured credit card of at least $300 with a local credit union or bank.

Wealth Hack Tools

Credit Karma

Cost: FREE

Most sites on the Internet will charge you to see your credit score. But Credit Karma allows you to accurately track your credit, ensure no unknown activity is happening, and watch your credit score go up! The app provides notifications when something important happens on your credit report and automatically updates every two weeks. It also has a handy report card that shows where your credit stacks up against the averages.

Quizzle

Cost: FREE

Quizzle is the only place on the web where you can get a free VantageScore credit score and an Equifax credit report – every six months. You won't find this combination anywhere else on the web. Also, when they pull your credit report it's considered a soft inquiry, which means it will not hurt your score.

Not only do they provide you with a credit score and report every six months with your free Quizzle account, they also provide other valuable freebies including credit card recommendations, home loan recommendations, a free home value estimate, and updates to all of your credit builder tools.

Myfico

Cost: FREE (but requires myFICO account to operate

The FICO score is the standard measurement that lenders use to assess your creditworthiness. This app allows you to view and monitor your FICO score with full credit reports from all three credit bureaus. You have a lot of options with this app, including the ability to set targets, track changes in your credit, and get notifications when something fraudulent happens on your credit so that you can act quickly. They even include educational content so you can become more familiar with credit and how it works. You will need a myFICO account to access these benefits, which will cost you $4.95 the first month, and then $14.95 per month.

> **Loan Shark —Loan Calculator**
>
> Cost: FREE
>
> Loan Shark is one of the best credit apps available and suited for those looking at car shopping, loan shopping, or just looking for ways to save money. It allows you to look at different rates and their payoff timelines to see where you get the best bang for your buck. I use this app to look at how much I need to pay per month on a loan in order to pay it off in a certain amount of time.
>
> For example, you can calculate the effect of paying an additional payment each year on your mortgage, or how much in interest you will pay on that car loan, or how long it will take to pay off those credit cards. This handy app can save you hundreds of dollars!

Wrap Up

Now you know how to win at the credit game. Remember, only use credit to increase your net worth. Credit used any other way can be destructive and endorse a lifestyle you can't sustain. Make sure that you keep an eye on your credit report and work to keep that score as high as possible, so it is there when you need to start purchasing IPAs.

Advice from Millennials

Name: Jane
Age: 26
Occupation/Job Title: Individual Investor Specialist
Annual Income: $40,000
Family Size: 1
Where do you live? Des Moines, IA
Do you currently own or rent your home? Rent

What's your credit score? When was the last time you checked your credit score?

770 according to www.creditsesame.com, updated on September 4, 2014.

How many credit cards do you have? Do you pay the balance each month?

One credit card. I pay the full balance the majority of the time and when I don't pay the full amount I'll pay over the minimum.

Do you believe there is such a thing as "good debt"? Why?

Yes, I don't believe that debt is inherently all good or all bad. How we use or abuse debt is what makes it good or bad. For example, purchasing a home is looked at as a smart financial decision, and as long as you're purchasing a home within your means and can afford the payments, I would consider that a good use of debt. Also, this decision could potentially have a huge impact in increasing your credit score, assuming you don't become delinquent on your mortgage.

In your opinion, how important is your credit score in becoming financially stable? Why?

It is an important factor, but it is not the most important piece of someone's financial picture. Taking a look at someone's whole financial picture is much more important than just taking into consideration their credit score. Credit score essentially evaluates someone's ability to pay debts on time and manage their debt load. It doesn't evaluate someone's ability to save, invest, career growth, their financial education, or knowledge.

Some financial gurus recommend paying cash for everything and not using credit, do you agree? Why or why not?

I agree and disagree; this is a difficult one because some individuals can handle credit and some cannot. For individuals that tend to abuse their credit cards and have a tendency to overextend themselves on credit, I would recommend them paying cash for everything. You also have to take into consideration an individual's personal goals. If someone wants to own their own home someday, the chances of them being able to pay for their home in cash is very unlikely.

The fact is that credit is still widely used to purchase a home, get a job, even to rent an apartment. Paying cash for some things is a great idea, but in reality, avoiding credit altogether may hinder some individuals from achieving certain financial goals.

As a financial advisor, do you have to discuss client's credit when looking at long-term goals? Why or why not?

I'm technically not a financial advisor, but if I were I would discuss a client's credit only if credit scores would impact one of their long-term goals. Debts are something that can impact a client's long-term goal, so it would be appropriate to discuss the subject with them.

My friend has a lot of debt. What is the best way to help?

Make a realistic plan. Dave Ramsey's snowballing debt concept can be very effective for someone that is motivated and disciplined enough to stick with this plan. The other key factor is making sure this is doable in their budget. If someone is struggling to pay their rent or pay for food, other issues need to be addressed before the debt, especially if it's unsecured debt. Prioritizing debts and making a plan that works with your budget is essential.

What's the single best way to rebuild your credit? Why?

Paying on time and in full, assuming you have credit cards and don't abuse them. These two factors alone make up 65% of someone's credit score. Also, checking your credit report annually is very important because there could potentially be incorrect information on your report that could be negatively impacting your score. Not checking your report at least yearly could have negative impacts.

What single piece of financial advice has made the largest impact in your life?

Simplicity. Our culture tends to over complicate things and purchase things that aren't really necessary. Simplify your budget and don't purchase items you don't need.

What advice do you have for people trying to build or repair their credit?

Patience. Rebuilding credit doesn't happen overnight; it takes a lot of time and effort. Make a plan and stick to it, and in the long run if you are doing positive steps to improve your credit, it will pay off.

8
JUST MAKE MORE MONEY

Our success and potential is not determined by talent or ability, knowledge or money, race or gender, or even circumstance or setting – it is created, developed, and determined from within ourselves.

Matthew V. Toone

Everyone is a genius. But if you judge a fish on its ability to climb a tree, it will live its whole life believing that it is stupid.

Albert Einstein

I truly believe that within each person is the ability to become great. Despite backgrounds, experience, skills, talents, or disabilities, we all can change our current situation to do something better with our lives. The LAZ Lifestyle builds the foundation for your financial freedom on your most important asset: YOU!

Think back to those early jobs or mindless chores. My first jobs were rock-picking endless fields for my grandparents, working in apple orchards in 100-degree weather, cleaning out horse stables at 4:00 am, and gillnet fishing for salmon in Alaska. There are two ways to look at these jobs: I could hate each job or I could learn from each job. These jobs taught invaluable lessons of fortitude, entrepreneurism, hard work, and ultimately provided the motivation to look for a better way to make a living.

After researching and reading every personal finance book I could get my hands on, I consistently found that wealthy people didn't focus on saving in order to become wealthy; rather they focused on making more money and having their money work for them through IPAs.

To be honest, the idea of my money working for me was laughable. I was raised to believe that if I work hard, I can achieve whatever I set my mind to. The issue was no matter how hard I worked, I could never save up enough money to purchase IPAs. I quickly did the math on how long it would take me to save enough money to buy real estate in Spokane, WA, where housing prices are far below the national average. It still did not look good. It would take me almost three years at my (then) current salary to come up with a down payment to responsibly purchase a home. More out of necessity, I quickly realized that I needed to shift my focus from *saving* money to *making* money to speed up the timeline! The rest is history.

I want to clarify, I am not saying that saving money is bad; I just think we spend so much time focusing on saving that we stop looking for new ways to make money and challenge ourselves to grow and invest in our personal development.

Focus on Making More Money

One of my good friends always says, "Most people miss an opportunity because it is dressed in overalls and is hard work." We want things the easy way, a get-rich-quick plan that requires the least amount of work to get the most reward. But the truth is financial freedom takes sacrifice and tons of hard work to accomplish. There is a reason not everyone is financially free.

The LAZ Lifestyle requires a pivotal shift in the way you think about finances. I want you to stop focusing on simply keeping the money you do have and start focusing on the skills and talents you have that can make you more money. Stop thinking of how much money you need to save to purchase that IPA and look instead at how much you need to make.

I have heard it analogized with football in that making money is the offense and saving is your defense. Both are needed but when we only focus on one it makes it difficult to win the game (unless you are the 2012 Baltimore Ravens!).

Much of the financial education out there today focuses on savings, and rightfully so. Americans have a spending problem. Delayed gratification has been thrust aside for immediate results. Look at coaches these days in both college and pro-level sports. If you have back-to-back losing seasons, you are in jeopardy of losing your job. Funny, coach Mike Krzyzewski of the Duke Blue Devils is one of the greatest college basketball coaches ever, but in his first three seasons at Duke he was 38-47, not even winning half of his games (ACC Media Guide 2008). It would be interesting to see how he would have faired in today's society.

The prevalent goal of contemporary financial education is teaching you to be responsible with the money you do have. It never empowers you to develop your potential to make more money to attain financial freedom. But financial freedom only comes when you have sufficient passive income to cover your expenses so you are not reliant on employment to pay your bills. It would be hard to save your way to financial freedom (Hall 2015).

> ## Millennial Insight
>
> *Think about this – if a person makes $50k after taxes, the most that person can ever save in any given year is $50k. They can't save a penny more because they haven't earned a penny more. On the other hand, a person who is focused on building additional streams of income, whether they be passive or active, has unlimited potential in terms of the amount they can save ... The possibilities are endless for the person focused on expanding their annual income by developing diverse streams of income.*
>
> Brandon, 35

When you shift your focus to making money, you start to find opportunities all around you in small jobs, freelance or contract work, technical services, and many other ways to leverage your education and experience to generate more and more passive income. You are smart, talented, and unique. You have all of the tools, now let's put them to work.

Value of Multiple Income Streams

"What is an extra $1,000 a month going to do for me?" Let me tell you, it is so much more than you think.

Rather than rely on retirement accounts alone or some pension, Whitney and I have made it a priority in our life to develop multiple income streams that continue to generate income well into the future. Right now we have seven different streams including regular employment, photography business, photo booths, rental properties, realtor, business partnerships, and long-term real estate notes. This means that if any individual source fails, we have other ones to get us through.

Financial freedom is a daunting goal. Just thinking of the amount of money you will need can be overwhelming, especially when you're just beginning this journey. By diversifying your sources of income, you become more resilient to downturns in the market and have more options to increase funding of your IPA bucket for creating more passive income.

As you may have noticed, most of our current income streams are active income. The reality is that the fastest way to financial freedom is a mix of active and passive income, even if it is just a small additional amount of active income each month. It is important to understand the impact of bringing in an additional $1,000 per month and the effect it has on your bottom line. It might not seem like a lot, but it is difficult to generate that much income in that time period simply through investment vehicles, especially if you're already holding down a full-time job. For example, if you have your money in a savings account and were lucky enough to earn 1% interest on it, you would need to have $1,200,000 just to collect $1,000 per month. Similarly, if you have it in an investment that earns 10% interest, you would need to invest $120,000. But if you just find an additional income stream, you can do it in a few hours per week and with little or no money on your end.

Thus, earning extra income is the fastest way to have more money in your pocket. This sounds like a totally obvious statement, yet few people actually consider it, let alone *do* it. Of course you have to work for the money, but you would be surprised with the ways you creatively develop income streams that you can actually be passionate about.

Again, creating and maintaining various income sources does take time and work. Start by looking at replacing something in your life that does not create value with one activity that generates more income or develops your knowledge on a topic you are passionate about. For example, Whitney and I try to limit the amount of television we watch — you'd be amazed at how much time this frees up — and are always looking for opportunities to add another stream of income. You might find yourself working nights and weekends here and there in addition to working your day job, but remember, be uncomfortable now so you can be comfortable later.

Get to $10,000!

"Why $10,000?" Let me explain.

I was looking back on my journey at the point where I knew financial freedom was possible. It was the point when we had reached a net zero net worth and had $10,000 in our bank account. At that instance, the hard work and sacrifice was visible on our bank statement. We were so used to a life where we thought in $100 increments and that was our reality affecting our money mindset. We added a few income streams and we started to think in $1,000 increments. With the addition of some rentals and a better full-time job, we now thought in $10,000 increments. Since we made it that far, there is no reason we can't be thinking in terms of $100,000 increments. The $10,000 hurdle is not easy. You cannot just sacrifice for a couple months; it takes a shift in lifestyle and mindset to get to the $10,000 line.

I have challenged several clients that if they could just come up with $10,000, I would partner with them on an investment property. You know how many of them have taken me up on that offer? Zero. Zilch. Nada. They were so motivated to purchase IPAs and live the LAZ Lifestyle, but when the rubber hit the road, they were not willing to sacrifice and make changes in their life to save and earn their way to $10,000.

Now for some people, $10,000 is easy. I applaud you. But for you, I challenge you to make that number $50,000. It needs to be enough money that requires you to make a lifestyle shift. Now, let's look at ways to develop your potential and get to $10,000.

The Next Donald Trump

I have invested years of my life and hundreds of thousands of dollars into an education for a career I wasn't even sure that I wanted. For all of you experiencing my same remorse, we have a WMA (Wrong Majors Anonymous) meeting the third Friday of each month.

There are a select few out there who actually stuck with their college career path, love what they do, and can see doing it the rest of their life. To the other 99% of the population, how do you change things? You are blessed with a set of skills and talents that make you unique. Your education, experience, and network equip you with the necessary skills to start making more money. We just need to start by identifying them, writing them down, and assessing how they will work for you.

For example, I was working at a local nonprofit and Whitney had just started her Master's in Teaching (yes, another investment in education) and all of her classes were at night. I would sit at home and scour Zillow and send house options to friends who were looking to purchase a home. So, I decided to do a skill and resource assessment to see what opportunities I could pursue. When I did this exercise I noted the following:

1. JD/MBA
2. Licensed to practice law in Washington
3. Experience renovating homes
4. Passion for finding real estate deals
5. Experience working with people
6. Training and experience writing (specifically grant writing)
7. Local connections to different industries
8. Experience starting new businesses

Whitney quickly suggested I should become a realtor. I looked into the requirements and found that they waived all of the classes because of my law degree and I just had to take the exam. The following week, I signed up, took the exam and passed. I was ready to be the next Donald Trump!

Prior to that point, the thought of finding part-time or supplemental work seemed overwhelming because, honestly, I was busy enough with my full-time job and wasn't sure where to look. But by identifying the skills I already had and understanding what I was passionate about, I was able to narrow down the options and have a focused search for opportunities to generate additional income. What skills do you have? List them in Worksheet 11.

Worksheet 11. List of skills to generate additional income.

1. _____

2. _____

3. _____

4. _____

5. _____

Are there moneymaking opportunities that fit both your passions and your skills? Remember to think creatively about your options. Can you build an amazing birdhouse? Let's sell it on Etsy or eBay. Can you write like John Grisham? Then see if there are contract or freelance work opportunities out there. Are you an automotive genius? Let's see if you can't moonlight in auto repair or fix up old cars and sell them.

You get my point. Every skill and passion can be turned into something that generates income. It just takes some imagination. Remember, money is just an exchange for value. Create value and you will make money.

For example, there is a website called Zaarly that connects people offering random services (like walking a dog, being a personal assistant for a day, giving guitar lessons, etc.) with customers that are in need of the service. With today's technology there are limitless opportunities to find additional income. Start small and grow.

Invest in Yourself

Maybe you completed this skills and resource assessment and found that you lack the education or experience or network to do anything else. Don't worry; Rome wasn't built in a day. You have time to start and begin educating yourself on areas of interest.

A wise person once asked me what I thought was the greatest investment, one that can withstand any recession and exponentially increase your income.

I responded, "Real estate of course because you can still have cash flow in a recession, it appreciates in value, you get great tax savings that directly affect your bottom line…" (It was a long winded answer.)

"Nope," he responded.

"It must be stocks then because of their historical gain over time. Or maybe it is gold or silver."

He shook his head. "The greatest investment is in yourself."

"What? I have the student loans to prove that it was not a good investment."

"The bank can take back your real estate. The stock market can crash. But no one can take away what you have learned."

This was an important lesson for me. It reinforced the power of education and knowledge. Those diplomas on the wall have gotten me to this point and no one can ever take that away.

Always challenge yourself to find new educational opportunities through secondary education, local classes, online classes, subscriptions or any other medium on topics that interest you. This is where you can continue to grow and learn.

Start by contacting your local community college for available classes or look online at www.udemy.com or The Khan Academy to find topics of interest and spend 30 minutes a day reading articles or watching videos. Colleges and universities are offering more online classes for you to get an education or even certifications. You will find that 30 minutes turns into one hour, then two. Through education, your passion may grow.

What Do You Want to Be When You Grow Up?

The infamous question we are all asked from a young age: what do you want to be when you grow up? As kids, we probably responded with ambitious jobs, such as an astronaut, the President of the United States, a dancer, firefighter, and the list of amazing opportunities goes on and on. But as we get older, something (and I'm not sure what it is) tells us it's too hard or unrealistic to be any of those things, so we become sales consultants, bank tellers, and any other run-of-the-mill job you think should be plugged into this list.

Don't get me wrong, I am not saying these jobs are any less admirable, but when we were growing up they weren't what we dreamed about becoming. You wanted to be a cowboy not a bank manager, don't kid yourself.

Even in our adult lives, the first question most people will ask you is: what do you do for a living? The issue with this question is that it allows what we do to define who we are. I think we need to flip-flop this idea and let who we are dictate what we do. The first step to finding ways to make more money is knowing who you are and who you want to be. Someone may be a doctor or lawyer, but isn't a father or mother or traveler or mountain biker a better description of who they actually are?

Tim Ferriss discusses the idea of letting your job define you. In his book, *The 4-Hour Workweek*, Ferriss said he is tired of having job descriptions be self-descriptions, and I couldn't agree more (Ferriss 2007). Just because I work as an Economic Developer doesn't mean that is who I am.

So, rather than ask you what you want to be when you grow up, I want to ask you, who do you want to be when you grow up? In Worksheet 12, write down who it is that you want to be when you grow up.

Worksheet 12. List of potential role models.

1. _____

2. _____

3. _____

4. _____

5. _____

I talk to people in their 60s who still don't know who they really are except what their job has defined for them. So you don't have to write down a lot, I just want you to start thinking about who you are now and who you want to be moving forward.

Think Like a Kid

The LAZ Lifestyle is not normal. Many people will laugh at you or tell you how risky this will be, without ever looking into it themselves. Somehow, the idea that you can follow your passion and still be financially free is too good to be true. In society, we have it all backwards. If you are doing what you love, we call that a hobby. If you are doing something for money, we call it work. Why does it seem so impossible to mesh the two so that your passion can help contribute to your bottom line and ultimately your financial freedom?

The issue is that we start out as kids wanting to be artists, athletes, movie stars, and we end up stuck behind a desk crunching numbers and punching a clock for 30 years. The kid version of yourself would punch you if they saw you now.

In the movie *The Hottest State* with Ethan Hawke, the characters have the following conversation:

"'Don't you find it odd,' she continued, 'that when you're a kid, everyone, all the world, encourages you to follow your dreams. But when you're older, somehow they act offended if you even try.'"

We are stripped of our creativity, passion, and inspiration as we get older and become confined to what we should be doing. We forget to think for ourselves. Reality backs us into a corner where it limits what we think is possible. Society tells us no so many times that we start to believe it. My wife was a great example of this. Even though she had a natural gift for photography, she never thought it was realistic or lucrative enough to actually be considered anything other than a hobby. She finally shifted her mindset and is now one of the top wedding photographers in our city, making more than a respectable income. This happens so often, but why?

In the late-1960s, George Land conducted an experiment to test the divergent thinking abilities of the same 1,600 school children between the ages of 3 and 5, 8 and 10, and finally 13 and 15 (Land and Jarman 1998). The experiment simply gave the kids a paperclip and asked them to come up with as many uses for it as they could.

Between the ages of 3–5, 98% of the group ranked as divergent thinking geniuses. By age ten only 30% of the same group of students qualified to such a level (Land and Jarman1998). By age fifteen, only 10% of the kids were thinking at a genius level of divergence (Land and Jarman1998). Then the same test was given to 200,000 adults where only 2% tested at the genius level (Land and Jarman1998).

The lesson appears clear that creativity and thinking outside the box may be a learned behavior. It is evident that the way we educate kids seems to be great at encouraging linear thinking—memorization, multiple choice selection, and repetition—but fails to teach or encourage creativity in the exercises.

Let's reflect on this a moment. From a young age, you have been trained to NOT think for yourself or be creative or innovative. You are told 3+3 = 6 and that a box is a box, and you are rewarded for getting the right answer. If you come up with anything else you are wrong. But what if I told you that a box is not a box? Or 4 plus 2 also equals 6? Let's try an exercise. In Worksheet 13, I want you to list all of the things you can do with a pencil:

Worksheet 13. Exercise to list of all possible uses for a pencil.

1. _____

2. _____

3. _____

4. _____

5. _____

Could you come up with five uses, besides writing? If you did, was it more difficult than you thought?

Your brain has been trained to see things as they are, not what they can be. You need to begin to retrain your brain to think like you did when you were a kid when there were no wrong answers and anything was possible, even if it sounds ridiculous or crazy!

Without creativity, it is hard to imagine a new way of doing things. It makes it impossible to think outside the box and find that new career or second source of income. Again, most people find structure to be comfortable, but we need to break out of that comfort zone to tie what you are passionate about with a way to make more money. What a great combination!

Millennial Insight

I hated my job. I dreaded waking up the next morning to go to work. I realized I had started settling for work instead of following my passion of working with animals. I quit my job to start a dog walking business and have never looked back.

Nick, 26

This creativity drain happened to me at one point as well. I wanted to be an architect and build amazing buildings that everyone would recognize.

But as I got further along in school, I kept getting pushed further and further into law with each tuition payment, and the next thing I knew I had invested $150,000 in a legal education.

Why?

Being a famous architect is too hard. There are already too many architects.

The excuses came faster than I could reason otherwise, and before I knew it I was headed down a completely different path. Don't get me wrong, I know there is practicality in reality and you may have circumstances that force you into a specific field, but if you are truly unhappy with where you are at, let's start looking at different ways to stretch your comfort zone to find what truly makes you happy.

It's time to live by what Steve Jobs stated in his commencement address to the class of 2005 at Stanford: "Your work is going to fill a large part of your life, and the only way to be truly satisfied is to do what you believe is great work. And the only way to do great work is to love what you do. If you haven't found it yet, keep looking. Don't settle. As with all matters of the heart, you'll know when you find it."

How to Find Your Passion

If you could do anything for work today, what would it be?

This is actually a harder question to answer than most people think. First, it assumes that you will be working, so people think of only the things that can make a "safe" income. And second, most people have had their passion and dreams beaten out of them by reality. So here are some exercises to get you out of your reality and have you thinking like a kid again.

In an article in Entrepreneur Magazine, author Lisa Girard suggested the following exercises to help jump-start your search to find that passion:

Exercise 1—Revisit your childhood. What did you love to do? (Girard 2014)

Think back to when you were a child. What types of foods, activities, and experiences do you remember enjoying?

"It's amazing how disconnected we become to the things that brought us the most joy in favor of what's practical," says Rob Levit, an Annapolis,

Md.-based creativity expert, speaker and business consultant (Girard 2014).

The article references Frank Lloyd Wright, America's greatest architect, and how he played with wooden blocks all through childhood and perhaps well past it (Girard 2014).

"Research shows that there is much to be discovered in play, even as adults," Levit says (Girard 2014). Think back to some of those activities and see if they can work in your life now. Are you still excited about building things? Writing? Drawing?

Exercise 2—Develop a personal "creativity board."

The concept of a creativity board allows you to work from the center out. So in the middle, you would have the words "New Career" or "New Business" and find images, quotes, and ideas revolving around a new career or business (Girard 2014).

Your board will continue to grow and evolve, as you get more and more creative. Continue to add to and modify your board.

Exercise 3—Emulate who you want to be (Girard 2014).

Is there someone out there doing what you want to do? Research them. Contact them. Have coffee, lunch, or drinks with them. Find out more about how they got to where they are. Most people are open to discuss or advise others on their experiences if you are genuinely interested.

I knew real estate was my passion, but I wasn't sure exactly what that looked like. So I contacted as many people as possible that were doing what I thought I wanted to do. I was able to weed through the options to find that "buy and hold" investing fit the bill for me. It was much easier making a decision after seeing it in practice.

Everything sounds good until you start doing it. Maybe it requires a lot of late nights and travel. Maybe it doesn't allow you to interact with people on a daily basis, like you thought it would. This exercise allows you to learn from others' experiences to find your passion.

Exercise 4—Start doing what you love (Girard 2014).

People analyze too much and many ideas or passions never see the light of day, according to Cath Duncan, a Calgary, Canada-based creativity expert and life coach who works with entrepreneurs and other professionals (Girard 2014).

"She recommends doing what you enjoy — even if you haven't yet figured out how to monetize it. Test what it might be like to work in an area you're passionate about… ask for feedback that will help you develop and refine a business plan (Girard 2014)."

This is a good way to just try something and become a trigger-puller who makes things happen. It may be very uncomfortable, but that's the goal here. You never know unless you try.

Exercise 5—Take a mental vacation and change your lens (Girard 2014).

We all need a break from the day-to-day routine to start thinking creatively. Whether it's a walk in the park, bike ride, or a road trip, you need to get out to get your mind thinking differently.

Levit suggests that after taking a mental vacation that you come back to a journal and write down any business ideas that come to mind (Girard 2014).

"You'll be amazed at how refreshed your ideas are," Levit says. "Looking at beautiful things—art and nature—creates connections that we often neglect to notice. Notice them, capture them in writing, and use them (Girard 2014)."

I never used to appreciate art, especially modern art. I was of the opinion that if I could create it myself, it wasn't art. I was walking through a local art event in Spokane and saw a bronzed dollar bill on a small plate. Normally, I look at this as a waste of time and space at an exhibit let alone $1, but I realized that I was only looking at the art through my everyday lens; the practical, must-fit-in-the-box lens that works so well in business. By shifting my view, the world became alive as I found "art" everywhere. The world was no longer limited by what I thought and understood.

Push yourself to get out of your normal train of thought and look at the world differently. Literally stop to smell the roses and appreciate the beauty all around you. You need to drop the imposed structure that society puts on your life and think back to when you were building forts as a kid or doing something simply because you loved it. This will free up your mind to start finding opportunities that you may be passionate about.

So, what excites you?

Helping others?

Real Estate?

Singing?

Teaching?

As we start narrowing in on what you are passionate about, we can start finding new ways to generate income.

Requirements for Sources of Extra Income

"I don't have the time!"

How are you going to find the time to make extra income when you are already working a full-time or two part-time jobs? You have to find a balance between schedule and quality of life. So when looking to add extra income, try to find income streams that fit the following criteria:

Flexible: It must work around your current schedule; you cannot be two places at once. Your day job might be from 8–5, so you need to find something before or after work or see if you can just work four days a week. You need to be able to call the shots.

Scalable: Find income streams that can grow without requiring more and more of your time. For example, a business can leverage more employees to meet increased demand and sell more products, making you more money. Or as a Realtor, I can hire an assistant to decrease the amount of time I spend on paperwork and follow-up so I can spend more time with the client since I can only work on nights and weekends.

Valuable: The extra income needs to be worth your time. This is where the balance comes in between working to acquire IPAs and a quality of life you enjoy. If the income is too low, wait and look for a better opportunity. You are looking for more bang for the buck, so try not to find a job at local convenience or grocery store making minimum wage. Remember to leverage your talents and skills to find higher paying work.

Responsible: You need to make sure your venture does not require a large investment on your end. I look for low-cost startups or activities that require little investment of my time but result in increased cash flow. You don't want to put yourself in a worse situation than when you started.

Learnable: Try to find something that advances your learning in a field of interest. Work is an opportunity to learn another industry or create a business in one. Always look for opportunities to learn.

Ideas for Making Extra Money

Start to think of your skills and talents that people would consider a value. Businesses are created because of problems, not solutions. For when there are no problems, no business will be needed to solve them. Let's keep this simple. There are some easy ways to start creating streams of income while you still have that full-time job. Remember, it is all about the IPAs.

Leverage Your Skills

Do you know a second language? Can you fix a bike? Do you play musical instruments or have experience playing sports? These are all skills that you can leverage to make money. You can be a tutor, coach, music instructor, and the list goes on and on. You can access a market on Craigslist, Facebook, local colleges, or even in the paper. Simply write one paragraph about your experience and what services you are offering and post it. This can be an easy way to make money on your schedule.

Find the Odds and Ends Jobs

With the advent of the Internet came opportunities to connect with people. You can use this to assist people who are willing to pay to have their dog walked, house cleaned, yard work, groceries picked up, you name it and it's out there. By simply spreading the word, you will find that usually more than just one person needs the service. Companies like Uber and Lyft allow you to use your vehicle to make money driving people around. There is no limit to the possibilities, just make sure they fit into your schedule.

Make Stuff

Another option is to take that birdhouse or scarf that you made and sell it over the internet on sites like Etsy and Ebay where people go to find handmade crafts and knickknacks. This allows you to sell your jewelry, artwork, and other crafts. Then there are websites like Cafepress.com that open up a new way to make T-shirts and products with custom words or graphics. Craigslist is another market to sell stuff on.

My dad uses eBay to make additional stream of income. He will go to garage sales locally and turn around and list the product on Ebay for a profit. He loves the thrill of finding hidden gems in the pile of rubbish at garage sales to make some extra money.

Freelance Opportunities

New sites such as www.flexjobs.com have exclusively telecommuting and freelance jobs with flexible schedule positions that would allow for the possibility of secondary income through such skills as writing, graphic design, grant writing, marketing, and many more. You have already invested in that pricey education, now put it to work for you. Also, the website Fiverr.com lets people offer many different types of services for just $5. Take a look; you will be amazed at all of the offerings.

Share Some Knowledge

There are sites like Udemy and Skillshare that act as a marketplace for knowledge allowing you to setup and teach classes online to students of all ages. They pay to participate in the class and the types of classes are endless. It takes some time to set it up initially but operates smoothly when in place. This is also a great way to give back and offer your experience so others can learn and benefit. These are just some of the many options to start creating additional streams of income. You never know what these small sources of income can lead to.

LAZ Lifestyle Moves

- Get to $10,000 challenge. Find ways to get $10,000 in your savings account.
- Write down three things you could cut out of your schedule that do not add value and see how much time it will free up.

- Create a list of who you want to be when you "grow up."
- Complete a skills assessment to get a baseline of where you are at and what you could qualify for.
- Spend 30 minutes each day researching opportunities that fit your skill set.

Wrap Up

You are capable of doing great things. You are talented, driven, educated and ready to make your mark on the world. You need to start thinking outside the box and look for the opportunities around you to add streams of income. By starting with what you are passionate about, you can craft your activities, research, and steps for getting there. How great would it be if you not only loved your work, but were compensated for it as well?

Advice from Millennials

Name: Jake
Age: 28
Occupation/Job Title: CFO
Annual Income: $120,000
Family Size: 1
Where do you live? Spokane, WA
Do you currently own or rent your home? Rent

How did you get to the position you are now?

A thoughtful and deliberate pursuit of goals. I figured out early in college that I wanted to pursue a career in investing. This path ended up being a fairly long road for me. Even though I figured out what I wanted to do there was no immediate way to accomplish this goal. Investment analysis and management is extremely competitive. In order for me to get to where I wanted to be I had to: 1) take a job for two years in an accounting while the financial crisis subsided, 2) agree to work for free for two years as an equity analyst for a start-up hedge fund, and 3) take a job in a role that offered both investment analysis work along with some accounting. The combination of these three experiences have opened the door to Columbia Business School. It's not that one particular experience, internship, or job set the stage, but more that each step towards achieving my long-term goals.

Are you a planner or a ready-fire-aim kind of guy? Why?

Long-term planner by nature. Some things are obviously out of our control but I think where we are is often a reflection of the choices we've made. I couldn't have obtained my apprenticeship without taking the time to get to know the managing partner. I wouldn't have been capable of my current role as CFO without both the experience in public accounting and my time as an investment analyst. And I don't believe I could have been accepted into Columbia without the combination of all three. Had I chose to stay in public accounting my career would look very different than it does today; not better or worse, just different.

What motivates you to keep educating yourself?

The pursuit of my goals. Planners are constantly evaluating and assessing where they are now in relation to their goals. The way one thinks about success and defines their goals also makes a difference in the pursuit of those goals. My long-term goal is not defined by a title or sum of money, rather a focus on learning and growing knowing that change is inevitable.

Are you passionate about your work? How do you know?

Yes. You know when it doesn't feel like work anymore, when you go to bed with an eagerness for tomorrow. It's a feeling of engagement and liveliness that can't help but permeate all facets of your life.

What are things you do to stay current on your industry?

Try to read or listen to audiobooks as much as possible. I try to read topics outside of my functional area of investing, whether it be about education or entrepreneurship. We are fortunate to live in a time where we have such easy access to incredible content.

What do you think the benefit of continuing education is?

Education is all about return on investment. What can I learn today that will add value in the future and how can I get this in the fastest and most reasonable way. For me all of my experience has been focused on technical knowledge of accounting and finance, so pursuing further education is about filling in the gaps.

I want to learn about business strategy and marketing. Why do companies pursue organic growth vs. acquisition? Why are certain marketing campaigns more effective than others? How does a company create the intangible asset of a brand that translates into pricing power and better long-term economics? These are questions that I hope to understand in greater detail.

What is your favorite business or finance book? Why?

I'd say *Fooling Some of the People All the Time* by David Einhorn is one of my all-time favorites. His book not only raised the bar for analytical due diligence but also for the courage it takes to be a whistleblower. Speaking out against powerful people within large companies takes an extraordinary amount of courage and fortitude. His battle against one particular company took years to come to fruition not to mention a considerable amount of public ridicule. One day I hope to do this kind of work.

Who helped you get to where you are today? How?

David Pointer — former supervisor and mentor. Dave helped me in three ways. First, he gave me the opportunity to join his company and work alongside him during the early stages of the fund. This investment analysis experience was invaluable for my career. Secondly, Dave provided critical feedback along the way. This feedback was both professional and personal. He clearly pointed out the areas that I needed to work on. This sort of honest and transparent assessment eventually led to serious personal growth. Having someone who challenges you and then offers the willingness to support you is critical to success. Lastly, Dave has never stopped investing in me, whether it's a phone call on my way to work or a Saturday afternoon to work on a letter of recommendation. I hope his selfless attitude and willingness to help others has rubbed off on me.

What is your benchmark of success? Have you reached it?

Consistent growth. Yes and no. There is no end necessarily but you are either moving in the right direction or not. I feel like I've done a decent job but I believe that this is only the beginning.

What financial advice has made the largest impact for you?

Be greedy when others are fearful and be fearful when others are greedy. Being contrarian is counterintuitive, but I know no better way to achieve better than average long-term results.

What advice do you have about continuing your education?

Read as much as you possibly can from those who have been successful before you in your area of interest. There are so many good books that are filled with mistakes you don't have to make along the way if you take the time to read them. Also take the time to meet with people who could provide you with additional insight or perspective. Most people have no problem talking about what they've done; use those opportunities to gather additional information and to broaden your network. One of my biggest mistakes in my career is that I undervalued the "networking" factor. More often than not, those that get the opportunities are those who are connected to the right people.

9

REAL ESTATE: THE FORGOTTEN INVESTMENT VEHICLE

Real estate investing, even on a very small scale, remains a tried and true means of building an individual's cash flow and wealth.

Robert Kiyosaki

Now, one thing I tell everyone is learn about real estate. Repeat after me: real estate provides the highest returns, the greatest values and the least risk.

Armstrong Williams

My head was spinning; I felt sick to my stomach. I was less than 48 hours away from closing on my first house flip project, but something was wrong. I was rifling through the garbage that the prior owner, a complete hoarder, had left behind. With gloves on and garbage bag in hand, I fought the foul stench and tossed piece after piece into the bag as it now sagged to the floor under the weight.

I had been doing this for more than 30 minutes and you wouldn't have known I had been there. This wasn't right. I was in over my head, literally. There was so much garbage.

I called the realtor and told him we couldn't go through with the purchase. Our $1,000 earnest money payment was forfeited, and my first attempt at a flip by myself failed before it even began. The optimist in me said I should cut my losses before losing even more money, but the pessimist in me said I failed from the get-go, that I didn't know what I was doing. I vowed then and there to learn all aspects of this real estate business before trying my hand at flipping again.

Fast forward three years. I have flipped three houses and have 20 rental units ranging from single-family homes to commercial property. It would have been easy to give up initially and say this real estate game wasn't for me. But by learning from the situation, I was able to grow and am now more educated about each transaction. I also know what I'm looking for *before* I pull the trigger on a property.

I am skeptical about "too good to be true" deals and am still learning from each transaction. But like John Maxwell so eloquently put it, "Fail early, fail often, but always fail forward." I took those words to heart and have not looked back.

"I Want to Work from the Beach"

This statement has directed every endeavor since Whitney and I began living an LAZ Lifestyle. (Coincidentally, working from a beach sounds LAZy). What I mean by "work from a beach" investing is that when evaluating a business or investment venture, my first question is, "Can I eventually operate this from a beach?"

For me, this mentality's origin dates back to a sunny day on a beach in Vernazza, Italy. Staring out over the vast Liguarian Sea as the sun sank into the water, sipping on Italian white wine, Whit asked, "Do we have to leave?"

Such a simple question with such a profound impact.

Of course, we did have to leave. We were running short on money and had to go home to get back to work. But it made me think: what if we weren't running short on money and work could be handled via the Internet? It was a long flight back, which gave me time to realize where we had to target our efforts from that point forward. We had to find viable businesses and investments that didn't require us to physically be there to make money (also known as passive income).

At that time, I was managing a portfolio of over 400 rental units, both as a property manager and an asset manager. I poured over the financials for cash flow, analyzing the expenses down to the cost of cleaning materials. They were making money each month from rental income and I began to notice the properties were increasing in value as well. The owners were making a significant income through proper management and all they had to do was review the financials. They could easily do that from a beach if needed.

How It All Began

It was mid-summer in 2006 and houses were flying off the market at or over list price. Whitney and I were planning to get married that December and thought homeownership was for us. I knew nothing about the process or why we should even own a house, but all of our friends were buying so we thought it would be a good idea. (NOTE: "Everybody is doing it!" is never a good investment justification!)

I was just starting law school and was unemployed while Whitney was coaching volleyball and had been employed for less than a year. We didn't think we could even qualify for a loan, but then again it was 2006. (I should have known something was wrong when unemployed persons were getting loans.)

We got what the bank called a "Don't Ask, Don't Tell Loan," another giant red flag we failed to notice. Essentially, if we could come up with 5% down, we could use stated income to qualify for the loan. Luckily, I had just gotten back from commercial salmon fishing in Alaska and we had the cash down payment in hand. Homeownership was within our reach!

We found a small 3 bedroom/1 bathroom house near a park and it was perfect. Well, almost perfect. It needed some work, but we thought we could put our touch on it and make it a home. We paid $96,000 after successfully outbidding two other offers. We captured our entry over the threshold from the Astroturf-lined front porch. I wouldn't have had it any other way. We tackled projects ranging from landscaping to opening up walls and putting in new kitchen cabinets. Unfortunately, we learned the hard way on most of them.

Not long after moving in, my parents started getting into flipping houses (just like you see on HGTV, but with a little less drama). I helped them on the first one and fell in love with the process. It was a 4 bedroom/1 bathroom, 100-year-old, Craftsman-style house that needed to be brought into the 21st century. But at $60,000, it had quite a bit of room for improvement.

We had a great realtor who found the home for us and we went to work. I don't know if it was the country music, the hot summer sun, or the beer in the fridge, but there was something about controlling what I did and working hard to make change happen that was exhilarating.

I was hooked. I loved the finding, negotiating, renovating, and even the selling of the home.

The first project was successful as we sold the home for $120,000 less than 120 days after we bought it, to a young couple trying to find their dream home. Overall, we made a $25,000 profit and were eager to move on to another home.

In that first flip project, I obviously learned many basics of home repair, but I learned a much more valuable lesson: I could invest in something where I could control (or at least feel like I could control) the outcome. My parents and I took a house worth $60,000 and, in less than 120 days, we made it worth $120,000. I realized I could add value to make money, something I couldn't say about my retirement accounts. In fact, I couldn't even tell you where my retirement accounts were invested.

I was addicted to real estate and, ultimately, the lifestyle it could provide. But I was attending law school and only working part-time, so it was difficult to build up the cash needed to invest in a flip project. We needed a different strategy to get started.

In 2010, Whitney and I decided to purchase a flip home to move into. I had just gotten my realtor's license and was busy combing through the Multiple Listing Service available only to realtors. Whitney had no intention of moving but said that if I found a house that was larger, in a better area, and had a smaller monthly payment then she would move. I'm pretty sure we both thought finding a house that met her criteria would be impossible, but I was determined.

Three days later, I found a bank-owned property that was 2 bedrooms/1 bathroom on the main floor with an unfinished attic and basement for

$52,000 in an up-and-coming area of town. We put in an offer the day the house was listed and, hours later, it was accepted. We kept our first home as a rental and moved into the new, flip property.

We lived in the house for over a year, gutting it and completely remodeling every square inch of the place. By the time it was done, it was perfect. But since the plan was to build cash through buying and selling these residences, it was time to sell and move on. We bought the house for $52,000 and put $40,000 into renovations when all was said and done. We sold it for $147,000 for a profit of $55,000 before taxes and closing costs.

We immediately reinvested the money into another house about a mile away. It was a Housing and Urban Development (HUD) foreclosure that needed some updating. It was a large 4 bedroom/2 bathroom Craftsman-style house with over 2,700 square feet. It had a closed-off living space but a ton of character that only an early 1900's house could have, such as French doors into the living room, beautiful hardwood floors, and large base and crown molding.

We flipped the entire house in four weeks *before* we moved in, learning from the previous house how hard it was to live in a construction zone. It was a 4-week whirlwind. I vividly remember painting the front door at 3 AM the day before we were scheduled to move in.

We purchased the house for $82,000 and have put roughly $25,000 into it. We are still currently living there but recently had it appraised for $167,000.

Now having equity in our homes, we turned to purchasing rentals. We acquired our first rental, a triplex with two 1 bedroom/1 bathroom units and one 2 bedroom/1 bathroom unit. The house had sold in 2007 for $150,000, and I noticed that units were being rented for way less than the market rate. We negotiated the deal and closed at a purchase price of $93,500. I immediately increased rents by $250 per month across the units. We used our savings and some equity to cover the 25% down payment required by the bank.

Less than a month later, we found another triplex close by that had market rents and was in great condition. I had just promised Whitney we would take a break from purchasing more properties, but we both knew we couldn't pass up another great deal. We negotiated with the sellers and they owner-financed the property with us putting 10% down. (Owner financing is when the seller carries the note for the property rather than a bank. You put a percentage down and pay at a negotiated rate and term for the length of the note. Usually, both parties require a third party escrow company to give and receive funds between the parties.) The market value was $135,000 and we were able to purchase it for $97,000.

These two triplex rentals cash flow $1,000 per month after paying all expenses. This was proof that passive income works.

Having seen success and tested demand in the area, we purchased a four-plex (four-unit house) nine months later consisting of two 1 bedroom/1 bathroom units and two 2 bedroom/1 bathroom units. This property was a foreclosure and had been vacant for over a year. The previous owner had tried to sell it for $215,000 before it went into foreclosure. We purchased the property for $128,000 and had to put about $10,000 into renovations. This one was a labor of love/hate because it had been vacant for so long and Spokane has very cold winters. Pipes were leaking and the electrical needed updating; it seemed like one issue would be fixed causing another to go bad. But we completed all the work in a month and had it rented in less than two weeks. It cash flows over $800 per month.

We have since moved on to purchasing commercial properties, such as office buildings and retail spaces. We use the same value analysis when making any of these purchases.

I tell you about our experiences because real estate investing definitely is a gradual process. Sometimes it is easy to get discouraged when you hear that someone has 1,000 units and wonder how he could have amassed such a portfolio. But my example shows that building a portfolio is a slow game that continually builds momentum.

Through this process, we have learned countless lessons and this chapter will dive deeper into the benefits, selection criteria, financing, management, and developing an exit strategy for real estate. This is a cursory overview but will outline a plan you can use to acquire long-term real estate without having to field calls at 2:00 am that the toilet is leaking in one of your units.

Why Own Real Estate?

Most people I talk to think it is too hard or overwhelming to get started in real estate. They don't want to get the late-night phone call to fix a toilet or deal with angry tenants. I agree, I don't like dealing with those calls either. But if it was easy everyone would be doing it. The key is to minimize these issues.

The real problem is that you will read this book or attend a real estate conference and be motivated to get started, but Monday will roll around and you have done nothing. And the longer it takes, the harder it gets to begin. Too many people suffer from analysis paralysis; you need to become a "trigger puller." I must clarify, I don't want you to become an impulsive real estate buyer chasing shiny objects; I want you to pull the trigger after due diligence and financial calculations tell you that it is a good deal. The only way to know what will work is to try it.

I have lost out on several opportunities because I didn't pull the trigger soon enough. Whitney and I developed a few mottos that we live by: if we want to renovate something, we put a hole in the wall so we are forced to make it happen; or if we want to travel, we book the airplane tickets. Somehow we always find a way to make it work after that. Real estate is no different.

Here are the reasons why you should use real estate to create your LAZ Lifestyle: (*P.S. I am not a CPA, so please consult your tax advisor or attorney on these topics.*)

Cash Flow

This is the major reason why I invest in long-term rental properties. Cash flow is the amount of money you have coming in after all expenses are taken out—it's basically the amount of money left over each month, your profit. What's awesome about rentals is that you get the cash flow *and* your tenants are paying down your mortgage each month. It's a win-win. This monthly income allows you to operate your properties successfully from anywhere with good property management.

Depreciation

Not many people understand depreciation. You don't receive any cash, yet it saves you money. Basically, the government understands that real estate breaks down over time, and they allow you to depreciate your building and take a tax deduction each year for the value lost. It helps offset most of the income produced from the property.

For example, let's say I purchase a triplex for $200,000 and my net annual cash flow is $6,000. Normally, this cash flow is taxable as a Schedule E on my income taxes for that year. But because of this gift of depreciation, I will not have to pay a thing. Why, you ask? The IRS allows me to depreciate my building over the course of 27.5 years, or $7,272.73 each year (IRS 2013). So on my tax return, I actually lost $1,272.73!

In case you're still confused, let's clarify: I collected and put $6,000 into my pocket from *income* from the rental property, and I don't have to pay taxes on it. In fact, I actually lost $1,272.73 (on paper) which helps decrease any other income that I have and, ultimately, my overall tax bill. So I get to collect the $6,000 per year and not pay taxes on it. Gotta love depreciation!

Appreciation

Appreciation is the icing on the cake for investing in real estate. Appreciation is the value increase of your property over time. For instance, I bought a duplex for $150,000 in 2000, and it is now worth $200,000. I gained $50,000 in value from appreciation while tenants paid down my mortgage (and I collected nearly tax-free cash flow). What a great investment vehicle! Ultimately, I would never recommend buying an investment property based on potential appreciation, but it is a fun payoff when you do decide to sell!

Leverage

There is no better investment than real estate to leverage the cash that you have. For example, to purchase a $250,000 four-plex, I need to have a 25% down payment (or $62,500). The lender picks up the rest. So for $62,500, I can own a property worth $250,000 and get the benefits of depreciation, cash flow, and possibly appreciation. For those looking at primary residences, it is even better. You can now buy a home for 3.5–5% down so you get to leverage your dollar 20 to 1. So for every $1 I contribute, the bank will give me $20. On top of that, I get to keep all of the cash flow and depreciation benefits.

Real Estate to Grow Wealth

The real estate investment I am promoting is long-term "buy and hold" rentals, which are perfect for millennials looking towards the future.

Again, it has to be a business that we can "do from a beach," so short-term flips like you see on HGTV don't fit the model because I have to be there for them to work.

With a long-term rental, we could develop monthly cash flow, tax savings, and possible appreciation. The downside to this approach is that you need cash to make most deals happen. Much of what you see on TV is the short-term flip project to create cash quickly. But beware! It is not as glamorous as it looks on TV. When you are sweating in an attic with no air conditioning or scrubbing a mold-infested basement, you start really wondering if it is all worth it.

Another major downside to flipping houses is how the IRS treats it. With a short-term flip, you must pay a short-term capital gains tax of up to 40% on any profits realized (IRS 2016).

But for long-term real estate, if you hang on to that same house for more than a year, you qualify for a long-term capital gains rate of up to 20%. Even better, if you live in the house for two of the last five years, you qualify for an exemption of $250,000 for single individuals and $500,000 for married couples. This means that if you purchase a place and move in for two years and then sell it, you will pay no capital gains tax up to the exemption amount.

It is important to look at your tax bracket before flipping, as individuals in the 10–15% tax bracket actually pay 0% capital gains tax regardless of how quickly they sell the house. However, the rules change more often than the Seattle Mariners' starting lineup, so make sure you consult your tax advisor before you begin a flip project.

To summarize, when I talk about real estate investing, I am referring to long-term single and multifamily rentals. Again, it would be hard to run a house flip project from a beach. We are trying to create a *lifestyle*, not merely a fun vacation.

The Process

The LAZ Lifestyle is all about processes to simplify and automate your life. Here is the 8-step process to finding your new home or rental property:

1. Educate yourself on real estate, pricing, and locations.

2. Find a realtor (or become one if you plan on purchasing many properties!).

3. Set your criteria and follow it.

4. Trust the numbers.

5. Conduct due diligence.

6. Find the right financing.

7. Decide whether or not you want to manage it yourself.

8. Know your exit strategy.

Now let's dive into each step and you will be ready to buy your first property!

Starting Point: Education

I started my real estate career off on the wrong foot, $1,000 in the hole. I failed to get educated. I was trying to be Donald Trump when I didn't know the difference between After-Repair-Value and Loan-to-Value. They make it look so easy on TV.

Before we examine what to look for in a property, how to finance, how to manage it, and how to grow your wealth, I want you to research and educate yourself on real estate in general.

Read books. Listen to Podcasts. Watch HGTV or DIY to understand the renovation and negotiation process for purchasing. The best resource I've found so far is www.biggerpockets.com (Biggerpockets 2015). They are a wealth of information with podcasts, articles, message boards, and a host of other resources on every type of real estate investment. You can use their forum to talk to other real estate investors about any topic of concern and connect with local investors.

Really dive into this education aspect but understand you will never learn it all, so at some point you need to just try it. You will learn far more in the purchase of your first property than any article or book can teach you. Trust me.

Find a Realtor (or Become One!)

Of course I had to put a section in the book about hiring a realtor. The truth is that a good realtor is an invaluable resource for current market trends, pricing, and available inventory.

I think of real estate a lot like your retirement accounts. Would you just go and pick stocks and build your portfolio without getting a professional opinion? If so, Zillow may be all you need to build your real estate empire. But for most people, it helps to have an expert who is working in the field every day advising and consulting on where to put your investment.

So how do you find a realtor? Start by asking friends for recommendations (everyone seems to know a realtor.) Then interview the realtor to make sure you are on the same page with seeing houses, timing, expertise, etc. Here are some questions to ask:

1. Why did you become a realtor?
2. How long have you been a realtor? In the (your city) market?
3. Do you work full or part-time as a realtor?
4. What services do you provide or why should I hire you?
5. What percentage of your clients are buyers vs. sellers?
6. How many transactions did you close this year?
7. Do you own any rental properties of your own?
8. Have you closed a transaction on a bank-owned property? Short sale?
9. Do you have three other investor clients that I can talk to as references?
10 What haven't I asked you that I need to know?

Take your time finding a realtor. He or she can be an integral part of your team moving forward.

Perfect Property Criteria

A piece of advice I was given early on was "focus and narrow down what you want to invest in." It doesn't mean that this can't change, but there is always a deal out there and you will drive yourself crazy if you don't narrow the focus. You need to avoid the "shiny object" syndrome.

Our first house was near a park and I really liked the location as an up-and-coming area because of its proximity to downtown and affordable rental rates. Thus, I wanted properties within a half mile radius of this location that were under four units (easier to finance) that I could pay less than $35,000 per unit. Now when anything comes on the market fitting that bill, we look at it and make an offer.

You can use the following analysis whether your investment is going to be your primary residence or a rental. You want to make sure to buy a property with instant equity and be able to sell for the highest value.

It is important to narrow down your focus to the types and location of properties that you want to invest in. It doesn't mean that you don't entertain other opportunities or even change these criteria later on, but it means that you develop your bread and butter so when a property comes up within that criteria, you know if it is a good deal and can act quickly. For example, I have some rules that I use (these are simply for reference, as you develop your investing rules as you continue to grow your IPAs):

- **The Starbucks rule.** Any property that I invest in needs to be within a 10-minute drive of a Starbucks. I have concluded that since Starbucks (not a franchisee) own all of their stores, they have put far more time and research into understanding the demographics and locations that best fit their target market. They take into account incomes, population, and clientele that frequent coffee shops. I just piggyback on their research.

- **No Busy Streets.** I never like to buy a residential property located on a busy street or main arterial. My only exception is a larger (20 unit or more) apartment complex. These are difficult to sell and create an obstacle you always have to overcome, yet can't do anything about, when leasing or selling the property. I can change the sinks and flooring of a house, but I can't change the busy street it is on. You've heard it said time and again, "location, location, location."

- **Don't be Awkward.** I can't stand buying an "awkward" house. Let me explain. If I walk into a house and think the layout is awkward and can't be fixed for a reasonable price, then I don't buy it. For example, the fridge doesn't fit in the kitchen, or you have to go through a bedroom to get to the only bathroom in the house. There is too much inventory to purchase something that most people won't like. You ultimately have to convince someone to rent or buy it, so make it easy on yourself.

- **Find TLC Properties.** I always look for properties that I can put sweat equity into either through actual improvements to the property or managing the property better to allow me to increase the rents. The key is to really understand the rental market in your area, which means you know how much a studio, 1 bed, 2 bed, and 3 bed unit rents for, so when you see an undervalued property, you can jump on it and make a profit from the get-go.

It is imperative that you have some screening criteria for purchasing rentals. The rules I use have kept me from purchasing properties that might have been gems, but it has saved me from far more bad purchases.

In addition to my personal rules listed above, here are some more industry-recognized rules that I apply as well:

- **1% Rule** (Boone 2013). This rule is simple and helps me weed through a lot of properties. What it requires is that your gross rental income is higher than 1% of the purchase price. So if I am looking at a 6-unit apartment building with gross rents of $2,000 per month, then I will not pay more than $200,000 for the building. This is always my first screening criterion.

- **Cap Rate.** The capitalization rate (cap rate) helps you determine whether you are getting a good deal on a property. It looks even closer at the deal than the 1% rule. I never like to purchase a property for less than an 8% cap rate unless it has some other possible use, such as an additional buildable lot or it's in an up-and-coming area. You calculate the cap rate of a property with this equation:

  Net Operating Income ÷ Purchase Price = Cap Rate
  (Kimmins 2015)

  For example, let's use the previous example of me purchasing a 6-unit apartment building for $200,000. Let's assume, the net operating income is $18,000, which would make our cap rate 9%. So it would pass my cap rate requirement. For residential properties, you want the cap rate to be above 8%, and I rarely buy unless I can get a 10% cap rate or higher.

- **50% Expenses Rule** (Turner 2013). What this rule assumes is that your expenses will be 50% of the gross rents. This takes into account monthly costs and future repairs. This helps you figure out your net operating income easily for better calculations on the property. Again, this is a general rule, but it will help you when determining your cap rate. For example, like the property above, gross rent is $3,000 so our monthly net operating income is $1,500 and our annual net operating income is $18,000.

- **Cash on Cash Return.** This important number helps you determine how much of a return you are actually getting based on the cash you put into the deal. Here is the equation we use:

$$\text{Net Operating Income} \div \text{Total Cash Invested} = \text{Cash-on-Cash Return (Schmidt 2013)}$$

So, if we put 20% down on the 6-unit apartment above, we would have $60,000 into the property. Our mortgage payment is $1,000 per month so we subtract that from our net operating income for an annual cash flow of $6,000. We can expect to have a cash-on-cash return of 10%. Much better than bank saving accounts right now!

- **$150 per Door.** This is the final rule. I like the numbers, but I need to have monthly cash flow of at least $150 per door. So for a four-plex, I need monthly cash flow (that's after all expenses, including the mortgage, are taken out) of $600 per month. This keeps the property profitable from day one.

Look at the Numbers!

Let's walk through a typical property evaluation. Here we have a brick four-plex that just came on the market. It needs a little TLC but is fully rented and brings in gross rents of $2,300 per month. The owner is retiring and wants to sell the property for $230,000. I will need 25% down to make this purchase with the rest of the financing in the form of a mortgage from a local credit union. Of course, it is within 10 minutes of a Starbucks, not on a busy street, and has a good layout. This property meets all of our criteria for a potential investment. Now we need to really break down the numbers. Here is the step-by-step process:

1. **Calculate the Monthly Gross Income.** For starters, never believe the numbers that the seller is giving you unless they are actual rents. He or she is trying to sell the property for the most they can get so those numbers are often much higher than market

rents. I use the traditional lease marketing sites like Craigslist. com, local newspapers, Zillow, local Multiple Listing Service, and other geographic-specific tools. Let's say we realize that all of the rents are under market and we could actually increase total gross rents to $2,600 per month.

2. **Calculate the Monthly Expenses.** The 50% rule is a good screening tool but you really need to get a more accurate number before purchasing or even putting an offer on the property. Monthly expenses include: property taxes, insurance, property management, mortgage, vacancy, and repairs. I like to include reserves that cover improvements as well.

- **Property taxes.** You can find this cost on your local tax assessor's website and divide by 12 to get the monthly amount. You can also contest your tax-assessed value if you think it is wrong. For example, we bought a triplex for $93,500 but it was tax assessed for $150,000. By petitioning to reduce the taxed value, we saved almost $70 per month.

- **Insurance.** Get a quote from your current provider and compare the rate with another company. This will give you a good idea of what to pay for properties moving forward. Be sure to ask for a landlord policy that covers the building but not the personal property. I always talk to my renters about renter's insurance because it is so affordable and can cover them in the case of a fire.

- **Property Management.** I currently manage all of our properties, but you still want to buy a property that makes enough cash flow to hire a property manager if needed. Use 10% of gross rents for your estimate for this cost. This is a key to making this a passive investment that you monitor from a beach. Even if you manage your properties now, you need to be able to have a third party manager take over down the road.

- **Financing.** You can use online mortgage calculators based on quoted rates to get an estimate of the mortgage cost. Zillow has a great payment calculator that allows you to accurately calculate your mortgage payment even if it is private money with higher rates and interest-only payments.

- **Vacancy.** You always have to include this. No matter how nice you are or great your properties are, people will move.

You can use whatever percentage you want but ensure that it is at least 5% of gross rents. (I am always more conservative and stay closer to 8%.) You will be able to get more specific with this number as you get more properties.

- **Repairs.** Always over-estimate this number even if the property is "turn key." You just never know what issues will arise. For new construction I keep this rate around 5%, but for older homes I use 10–25% (and higher, if needed) to cover the cost of improvements.

3. **Calculate Net Cash Flow.** In order to make this calculation, you simply take the revenue and subtract the expenses to get the net cash flow. If you just want the net operating income, take the financing cost out of the expenses and then subtract the updated expenses from the revenue.

Here's what it looks like in numeric form (Table 5):

Table 5. Example monthly budget.

Monthly Budget	
Revenue	
Gross Rents:	**$2,600**
Expenses	
Property Taxes:	$150
Insurance:	$100
Management:	$260
Vacancy:	$230
Repairs:	$230
Total Expenses:	**$1,070**
Monthly NOI:	**$1,530**
Annual NOI:	**$18,360**
Debt Service	$900
Net Cash Flow	**$630**
Annual Cash Flow	**$7,560**
Cap Rate	$18,360 ÷ $230,000 = **8%**
Cash on Cash	$7,560 ÷ $57,500 = **13%**

How Do I Pay for This?

"Great, I found the property, how do I pay for it? I don't have $230,000!"

I have heard this hundreds of times and it can no longer be an excuse. True, you do need money to make this happen. And the more money you can bring to the table, the better numbers will look, but there are several ways to make deals happen.

It is important to know the basic areas those lenders or investors will focus on before lending you the money.

- **Income Verification.** This is easy for a person with a W-2 income, but for those that are self-employed, you will need two years of tax returns to prove your income.

- **Debt-to-Income (DTI).** This calculation looks at the percentage of your monthly debt payments on your credit report compared to your gross monthly income. If your monthly debt payments are $500 and your gross monthly income is $2,500, then your DTI is 20%. The lender then adds the new payment amount to your existing debt and makes sure the new calculation is less than 43%. Some banks may go higher.

- **Credit Score.** Banks want to see above a 620 credit score for you to qualify and above 700–720 to get great rates.

- **Loan-to-Value (LTV).** This is the percentage of the new loan compared to the value of the property. For example, if a bank will only lend up to 80% LTV and the value of the property is $100,000, then the bank will only lend $80,000. On a primary residence, this can be up to 97% while a rental will be no higher than 75%, likely 70%.

Next, let's look at some of the financing options available when purchasing property:

Banks and Credit Unions.

Banks and Credit Unions are the most traditional way to get financing for your property purchases. It is a formal process of meeting with a lender and qualifying for the loan. They assess your income, debt, and credit score.

To purchase a property with 1–4 units (5 or more units will require a commercial loan), you will need 25–30% down, and you will get a very competitive rate. For example, we purchased the triplex for $93,500. We put $23,375 as a down payment with a 30-year term and 5.25% interest from a local credit union. We got a very competitive rate, but it did require a lot of cash to make the deal happen.

The main issue with this type of financing is that you are limited, with a few exceptions, on the number of mortgages the bank or credit union can issue to you (in many cases, you are limited to four mortgages.) For example, we currently have three mortgages on properties, so even if we qualify normally, we could only get one more mortgage through a bank.

Banks and credit unions can be a great place to start your purchasing process and almost always offer the best rates. Here are some important terms you might hear your lenders use:

- **Fixed Rate Mortgage.** Interest rate stays the same for the entire mortgage period no matter what the economy does.

- **Adjustable Rate Mortgage (ARM).** The interest rate is usually lower than a 30-year fixed rate mortgage but can adjust and is variable based on market conditions. This is a great option if you do not plan on being in your home for a long period of time.

- **Amortization.** When you get a loan, the payment is broken down according to the term of the loan so that it balances out at zero on the last payment. The longer the term the smaller the payment. These payments are shown on the amortization schedule. This becomes important when you have balloon payments (date when the entire balance is due) involved because a longer amortization period results in a lower monthly payment. Just a thought.

- **Points.** Points are simply prepaid interest and may be deducted on your taxes. These can be purchased to decrease the interest rate. Be sure to ask your lender if you are purchasing points or if you should.

- **Property Mortgage Insurance (PMI).** Because of the credit crisis of the Great Recession, lenders are requiring PMI if your

Loan-To-Value is higher than 80%. It does not contribute to your principal (a waste if you ask me), but it compensates a lender if your loan is foreclosed on. For conventional loans, when you can show a 80% LTV it can be removed, while FHA Loans require it for the life of the loan.

Cons	Pros
- Large amount of cash needed - Limited to four mortgages (few exceptions)	- Great rates - Up to 30-year terms - Predictable qualification criteria - Most traditional route

Owner/Seller Financing

Seller financing is basically where the seller becomes the bank. You pay a percentage down, usually 20% (you can negotiate this), and the seller finances the remaining balance at a negotiated rate. Typically, you use a third party escrow company for all payments and a closing company for proper execution of closing documents. If you default, the seller can take possession of the property again.

Cons	Pros
- Usually has a balloon payment (entire balance due at a defined time) - Servicing fees through an escrow company	- Don't require bank qualifications - Negotiable down payment and interest rate - Lower closing costs - Debt does not show up on your credit report

Lease to Own

This is a great option for people interested in owning real estate but who don't have the credit or the down payment to purchase in more traditional ways. It allows you to negotiate the purchase price in advance and lease the property for a negotiated time period with the option of purchasing when that time expires. Usually a percentage of your lease payments gets credited towards the purchase price and the seller requires a larger down payment in exchange for the option.

Cons	Pros
- Can lose down payment if you are not able to exercise the purchase option - Paying rent payments to owner for term of lease - Do not actually own the property	- Secures a house with option to purchase later - Inexpensive to get home - Allows you to build your credit & save a down payment - Owner still responsible for maintenance to the home

Home Equity

Eureka! This financing vehicle jump-started our real estate investing and allowed us to access large amounts of cash for down payments without having to move and sell our home.

A home equity line of credit is like a big credit card that is secured by the equity in your home. You only pay on the balance that you have outstanding. It is interest only and usually has a low interest rate. Beware. These rates can adjust as market rates increase.

A home equity loan is a second mortgage where you pay a fixed amount for a fixed time period and you receive all of the money at closing. Again, they use the equity in the home, but if you do not need the money right away, you are paying interest on money sitting in your bank account.

I prefer lines of credit because of the low interest rate and the revolving nature of the loan, so you are only paying for what you use. We used our line of credit as down payments for purchases both with a traditional mortgage or owner financing options.

Cons	Pros
- Takes equity out of residence (which means less profit when you sell it) - Rates may be variable - Qualification requirements	- Allows you to use equity to make money work for you - Low interest rates (cheapest money out there!) - Flexible terms

Hard Money/Private Money

Hard money/private money is financing from an individual or entity with higher rates and fees, but with limited qualification criteria and short-term loans.

I call this "flipping financing." It is meant to be short term and has high interest rates to compensate the lender for the risk. These rates range from 8–17% with terms of six months to three years on average. This type of lending can come in handy on properties that don't qualify for a typical mortgage because of the repairs needed. Some hard moneylenders will even finance the repair costs of the property as well. In essence, they are not lending based on your qualifications, but on the project itself. *Because if you can't make the payments, they will get the property back.*

For example, we used this financing for flipping homes or buying rentals that needed some work. To be more specific, we used private money to buy the home, fix it up, and then refinance it with a traditional lender once it qualifies for a mortgage.

Beware of refinancing, as many banks have a seasoning requirement of up to six months, meaning you cannot refinance until you have owned the property for six months or more. This definitely plays into your cost calculations for the property.

These lenders are not difficult to find in your community. So if moneylenders tell you "no," you should probably re-evaluate the project.

Cons	Pros
- High interest rates - Shorter terms - High closing cost fees	- Fast closings - Able to buy properties in need of significant repairs - Short-term project

Partnerships

There may be projects that are more risky or require more capital, in which case a partnership can be the perfect vehicle. Both partners put up the necessary capital and take out a loan for the property. I will discuss partnerships more in depth in the next chapter, but know that this can be a good option for certain projects. The idea here is that you would rather have 50% of a lot of properties than 100% of a few.

Cons	Pros
- Lose having complete control of the property - More difficult to do cash-out refinances - Partners can be unpredictable	- Mitigates the risk and spreads it between two or more people - Qualify for larger properties - Valuable expertise from different partners

Due Diligence

Caveat Emptor. It means "Buyer Beware."

This phrase is the law regarding the purchase of real estate and basically means that you get what you pay for, so make sure you check out everything before signing on the dotted line.

This often-overlooked step in the process is the most crucial. Due diligence includes the physical inspection of the property and the visual inspection of the financials and information provided by the seller. Your realtor should be able to refer a trusted home inspector for you.

Millennial Insight

I made the mistake of not walking through each unit in a triplex I wanted to buy. We closed on the property and not more than two days later, I got a call there was a small leak. I walked into the unit and not only was there a leak but there was mold and water damage throughout the unit. Next time, I will put on my overalls and grab a flashlight to search every square inch.

Lauren, 31

For every home, I always recommend you hire a professional home inspector and have your contractor (if you have one) walk through the property with you. You want to take note of major items, such as the condition of the roof, foundation, windows, electrical, and plumbing. Of course you want the countertops to look good too but those are cosmetic changes that are easier to make.

Next, you want to verify all of the information that has been provided. Check the utilities and their average costs with the local providers, make sure permits were pulled if visible renovations were completed, verify everything on your contract is included (e.g., like sprinkler systems), and make sure there are no assessments against the property. If it is a rental, then you are also going to verify the leases and any vendor contracts related to the property.

I could write an entire book on due diligence, but for overview purposes, be sure to verify all information and conduct thorough inspections of the property.

To Be or Not to Be a Landlord

The decision to be a landlord should not be taken lightly. The LAZ Lifestyle requires that you have a property manager at some point, but much like McDonald's makes their employees start out flipping burgers and work their way up, it isn't the worst idea to see what property managers do. It can help as you oversee them in the future.

I self-managed our units for the first two years until we became part-owners of a property management company to do that for us. I tried to find a company to oversee our units but was not impressed when I started looking. I soon found that it was difficult to find a person or company that cared about the property as much as I did. I realized not all property managers are trustworthy, and you really need the right person protecting your investment.

It is imperative to interview the right manager or management company until you find the right fit. Here are some questions to ask a potential property manager:

1. How long has your company been in business?
2. How many properties do you manage?
3. How many staff members do you have and what are their job functions?
4. Where are most of the properties located?
5. What other properties do you manage in my neighborhood/area?
6. What criteria do you use to screen tenants?
7. How do you ensure rents are at market rate?
8. How do you market a vacant property?
9. What is the average length of time it takes to fill a vacancy?
10. What percentage of tenants do you have to evict?
11. What are your management fees?
12. How long does it take to turn over a unit when a tenant moves out?
13. How will you communicate with me? Tenants?
14. How often will you physically be at my property?
15. If I sell, do I have to list my property with you?

These are just a few questions, but it is important that you feel confident in the property manager. Once you hire a property manager, your work is not over. You still need to check in periodically and make sure they are doing what they promised and keeping up your property.

But once you find the right property management company, you will just have to check the financials from the beach!

Develop Your Exit Strategy

Before diving head first into real estate, you need to understand your exit strategy. Are you going to sell off all of the properties? Are you going to sell them off as owner finance only so you can carry the real estate note on them? Are you going to consolidate them into larger properties?

It feels odd thinking of the end before you start, but it makes a difference. When you purchase your primary residence home, for example, it helps if you know if you are going to be there two years or ten years. You will get a different mortgage, you will have to buy at a better price to cover closing costs when you sell, and the improvements you make need to adjust closer to market demand rather than your custom style.

For example, our personal exit strategy is to sell all of the rentals on owner finance notes only so that we can keep the monthly income and make a percentage on our money. It defers the tax bill to a degree and gives us steady income through "retirement." You don't have to have all the answers for your exit, but at least think of what your plan for each property is. It may change, but having a better idea before you purchase a property will help protect against foreseeable risks.

LAZ Lifestyle Moves

- Read *Rich Dad Poor Dad* and one other real estate investment book of your choice.
- Listen to at least 20 podcasts on different topics on www.biggerpockets.com.
- Meet with three realtors in your area.
- Talk to a lender at your current bank to see what mortgage amount you qualify for.
- Practice the 8 steps listed above on a hypothetical property that is currently listed for sale.

Wealth Hack Tools

Bigger Pockets

http://www.biggerpockets.com

This is a one-stop resource for real estate investors. It has podcasts, a blog, articles, investment calculators for rentals and flips, and a lively forum to ask your real estate investing questions. This is where your education should begin. I listen to every podcast and try to engage in the forums.

Appfolio

http://www.appfolio.com

This is the program I use. It has a setup fee and is $1 per unit per month. It is designed for a property management company and can help list units, background checks, collect rents, accounting, has an owner portal, and basically anything else you will ever need to manage a property. It has great support and can be customized to fit your individual portfolio's needs.

PayNearMe

http://www.paynearme.com

This great website allows your tenants to pay at a local 7/11 or family dollar and it gets directly deposited to your account, sends you a notification, and allows you to track their rent payments. No more accepting cash.

The Landlord App

http://www.thelandlordapp.com (for Android and iPhone)

The Landlord App has great information about managing a property. The program allows you to find tenants, schedule payments, manage rents, and it has a bill-pay feature for other bills. You can also track prices of other properties in the area to make sure you are keeping your rents at market value.

Wrap Up

Real estate can be the investment vehicle you need to be living the LAZ Lifestyle. It has great benefits, but it is important that you educate yourself on how it works, the terminology, financing options, and every aspect of real estate that you can. Then dive in; do your due diligence and start your investing career. Do not be afraid to reach out for help from local investors and try to find a mentor that can prevent you from learning lessons the hard way. Utilize sites like Biggerpockets and start asking questions on the forums and listening to podcasts. Take notes, soak it all in, and start looking for your first property.

Advice from Millennials

Name: Kate
Age: 32
Occupation: Project Manager, Interactive Web Design Company
Annual Income: $65,000
Family Size: 2
Where do you live? Salem, OR
Do you currently own or rent your home? Own

Why did you get started in real estate?

My husband and I got started in real estate by accident, really. We bought our first home in 2005 and wanted to sell it a few years later but we wouldn't have even broken even on it, so we decided to rent it instead. We have been lucky enough to have it rented ever since! After seeing that we could make a profit each month while having someone else pay down our mortgage, we decided to invest in a duplex property in 2012.

Do you currently work full time? What exactly do you do?

Yes, my husband and I both work full-time. I am a project manager for a web design company and he is a firefighter.

What is it like working full time and investing on the side? Which do you like more the job or the investing?

So far, we have been able to manage working full-time and having our real estate investments without a problem. My husband's work schedule is more flexible than mine, which helps, but most anything that comes up with our properties can usually be handled when we're done with our day jobs. We both like our full-time jobs for now, but are definitely starting to see how real estate investing can be addicting and are currently looking for another property!

How many units do you have? How many do you plan to acquire?

Counting the home we currently own and live in, we own four units. We are looking to partner with another couple on a 4–6 unit building next! Our long-term goal is still uncertain, but I envision us eventually owning between 15–20 units down the road.

Do you use a property management service? If so, why?

We don't use a professional property management company yet, but plan to do so if/when we acquire our next multi-unit property. What we have now is manageable between my husband and I, but once we add 4–6 more units and another investment partner into the mix, we will hire a property manager for that property. The reasons for this are mainly to ensure our quality of life is maintained, but also because it'll just be easier to not have to split up responsibilities with our other investor.

How do you finance your real estate deals?

Our first house was financed with a conventional loan (which has since been refinanced) and we were lucky enough to have our duplex be financed by the owner. To finance the 4–6 unit property we are currently looking for, we are using a personal line of credit we acquired as well as partnering with another investor.

What do you like about real estate? Don't like?

My favorite feature about real estate is that if worse comes to worst, we still have SOMETHING to show for our money and can sell the house (or even live in it.) Conversely, investing in stocks always intimidated me and felt more like gambling because you could invest your money and potentially have NOTHING left if it didn't pan out. My least favorite part of real estate are the unknowns that inevitably come up—whether that's dealing with a mouse problem in one of your houses or simply getting a property leased up—these issues always seem to happen when you feel like you don't have the time or money to deal with them. We somehow always manage to make it work, but it can sometimes feel daunting to deal with these issues on top of everything else going on in our lives!

Do you have an exit strategy for when you are ready to be done owning properties?

We are still kicking around ideas for our exit strategy, but will likely sell most of our units when we decide to retire and either use that money towards retirement or reinvest some (or all) of it, depending on how our finances look at that point.

What advice do you have for getting into real estate?

My biggest piece of advice would be to talk to other people who have invested in real estate and see what works for them and what doesn't. Also, make sure your investment makes sense on paper and is not something you're simply emotionally attached to! It's easy to have emotional attachments to certain properties and get wrapped up in their charm or location, but at the end of the day, real estate investing is a business.

What single piece of financial advice has made the largest impact in your life?

I don't remember who said it, but someone told me that the more you are consumed with money, the more it will consume you. This is so true. Once I started viewing money more like a game that I could play to my advantage, and the less I started counting every penny I made, the more I was able to let go and really move forward confidently with investing and seeing the bigger picture.

10
THINK LIKE AN ENTREPRENEUR

Entrepreneurship is living a few years of your life like most people won't so you can spend the rest of your life like most people can't.

Warren G. Tracy's student

People who say it takes money to make money are using the worst excuse ever. Create massive value for others by providing a solution where no other exists.

Matt Mickiewicz (Founder: Sitepoint, 99designs, and Flippa)

I had dabbled in garage sales, lemonade stands, and the occasional lawn-mowing job as a kid, but I wouldn't quite classify myself as a natural *entrepreneur*. My early income strictly came from working for someone else. It was the way that everyone got his or her money, so I thought. But it wasn't until I was working in 100-degree heat in an apple orchard in Othello, WA, that it hit me… I wasn't the one making money in this deal. I was only 16 years old, but I understood that the owners of the orchard were the ones making the real money. Don't get me wrong, I was grateful for the job, but I realized that I needed to have the control if I was ever going to have the money.

Fast-forward eight years. Whitney and I were living abroad in London, England. I was studying international law in a semester abroad program at the University of London while Whitney was crafting her skills as a photographer.

Whitney is a very talented photographer. Just to put it in perspective, my version of photography takes an object, makes sure that it fits in the screen, and I snap the photo. But not Whitney. She has an eye for it. She would duck under a tree, adjust for just the right lighting, and catch the same building with doves flying across as if rehearsed. She captured London and our travels throughout Europe in a way few people will ever see. It was skill that she had and quickly her pictures were gaining notoriety back home via her blog, Tampien Tandem.

Immediately upon returning home, she was hired to do family pictures for friends, then her first wedding, and viola, Flat 4 Photography was born. (We named it Flat 4 Photography after the flat that we lived in while in London). The photography was still more of just a hobby, as I was still attending law school full-time and she was working full-time at her dad's business. But her eye for detail and talent for capturing unique images quickly grew the business at a pace we could not have anticipated.

The concept that someone would pay you for doing something that you loved took hold in both of our lives. But for me, it wasn't until the addition of the photo booth to the Flat 4 Photography empire that I officially caught the entrepreneur bug. Trying to use and justify my spendy MBA degree, I was always looking for ways to drive traffic to Whitney's photography website (it was the least I could do to help). The traffic had to be organic and not feel forced through something that complimented the photography element.

One fateful day, Lindsay, Whitney's sister, approached us and suggested that we add a photo booth as a part of our business. Lindsay was an event planner at a successful event and catering company in Spokane and had just seen a photo booth the night before at a corporate event. She worked primarily with wedding clients and suggested we enter the wedding market since the only photo booth in town at the time was geared towards corporate events. We looked at pictures online and conducted tireless research on whether it could be successful in Spokane. After a few sleepless nights, we decided to take the plunge. Knowing we did not have much money and were scared to fail, we decided to first put out sensors using social media to see if this would be widely accepted before we ever purchased the booth.

We were amazed at the positive feedback. We booked five events before ever buying the booth.

Going in, we hoped that we could do 5–10 events a year to pay for a small vacation and have something to do with our down time. (I think back now and laugh about our expectations.) We have now been in business for six years, own two photo booths and one Instagram Booth, have four employees, while doing more than 400 events and generating over $300,000 in gross income. Not a bad little side gig.

It started with a passion and morphed into a legitimate business. On January 15, 2012, Whitney was able to stop full-time employment and dedicate her time to Flat 4 Photography. One small step towards financial freedom. The additional income allowed us to invest in IPAs and get to net zero much quicker than we ever thought possible.

Don't Quit Your Day Job

How many times have you been sitting at your office desk, thinking that if you were running the place things would be different? Or in a flash-in-a-pan moment, you have the next pet rock idea to make millions?

There is something alluring about having the next great idea or even just the control of your own destiny. Most will say you are crazy (I know they did with the photo booth purchase), or even foolish for leaving the security of a full-time salary for the unknown of a business. But you are ready to commit anyways. So, I know that you are ready to complete an Office Space-type ritual of destroying the copy machine in an open field with baseball bats as you give your notice, but stop and think bigger. I know you may hate punching a clock and listening to the rants and raves of your tyrannical boss, but stop and think bigger. Remember, active income is always a means to an end.

In order to live the LAZ Lifestyle, you need to have passive income. One of the fastest ways to get passive income is to develop multiple streams of active income. So, though we didn't always enjoy our day jobs, Whitney and I were able to leverage them to purchase and develop IPAs that generate passive income until we have enough to be financially free. I know you thought you could just quit your job, but that job will get you to the LAZ Lifestyle much quicker.

Where Do I Find The Time?

I don't have enough time.

I'm too busy.

I'll work on that later.

I started this book stating that to achieve the LAZ Lifestyle it would take hard work and sacrifice. While your friends are playing Modern Warfare or Madden 2040, you will be out working or educating yourself on investments or the next IPA purchase. Instead of learning the shortcuts on a video game or spending your hard-earned money each night at the next hot spot, you are reading and meeting with individuals that will influence your path in the future. The reality is that if the path were easy, everyone would be on it.

This is where your vision comes into play. When you start to doubt yourself, grab your vision, whether it is a written statement or just a picture, and stare long and hard at it. Repeat after me: *I am being uncomfortable now so I can be comfortable later.*

What you will start to find is that your time will now be filled with activities (and people) that move you towards your vision. I'm not saying you won't play video games ever again or waste your time in one way or another; I have just found that when you want something bad enough, you will make it a priority. Those who don't just don't want it bad enough. Time is such a finite resource that you must learn to value and not waste it on things that won't get you to your vision.

So start by carving out time in the morning, on your lunch break, or before you go to bed to start educating yourself on money, real estate, business, and basically anything you are passionate about. Each month, try to increase the amount of time you spend on this education. Slowly, it will start infiltrating every facet of your life and you will become hungry for more knowledge.

Like Catherine Cook said, "stop just thinking about it, and make it happen. When you're young is the best time to start your own business, as you do not have the responsibilities you will have when you're older. The worst that can happen if you fail now is that you have firsthand experience to make your next venture a success." Remember, *a journey of a thousand miles begins with a single step*. The process takes time and you are in it for the long haul.

Make Your Time Matter

I know nothing about business.

I don't have an MBA.

It's too risky.

Many people never explore the idea to start a business because they feel it is too risky, they simply don't have enough time, or they are not qualified to run a business. But I am going to let you in on a little secret: you are a business. Let me say that again. You are a business. You essentially trade your time (value) for compensation (money). See, you have been running a business this whole time and didn't even know it.

As we discussed previously, time is a finite resource that you must take advantage of to move forward. This is why business owners hire employees, so they can produce more in less time.

The LAZ Lifestyle requires that you get the most money for your time. Thus, if your day job pays well and allows you to save, then that could be your vehicle to passive income. If not, we need to start exploring other options to generate additional income because the more additional income you derive, the more IPAs and passive income you can start to generate. We are looking for an accelerated path that your day job alone might not be able to get you on. But even at that high-paying job, you may be making less than you think. So, let's look at your job and see what you are exchanging your time for.

In their book *Your Money or Your Life*, Vicki Robin and Joe Dominguez spend some time talking about valuing your time (2008). They suggest that you are a business and you are essentially trading your "life energy" for money (Robin and Dominguez 2008). Like any successful business, we need to look at the rate you are exchanging your energy for. For example, if you make $60,528 (2012 U.S. median income) working an estimated 50 hours per week (let's be honest, a 40-hour week is hard to come by), then you would be working for $23.28 per hour before taxes. If you are single, you will be at a marginal tax rate of 25%, resulting in a tax bill of around

$8,450 according to the TurboTax calculator. This means that your time is not valued at $23.28; instead, after tax, it is closer to $20 per hour. Not bad.

Robin and Dominquez actually push you to go a step further to look at how much additional time is spent in relation to work, such as commuting, costuming, meals, daily decompression, escape entertainment, and other job related activities (Robin and Dominguez 2008). For the sake of the example, let's assign arbitrary numbers:

Commuting: 30 min one way, gas, parking, etc. - $650/mth
Costuming: Work clothes - $100/mth
Meals: $15 a day (20 working days per month) - $300/mth
Daily Decompression: Coffee, working out, etc. - $200/mth
Entertainment: Conservatively - $250/mth
Other job related activities: $200/mth
Total: $1,700/mth (or $20,400 annually)

Now let's calculate your dollar-per-hour value: $60,528 – $8,450 – $20,400 = $31,678. Divide that by 2,600 hours to get $12.18 per hour. Yikes.

Despite thinking you are making $23.28 per hour at your "safe," salaried job, after you factor in the additional costs of going to and performing at work, you really are working for $12.18 an hour. These numbers will be different for everybody, but it illustrates the point of seeing the value of your time.

No wonder there is often little left over to put into savings and buy IPAs. Remember, you are in the business of trading your "life energy" for money. By understanding your real hourly wage, you can start to evaluate opportunities that can increase the amount of income you are really bringing in and find ways to get more compensation for your value. Sometimes, that "safe" job really doesn't pay what you think it does.

Where to Start

Starting a business is one of the best ways to generate an alternative source of income, whether it's a photography company or a custom furniture shop on Etsy. No matter what it is, it is time to start. We are going to walk through the IDEAtion process for starting a business that can help you take an idea and turn it into a business.

IDEAtion Process

Do you have that next million-dollar idea? If so, why have you not acted on it yet? Fear? Too much work? What is it that prevents great ideas from moving forward while the inventor of the Pet Rock sells more than 1.5 million rocks to become a millionaire?

The IDEAtion process is composed of four stages: Idea, Development, Evaluation, and the Ask. It helps you start with an idea and take it all the way to getting funded. It can be as simple as a dog-walking service that brings in an additional $500 per month or a 100-employee business, but either way it follows a similar process. So let's walk through it.

Idea

The first step is to develop an idea for your business. The foundational question you must start with is: *what problem are we going to solve?* Businesses are created to solve problems. For example, since we no longer have VHSs (90s kids know what those are), a VCR repairman is irrelevant and the business would fail. A more prolific example is Blockbuster Video. Back in the "old days," you used to get in the car and drive down to the video store to rent a movie. It was an event in itself as you hoped that the movie you wanted wasn't checked out yet. But with the advent of Netflix, CinemaNow, Amazon Prime, and On Demand, you can do all of that from the convenience of your couch, eliminating the need for Blockbuster.

You have a full or part-time job and limited resources so whether this business is going to make you an additional $1,000 per month or replace your existing income; you need to adhere to the following requirements:

1. You must be passionate or enjoy the idea. This is crucial.
2. Inexpensive startup costs (under $10,000, preferably).
3. Profitable or have the ability to be profitable.
4. Since you have a day job, the scheduling must be flexible.

If your business follows these criteria, you will be able to continue your day job and make additional income on the side. You want to start small with low overhead (monthly costs to operate) and flexibility. These conditions lend to service-related businesses but allow for other types as well.

As Cameron Johnson stated, "Put yourself out there. Get started, do something and start small—the lower your startup costs, the easier it is to find profitability. Create value for others, and you'll be rewarded."

For example, when I decided to start a real estate business, I made sure that it fell in the criteria we just discussed:

1. Passionate: I love working in real estate and when you talk to me, it is easy to tell. I enjoy reading about it, studying it, and promoting it.

2. Inexpensive: My startup costs were under $1,500. Have I spent more than that all together? Definitely. But it's important to remember you don't have to get everything at the beginning. Stick to the basics.

3. Profitable: My overhead was low and most of my expenses were incurred when I sold a property. With my fee structure, I made 100% on my commissions.

4. Flexible: Being a realtor requires that I am available on nights and weekends, which still allows me to have a day job while maintaining my real estate business.

We all have it within us to be great and come up with the next million-dollar idea or the next best dog-walking service. Just make sure you find opportunities that fit your necessary criteria. David Hauser advised that you should "always be on the lookout for new venture opportunities from the voids and challenges you experience in your life. Success is finding solutions in challenges that help others; money is secondary."

Development of Your Idea

Now that you have the idea, what do you do next? Research, research, research. Oh yeah, did I say research? You now need to move to the stage where you look at taking a brilliant idea and seeing if it will work.

One helpful tool that I used to examine all of the key areas of my businesses is what is known as a business canvas. The business canvas allows you to take a strategic look at your business so that you can understand how it works and make changes on the fly. Too often business plans are created and then put on the shelf to collect dust because they are so informal they are useless. The one-page design keeps only the most important information for you to review and update as needed. In the example below, they use the following categories: Key Partners, Key Activities, Key Resources, Value Propositions, Relationships, Channels, Customer Segments, Cost Structure, and Revenue Streams (Business Model Innovation Matters 2012) The one I would add to this page is Competitors. By understanding these key areas, you will know how your business will operate, function, compete, and ultimately make money.

Most banks will require a business to have an in-depth business plan explaining and predicting how the business will operate well into the future. But, the reality is that most businesses, or people for that matter, can't look that far into the future. This business canvas allows you to look at and assess where the business is now on one, single page. Even if you are just planning to start a small dog-walking service, it is still good practice to develop a business canvas. It forces you to research the viability of your business concept. You can find several different forms of the business canvas online with a simple search.

Once you have the operational side of the business taken care of, we move to the more daunting financial side. Will this business even make money? Fortunately, you aren't the first person to face this issue. Intuit created the Startup Financial Planner (Quickbooks 2016) that can help you calculate the actual cost for starting a business. It takes the data of what existing companies have spent to start similar types of businesses across the country. In an article in Inc. Magazine, Aaron Anders listed a few principles to consider if using the Startup Financial Planner:

- **Don't sugarcoat the numbers.** Make sure you try to use actual numbers for all of your startup expenses. The Planner looks at all numbers related to starting a business, including the expenses the business had before they actually opened. So you need to be realistic and err on the side of over-estimating (Anders 2014).

- **Prepare for year one.** The Planner helps with this. "After a user enters all the applicable costs into the fields as prompted, the tool generates a financial analysis that shows total costs for first year of business as well as a breakeven analysis with the specific number of months it'll take to recoup startup expenses and ongoing costs. Users can even see how their financial data compares to real businesses in their industry and state (Anders 2014)." These numbers can be used for reference or shared with the bank or investors.

- **Heed expert advice.** The Planners numbers are based on forecasting and do not guarantee success so talk with experts in areas of concern (Anders 2014). The SBA has local representatives at the Small Business Development Centers and local SCORE chapters of experienced individuals that can help you with the planning.

Now that you have the operations and financial pieces worked out, we need to see if anyone would be interested in your idea.

Evaluation of Idea

Perfect. You have the idea and have developed what it is going to look like. Now you need to examine whether it will work. Sure, your mom liked the idea, but we need to see if a broader market will buy your product or service. Barbara Corcoran, one of my favorite celebrities, said something that was so simple, yet so accurate relating to what the consumer wants.

Everybody wants what everybody wants—and nobody wants what nobody wants—is what I learned in selling 2 billion dollars of real estate over 30 years and is the dictum played out every week on Shark Tank, to both the viewers' and the entrepreneurs' delight. If you don't have enough demand for your product or for your service, you should dream up a way to create the illusion that there is (Corcoran 2015).

> **Millennial Insight**
>
> *We started our business on a shoestring budget. We didn't do much research and definitely didn't have a business plan. We learned a lot on the job and I wish we had spent a little more time evaluating the idea!*
>
> Craig, 32

This simple philosophy keys in on the consumer mindset. You must create a business that people want, as this will draw more people. For example, if you walk into a restaurant and you are the only person or couple there, are you more likely to stay or go find another place? Most people will go find another place. If a place is empty, we think it must not be good because nobody else is eating here. This concept is true across the board. So how do you determine if your idea is "in demand"?

To determine demand, one of the tools I did learn at business school was the importance of performing a SWOT analysis. SWOT stands for: Strengths, Weaknesses, Opportunities, and Threats (Mind Tools 2014). Strengths and Weaknesses are the internal factors within an organization while Opportunities and Threats are the external factors derived from the community, market, or societal factors. The website, www.mindtools.com, has free worksheets and more information and videos on how to conduct a SWOT analysis, but we will go over the basics. Let's look at each below.

Strengths

Strengths are the areas your business does well and where you have an advantage over your competitors. How are you doing it better than Acme Corp down the street? You need to know where you have the upper hand and the intangibles that aren't advantages, but a necessity to survive in the business. Here are some questions to ask:

- What are the advantages our business has or will have?
- What are things that we do better than anyone else?
- What unique or lowest-cost resources can you draw upon that others can't?
- What do people in your market see as your strengths?
- What is your organization's Unique Selling Proposition (USP) (Mindtools 2014)?

Think through the strength in terms of what the market or a consumer would think. Ask friends and family to give their objective opinion of the business concept. Google search the business idea in your area so you get an idea of the competition and if the market is saturated. Better to know now before moving forward.

Weaknesses

Weaknesses refer to the areas of the business that are lagging behind compared to competitors. Take a real good look at the weaknesses and find ways to improve this section over time. Here are some good questions to ask:

- What areas of the business need improvement?
- What part of the market should you avoid?

- What would consumers see as your weakness?
- What areas of the business is the competition better at? (Mindtools 2014)

By identifying the weaknesses, you can become more realistic about how to market and pitch your business to others.

Opportunities

Opportunities refer to the things that can happen outside of your business to affect its operations in a positive way. These can be investment in your business area by the government, new development from private developers, increase in population, change in regulations, etc. Start looking at external factors in your area and industry that can be an opportunity for your business. Here are some questions to ask:

- Is your city or region growing?
- What opportunities are there for your business?

Follow this closely through publications by the local business journal or paper that track proposed development. You can also look at things like the state liquor board for new applications for restaurants to see if any are being proposed for your area. You want to have your hand on the pulse of your community to know when the right time is to grow, what the population wants and be in tune with the consumer.

Threats

For every good side, there is a bad. Threats refer to the external factors that can negatively affect your business. Just like the Opportunities, you want to now look at those similar factors to see if they have a negative trend. Here are some questions :

- What obstacles do you face?
- What are your competitors doing?
- Are quality standards or specifications for your job, products, or services changing?
- Is changing technology threatening your position?
- Do you have bad debt or cash-flow problems?

- Could any of your weaknesses threaten your business? (Mindtools 2014)

The SWOT analysis allows you to look at your business concept from all angles and be both optimistic and pessimistic at the same time. It forces you to look short term and long term. This is a good evaluation tool. that allows you to move forward or decide that you need to review the development stage. Worksheet 14 is a sample template that you can use.

Worksheet 14. SWOT analysis template.

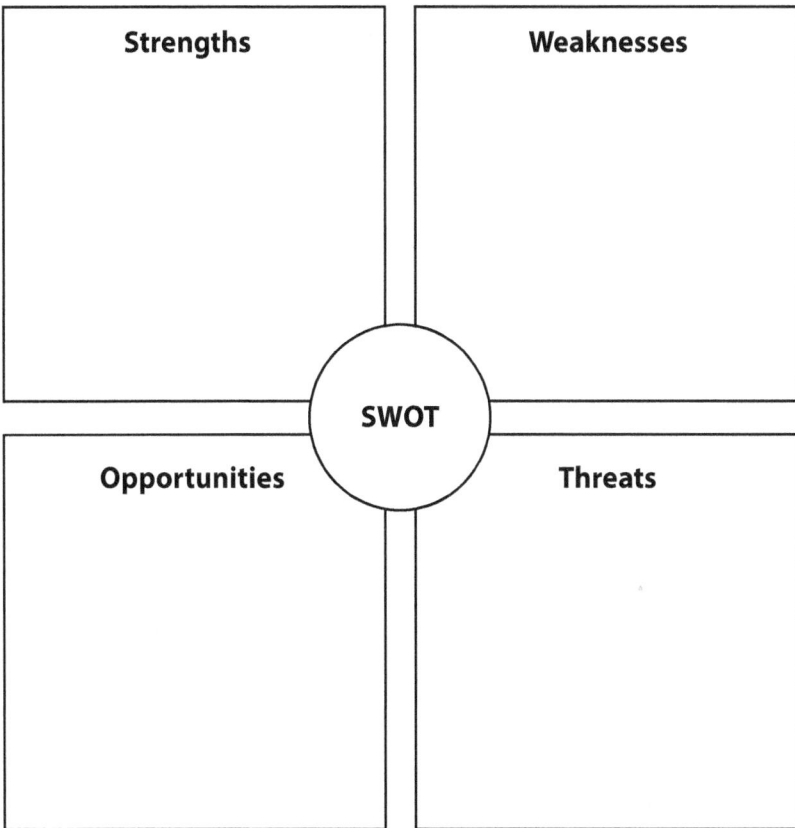

Strengths	Weaknesses

SWOT

Opportunities	Threats

Once you have hashed out the business canvas, you want to start presenting the idea to friends and family to get their feedback. Some of it will be informative and helpful and you will have to disregard other comments. But the more people that can provide feedback, the better you can understand consumer demand for the product or service. You are getting closer!

Ask for Money

Now comes the hardest part, asking for money. You have come up with a great idea and have it all mapped out but how are you going to pay for it? Last time you checked there was about $100 to your name and that was if all of the checks didn't go through at the same time. I will give you some some ideas for low cost startups, but even those take some money. If you are going to be an entrepreneur, you can't let a little thing like money stand in your way.

I will discuss several different options for finding funding, so put that lottery ticket away because, really, you have a better chance of becoming the President of the United States (1 in 10 million) than you do of winning the lottery (Khan 2012). Here are some options for getting your business started:

Bootstrapping

Cleverly, bootstrapping got its name from grabbing the boots by the straps and making it happen. This involves normal refuges of money requests (family, relatives, and friends) but it also includes your personal access to capital as well (credit cards, personal loans, cash in the bank, etc.) Any of these would be considered bootstrapping. This is how most businesses get their start.

When Whitney and I were looking at starting the photo booth business, we were able to get the necessary funds from family and from pre-booking events to buy our first booth. It was a stretch of faith (I mean, they were investing in a photo booth *of all things*) and without them we would not have gotten started, as no bank would lend us startup funds.

Partnerships

Partnerships can be a way for you to mitigate risk and bring expertise into the business in an area that you are less comfortable with. The concept that "more brains are better than one" plays out in the partnership arrangement…sometimes good and sometimes bad.

Partnerships are an interesting option. It is best to think of them as a double-edged sword. Many real estate and business investing books talk about using OPM or other people's money to finance your ventures. This is great but remember you will be in a working relationship. As I have found, things are great when they are great, but when they go bad, you need to be prepared.

As I mentioned earlier, we partnered to start a restaurant and bar in Spokane, WA. The deal did not make sense as strictly a real estate purchase, and, for my business partner, it did not make sense as just a restaurant venture. We decided to partner. Here are a few of the lessons I learned:

- **Think about creating an Entity.** Whether it is an LLC, S-Corp, or C-Corp (all different forms of corporate entities), you want to consider forming this before moving forward. You do not want to be operating this as simply a partnership. Not just for liability purposes, but for how you are going to operate the business.

- **Draft an ironclad Operating Agreement.** We spent weeks on the operating agreement and discussed thousands of possible scenarios. What if a partner dies? What if a partner can't afford to put more money into the business? What if a partner divorces? Who will be in charge of what? You need to go over multiple scenarios so you are comfortable if things go sideways.

- **Partner with a person with a different skillset.** My partner and I have different skillsets; I know the real estate and he knows the restaurant side. It doesn't mean that he doesn't give his opinion on real estate and I don't throw in a comment or two on the restaurant, but I let him do what he is good at and vice versa. It creates a good check and balance.

- **Have the end in mind.** Are you just partnering on this deal or investing for the next 30 years? Do they just want a return on their money or ownership of the business? You need to be thinking of your exit plan (same as in real estate) to ensure your goals are aligned. You do not want the boy band effect where one partner just leaves and you are left picking up the pieces to save the business.

- **Consider your relationships.** If everything goes well then this could be the best decision, but if you were friends before and things go badly, you may lose a close friend. A failing business venture has a way of destroying everything around it. If your business partner is a close friend, strongly consider and discuss the impact if things do go as planned.

Crowdfunding

As a rapidly emerging trend, the new way of lending is crowdfunding. The basic premise is to have multiple other people fund your loan request. It can be one person or it can be a thousand, giving anywhere from $25 to the entire amount. The rates of interest tend to be higher, but some sites will not require collateral for up to $35,000. This can be an easy way to get funds for startup costs.

For a brief understanding of raising capital, I will give you the 2-minute overview. Until recently, businesses could only solicit funds from "accredited investors" who are people who make more than $200,000 (or $300,000 together with a spouse) in each of the prior two years, and reasonably expects the same for the current year, OR has a net worth over $1 million, either alone or together with a spouse (excluding the value of the person's primary residence) …basically, the top 1% of the population (Investor. gov 2013). In order for a business to solicit funds from an "unaccredited investor" (every other poor schmuck), the business would need to issue lengthy disclosures about the riskiness of the investment, which can cost upwards of $25,000 for an attorney to draft. This 8-point font, all caps, single spaced, 100-page document has almost killed the unlucky few that have tried to read it. This requirement was put into law by Securities and Exchange Commission (SEC) regulations enacted in the prehistoric era in the 1933 Securities Act, or the "Blue Sky" laws, as they are better known (SEC 1933). The law was meant to protect grandma from buying blue sky in Montana with her retirement funds. The disclosures are meant to warn would-be investors of the dangers of an investment.

The SEC governs securities which Webster's dictionary defines as "a fungible, negotiable financial instrument that represents some type of financial value" (Merriam-Webster 2016a). Basically, if you are receiving a return of financial value for your contribution, a security is likely created.

As humans do, we have found some loopholes in the law; thus, crowdfunding was born. If no security is created, the disclosure rules do not apply.

The crowdfunding model started with Kiva, a company that gives out small, 0% interest loans to small businesses, and investors are only returned their principal invested. No return = no security. The bigger sources gaining notoriety are Kickstarter and Indiegogo (and every other variance that has since been created). These sites allow individuals to post videos and stories to request "gifts" (no need to repay) to fund their activities and, in return, they give them a pat on the back, a shout out, cup of coffee, or any other non-financial reward.

No one thought this would catch on, but since its inception, Kickstarter has successfully funded 81,213 projects to the tune of $1,619,357,633 (Kickstarter 2015). This is all money that does not need to be repaid by the requester. Again, you simply offer a token, gift, or gesture in return for the funds given by investors.

Certain activities and products have generated over $1 million from their crowdfunding campaigns. The most recent is the "10-year hoodie" that raised over $1,053,830 from 9,226 investors (Kickstarter 2015). The shirt is American made and designed for sustained quality. But it's just a sweatshirt. What are people thinking? This just proves that crowdfunding is a viable avenue to raise funds for a project or business.

If you have an idea that your friends, family, and network would support, this can be a great way to get the idea going. You will want to read more about the differences between the platforms. For instance, if you do not receive the total amount you were requesting on Kickstarter, then you get nothing, but on Indiegogo, you get to keep any of the money that you raise. It does take some work to put together the pitch but the reward can definitely be worth it.

Peer-to-Peer Lending

Now that you understand crowdfunding, peer-to-peer lending will be a walk in the park. Essentially, this is crowdfunding except you make money on your investment. For example, if I need $10,000, I can use peer-to-peer lending platforms to get investment from multiple investors in amounts as small as $25. It can be one person or it can be a thousand people giving anywhere from $25 up to the entire request. The rates of interest tend to be higher, but some sites like Lending Club and Prosper will not require collateral for up to $35,000. The host sites have invested in and completed all of the disclosure requirements, so the business and the investor do not have to worry. They are complying with the law.

These can be great ways to get started and get funding very quickly. You are assessed based on your credit and total income. You are assigned a grade and your interest rate is based on that grade. You are given terms as short as a year and up to five years to repay. We used this method to fund the down payment for a rental unit and, since there are no prepayment penalties, we simply pay it back like a normal bank loan.

If I had a crystal ball, this is where I see lending going in the future. A simple, clean platform that assesses your information in minutes rather than weeks and gets you funded quickly.

Preselling

Preselling is a method similar to crowdfunding. Basically, you offer your product or service through a gift card, early booking or something in the future at a discount for funds right now. For example, we pre-booked five photo booth events where we offered a discount for paying in full. We then took the money we received and bought the photo booth. The clients got a deal and we didn't have to borrow much money to buy our booth.

This can be a great method for product- or service-based businesses and has an underlying benefit of creating business loyalty and testing whether the market is ready for your idea. This can be an easy one to try to get feedback on. If you can't presell any of your services, you might want to revisit the evaluation phase to see if you are marketing your business correctly.

Traditional Bank or Credit Union Loans

You may be wondering why I didn't start with this option: the good ole bank and credit union on the street corner in almost every city in America. I think this is a viable option, but they have a tendency to not fund startups without significant collateral. Society has shifted from the relational banker to stats on a piece of paper. I have found that it is still important to get a relationship established with a local institution that can grow with you and, when you need the money the most for the once-in-a-lifetime deal, they can be that option for you.

To recap, they may not fund your initial startup project, but it will be important to establish a relationship with a local bank or credit union as you grow because they will be vital to acquiring IPAs down the road.

Remember, think longer term and think bigger. It may be a single-family home today and a 110-unit apartment down the road.

SBA Loans

A great product that was introduced through the Small Business Administration is SBA Loans designed to assist small businesses. These are loans provided by a local bank or credit union but are backed by the SBA, which decreases the risk for the bank. They do require collateralization, but are really good loans when looking to purchase real estate. Here are four of the main loan programs:

SBA Express Program: This program is designed to provide a quick response to your loan application, usually within 48 hours. SBA small business loans can be used for equipment purchases, expansion, owner-occupied real estate purchases, working capital, and more. The beauty of this loan is that there is an accelerated loan application response time and you have your choice of a fixed and variable rate with loan amounts up to $350,000.

7(a) Loan Program: This program is perfect for finding the capital your business needs to operate, expand, and succeed. It can be used to purchase new equipment, real estate expansion, or working capital. This is a more flexible loan that has a fixed and variable interest rate with longer loan terms and no balloon payments. You can get loans up to $5 million.

504 Loan Program: This program is designed to allow business owners to receive up to 90% financing for the purchase, construction, and renovation of owner-occupied real estate or for purchasing machinery and equipment. Again, you can get a fixed or variable rate with loan amounts up to $12 million.

USDA Loan Program: This program is designed to improve the economic and environmental climate specifically in rural areas. The USDA loan proceeds are used to develop and finance businesses in rural communities. If you qualify, (your business is in a designated rural area) then you get a fixed or variable rate with longer and favorable terms and interest rates (SBA 2014).

Home Equity

Home equity has been a game changer. We are able to use the equity from our homes at low interest rates to buy IPAs and repay and reuse again. Obviously, you must own the real estate to have this option, but if you own your home and do not want to sell but have equity in the property, you can go to your local bank or credit union or even online companies (Quicken Loans) to pull that equity out in the form of a fixed rate loan or a line of credit. Often referred to as a HELOC. Now, I don't want you to rush to bank and pull all of your equity out now. Remember the debt chapter: you should only use debt if you are buying something that produces income, not to go on vacation or buy that new car you've had your eye on. Understand that when you pull that equity out, you may have to bring money to the table when you go to sell. Understand the risk before moving forward.

Angel Funding or Venture Capital

Think Silicon Valley. Shark Tank. Tech startups. High growth businesses. Both Angel investors and venture capitalists are, for the most part, looking for equity positions in your company in exchange for cash. One of my favorite shows is Shark Tank where accredited investors hear pitches from businesses about their next great thing and the investors ask questions to decide if they want to invest. But all of the pitches start with the ask (i.e., 10% of my company for $100,000 or 25% of my company for $50,000). They are willing to give up part of their company in exchange for the finances and expertise to get to market.

This can be a great option for some larger, more scalable businesses where you need a significant injection of capital. I was always told to not worry about the money because, if you have a good investment, the money finds you.

Tell People...Grassroots Style

With any business, you need to learn to self-promote. You need to let your connections and network know that you have a business and are ready to work. The most powerful source of advertising will be word of mouth. Getting clients is hard, but keeping clients can be harder. You must create a customer experience with good communication, prompt responses, and a quality service or product. A good referral goes a long way.

Whitney handles the customer experience with Flat 4 Photography and has a policy of returning calls or emails within 24 hours. Countless times, the clients have booked our photo booth or her photography services simply because she was the first to respond. I can't stress enough the importance of communicating with the client and ensuring that they have a good experience. Just as good news and feedback travels fast, bad news and feedback travel even faster.

25 Businesses and Startups Under $10,000

Here are some ideas to get your brain thinking about new business ideas:

1. Real Estate Agent
2. Pet Groomer
3. Translator/Interpreter
4. Freelance Writer/Blogger
5. Bookkeeper
6. Photographer
7. House Cleaning
8. Virtual Assistant
9. Website Design
10. Etsy/Ebay dealer
11. Uber Driver
12. Home inspector
13. Massage therapy
14. Computer Repair
15. Dog Walking Services
16. Lawncare
17. Vending Machine Owner
18. Tutor
19. Consultant
20. Estate sale specialist
21. Personal trainer
22. Handyman
23. Franchise opportunity
24. Bicycle repair
25. Childcare

Wealth Hack Tools

Kickstarter

http://www.kickstarter.com

Kickstarter is a site where creative projects raise donation-based funding. These projects can range from new creative products, like an art installation, to a cool watch, to pre-selling a music album or book. It's less designed for businesses, causes, charities, or personal financing needs.

Indiegogo

http://www.indiegogo.com

While Kickstarter maintains a tighter focus and curates the creative projects approved on its site, Indiegogo approves donation-based fundraising campaigns for most anything — music, hobbyists, personal finance needs, charities, and whatever else you could think of (except investment). They have had international growth because of their flexibility, broad approach, and their early start in the industry.

Crowdrise

http://www.crowdrise.com

Crowdrise is a place for donation-based funding for causes and charity. They've attracted a community of do-gooders and fund all kinds of inspiring causes and needs. A unique points system on Crowdrise helps track and reveal how much charitable impact members and organizations are making.

Quirky

http://www.quirky.com

If you're an inventor, maker, or tinkerer of some kind, then Quirky is a place to collaborate and crowdfund for donation-based funding with a community of other like-minded folks. Their site digs deeper into helping the process of bringing an invention or product to life, allowing community participation in the process.

Lending Club

http://www.lendingclub.com

Lending Club offers unsecured (no collateral required) loans up to $35,000 on terms up to 60 months. The rates vary depending on your credit worthiness but can be funded quickly. There is a fee that is usually a percentage of the total loan amount and all payments must be ACH (automatically withdrawn from your bank account). They are growing at a rapid pace and think of this as an option for you moving forward.

Prosper

http://www.prosper.com

Same as Lending Club, but has some different algorithms for their credit worthiness rating. You will see the rates and terms fluctuate a little but very similar in all other regards.

Upstart

http://www.upstart.com

This is another peer-to-peer lending site but it is unique in that it values your education in their algorithm. You can borrow up to $25,000 with rates starting at 5.7% with no prepayment penalty. Finally, something that values that high-priced education!

Kabbage

http://www.kabbage.com

This is designed for existing businesses but allows them to borrow up to $100,000 by examining real-life data instead of just a credit score. You can use the money to buy inventory, equipment, marketing, staff, or even working capital. The fees can be high and range from 1–13.5% with shorter terms.

LAZ Lifestyle Moves

- Take 30 minutes and write down as many business ideas as you can that you would be interested in. Then run them through the business criteria and see how many emerge.

- Talk to five friends about ideas they have for a business.

- Start reading your local paper or business journal once a week to see what is arriving or needed in your community.

- If you do not know your community, take two hours this weekend to drive around and get to know your community.

- Use your smartphone or carry around a pen and paper to record any business ideas. Start a list and reference it for potential additional streams of income once per week.

Wrap Up

So do you think you are ready to take that idea and turn it into another stream of income? Make sure that it fits the criteria and you have taken the time to research, develop a business canvas and assess the financial projections. There is risk in business, but by taking the appropriate steps, we can work to mitigate the risk and start creating income. So next time you have that great idea, write it down and run it through the IDEAtion process. You never know where it may lead.

Advice from Millennials

Name: Ryan and Alissa
Age: 28, 27
Occupation/Job Title: Videographers
Annual Income: 60k
Family Size: 3 + 1 on the way…
Where do you live? Spokane Valley, WA
Do you currently own or rent your home? Rent

Do you own your own business? How long?

Yep. It'll be 4 years in January.

What's the business name? Was it hard coming up with it?

Ferguson Films. Not hard at all—seemed to flow and is hopefully easy to remember.

What industry are you in? Why did you choose that niche?

Video Production—mostly wedding cinematography. Video production has always been Ryan's passion, even through high school. We both are creatively minded people and enjoy the many avenues the industry brings.

How did you get the idea for your business?

Honestly, it started as a way to make additional money so that I could quit my job and stay home with our little girl. But it rapidly became a thriving business we wanted to make our primary source of income, so we worked towards making it just that.

Do you currently work another full-time job? If not, what made you commit full-time to your small business?

Used to—Ryan had another full-time job the first three years of our business. Ferguson Films kept growing, and the goal was to make it our primary income. In the last year of Ryan's full-time job, we were often turning down work for our business because there was just no time available. We knew, in order to make Ferguson Films thrive, we needed to commit and go all in. Ryan was able to go full-time for the business last January, and it's been so worth the three years of insane schedules and very late nights we went through.

How did you finance your business to get started?

Because Ryan had another full-time job, we chose to live on less, save up, and purchase equipment as we could. The nature of our industry allows us to build gear as we need it, so we made sure there was no initial debt involved while starting our business.

How do you market your business? What's effective?

We've tried a few strategies—blogs, shows, etc. At this point, our most effective tool is word of mouth. References from other vendors and previous clients are huge.

Social media is the best way for us to showcase what we do to large audiences. A friend of a friend happens to come across our work, and ends up liking what we do. That's really the most common way we get work.

What is the hardest part about your business?

Not having a consistent income—it's a little unnerving that our livelihood depends on whether we book projects, specifically weddings. Some book really late, others book early. Some months are full, others are bare.

You just never know in this industry, and each year is different in our experience so far.

What single piece of financial advice has made the largest impact in your life?

Do everything you can to avoid debt. Don't live outside your means. Set goals and work towards them. We continue to work towards where we want to be, and that means making sacrifices now to get there.

What advice do you have for those starting a business?

Ask yourself, "Is this my passion?" Do I want to do this above all else careerwise? If the answer is no or even maybe, I would rethink starting the business at all. It's hard work to have your own business. There are many hurdles involved and sacrifices to be made. We've had our share, and I'm sure we will experience many more. But the bottom line is, it's worth it to us. We love it. It allows us to exercise our excitement and love for creativity while providing the means to live. And *that* is a beautiful combination. So if you love it, go for it. Make it happen. It'll be worth it in the end.

11

NEW MILLENNIAL RETIREMENT PLAN: BUY IPAS

As far as your personal goals are and what you actually want to do with your life, it should never have to do with the government. You should never depend on the government for your retirement, your financial security, for anything. If you do, you're screwed.

Drew Carey

Don't let the opinions of the average man sway you. Dream, and he thinks you're crazy. Succeed, and he thinks you're lucky. Acquire wealth, and he thinks you're greedy. Pay no attention. He simply doesn't understand.

Robert G. Allen

The water rippled softly as I submerged my hand and the hot Mediterranean sun warmed my skin. I laid back with a glass of white wine in one hand and the newest John Grisham novel in the other as I reclined near the pool. We were staying in Santorini, Greece in a small cave house with a stunning view of Oia, the picturesque city below, along with the mammoth cliffs surrounding the island. Whitney and I had always wanted to go to Greece, and rather than wait until we retired, we decided to do it now.

She emerged from the dwelling, "This place is amazing! Why didn't we do it sooner?" She grabbed her glass of wine and snuggled in next to me as we both stared at the golden, red sun as it disappeared in the ocean water below. What an amazing experience!

On this particular trip, we travelled to Croatia, Montenegro, Greece, and the Netherlands. We returned home with enough memories to last a lifetime. Suffering from a little jet lag and too tired to cook, we decided to grab a pizza on our way home from the airport. Whitney called it in and I ran inside the pizza parlor to get it. A man about 65 years in age with a slight limp and distinct drawl in his voice greeted me as I entered while he tallied my total.

"That will be $12.50," he explained.

I accidentally tried to pay in Euros that I forgot to exchange at the airport, which prompted a conversation about our trip as I explained where we had gone.

"I have always wanted to go somewhere. I have never been outside the state," the older gentleman responded.

I couldn't believe it. Not outside the state? Washington is not that big. As I was thinking through the statement, a girl no more than 20 years old stormed over and started yelling, "This is all wrong. You rang in his order wrong and I have tried to explain this to you 30 times!!!" The older gentleman retreated back and started to respond but decided to remain silent. "Just go mop the floors then," the girl yelled and she rolled her eyes and walked away, forgetting I was even there.

The man slowly grabbed the mop, and with the most defeated look I have ever seen, he moved towards the back of the store and began mopping.

I couldn't help but think how terrible this whole situation was. I immediately felt sorry for him, but then my thoughts turned to "why?" Why had he not planned better to avoid this? How could he be this age and never have left the state? And why is a smart-ass 18-year-old bossing him around? This situation imprinted in my mind as a vivid illustration of what a lack of planning for the future can do to your life.

After all that, our pizza was burnt so we just threw it out, but the lesson I took away from that pizza shop has stuck with me. *I do not want that to be me.* I do not want that to be *you.* So how do we ensure this does not happen?

The reality is that Americans struggle when it comes to saving for retirement. The most recent data from the Employee Benefits Research Institute shows that more than one-third of workers have saved less than $1,000 (Gauba 2015). That is less than $1,000 to live on when they want to retire and start enjoying life. What inevitably happens is, like the older gentleman, these people have to keep working whether they want to or not. How do we avoid this? Let's start by talking about this crazy notion of retirement, or what I like to call "simply doing what you want to do every day." Let's not wait until 65!

Mark Singer once said, "I believe that the biggest mistake that most people make when it comes to their retirement is they do not plan for it. They take the same route as Alice in the story from Alice in Wonderland, in which the cat tells Alice that surely she will get somewhere as long as she walks long enough. It may not be exactly where you wanted to get to, but you certainly get somewhere."

What is Retirement Really?

Retirement. Retirement. Retirement. You say it enough times and pictures start to form in your mind of yourself walking slowly across a beach with a margarita in hand as the sun sets. But what is retirement, really?

The concept of retirement, as a common event in a person's life, can be traced back to 1889 when it was introduced by Otto von Bismarck of Germany as he promised Germans over 70 that the state would provide them with income (Hiemstra 1999). It reared its head in American culture when the Social Security Act was signed in 1935 in a similar attempt to assist the aging population. Social Security was designed as a "pay-as-you-go" system. Basically, this means that payroll taxes from current workers are used to pay the benefits for current retirees. This allows people to stop working and get new blood into the workforce, but there is an inherent flaw: What happens when the proportion of retirees grows far faster than the number of people working to support them (New Direction 2016)? It stops working. Similar to a parent whose income stops growing but they continue having kids. The solution is that the parent can either earn more or go into debt, or cut back on the amount of money available for each child. So played out, how long can this system last and how much will you actually be able to rely on it?

The Great Recession exposed this major flaw as retirement accounts were hit with devastating losses, forcing a great reliance on Social Security and exposing the fact that people simply did not have enough to live on and retire. Now instead of retiring, people are working longer just to survive, creating a backlog of available young workers to take their place.

This antiquated notion of retirement must be flipped on its head. Do you really want to wait until 65, 70, or 75 to actually start living? What if it is too late? I have a colleague that, along with his wife, saved and sacrificed to renovate and sustain a vacation rental that they wanted to retire to. My colleague was three months from retirement and his wife passed away suddenly. That life they had envisioned and saved all those years for was gone.

The new definition of retirement for the LAZ Lifestyle is simply being financially able to do what you want to do when you want to do it. This can be different for everyone, but please do not wait until you're 65 years old to start living your life!

Millennial Insight

How can I think of retirement when I barely pay my bills now? By understanding the skills I had, I was able to get a part-time gig writing and now every penny of that check goes into a retirement savings account.

Alex, 25

Millennials and Money

The previous section pleaded with you to start living, but I want to take a step back and ensure that you are doing so in a financially sustainable way. Again, as a millennial you are unique and different and require a different strategy than your parents. Your parents' retirement advice and information was designed to address their needs in an economy far different than the landscape of today's economy. They were basically taught to save money, invest in the stock market, and work for a company for 30–40 years while watching their money or pension grow. Then one day they could hope to retire around 65 years old after a long, career-oriented life. I don't know about you but that does not sound like a fun plan!

First of all, the idea of working one place for 30 years is a thing of the past. And the long-term notion of savings is lost on most Millennials. We need something we can work for *now* and reach in a reasonable amount of time. You need the Millennial Retirement Plan: Financial Freedom!

I have talked about the benefits of real estate and business ownership, but sometimes it is easy to overlook the greatest income stream of all: simply saving money. It is not sexy and moves at a snail's pace, but over the long term, you can utilize the power of compounding interest to grow your net worth.

Save Early, Save Often

You just completed college, have student loan debt up to your ears, a car loan on an old jalopy that could break down at any point, and you're struggling to get a burger-flipping position at a local burger joint. You may be asking, "How can I possibly invest?"

Save early, save often. Find ways to make more money, educate yourself on IPAs, and save so that when you see the right opportunity you are ready. Remember this LAZ plan is more than just a way to make more money, it is a lifestyle change where you look at every day as a challenge to learn more, earn more, and ultimately *live* more.

Small amounts of money can grow with the compounding interest. Albert Einstein referred to compounding interest as "the eighth wonder of the world." He went on to say that "he who understands it, earns it ... he who doesn't ... pays it."

But what does it look like in practice? Let's say you are 25 years old and have no retirement savings (this was not far from the truth for me). What if you started with $1,000 in your retirement account and saved $100 per month? Here's what it would look like 40 years from now (Table 6) when I am supposed to retire (we will use a modest 8% interest rate):

Table 6. Example amortization schedule for return on investment.

Year 1	$2,200.00
Year 5	$8,509.25
Year 10	$19,542.80
Year 20	$59,575.31
Year 40	$332,592.34

So, if we break down these numbers, you contributed $49,000 over the course of 40 years. But because of compounding interest, you now have $332,592.34. Who wouldn't love to have that? Can you carve $100 per month?

A very important factor to note is time. The sooner you start saving money, the better off you will be. For instance, look at the example in Table 7.

Table 7. Comparison savings schedule compounded over time.

Age	Sam	Joe
20	$10,000.00	$0
30	$21,589.25	$1,000.00
40	$46,609.47	$19,542.80
50	$100,626.57	$59,575.31
65	$319,204.49	$221,565.51

Sam decides to make one big deposit of $10,000 into a deferred-tax IRA at the age of 20 and never makes another monthly contribution. Joe waits until he is 30 to deposit $1,000 and then he deposits $100 per month until he is 65 years old. Assuming 8% interest, this is what each would have at age 65.

That is a difference of **$97,638.98**.

So start with $100 per month. Too much? Start with $25 per month. The amount is irrelevant. What is important is building the habit of saving money for a long-term purpose. I am not talking about saving to go on vacation. I am talking about the savings that allows you to not have to work anymore.

But first, you need to understand *how* your money grows to find the best ways to make it grow.

An easy way to see how long it takes your money to double is the "Rule of 72." You start by dividing 72 by the annual rate of return, so you get a rough estimate of how many years it will take for the initial investment to duplicate itself (Moss 2015). By understanding how your money grows, you can start plugging in returns on real estate, stocks, bonds, and other IPAs to see how quickly your money will grow.

> **Rule of 72**
> 72 ÷ Rate of Return = # of Years for Investment to Double

Your Number

Do you remember those commercials with people walking around with an orange dollar figure hovering over them? It was supposed to be their number for retirement, the amount of money they needed to save in order to survive while they were retired. What is your number? $1,500,000? $2,000,000?

$5,000,000? As this number gets larger and larger, so does the overwhelming task to generate that much money.

Why do we focus on the total amount of money we need to save in retirement? Financial advisors used the 4% rule to guide this decision. What is the 4% rule you ask? The 4% rule states that you will withdraw 4% of your total number each year so, without any increase or decrease of that number, you could survive on that amount of money for 25 years. This was great for our parents' and grandparents' generations, but we are living longer and longer and wanting to retire earlier and earlier.

What I propose is that we look at a different number. We look not at the total nest egg number but the monthly income we need in retirement. So instead of $5,000,000 total, we need $10,000 per month. Which number seems more achievable?

By shifting the focus to generating IPAs for a certain monthly income, we create a scenario, if done right, that allows us to have inflation-adjusting income whether we live 25 years after retirement or 100 years. By focusing on monthly income, we can plan to purchase the IPAs that get us to financial freedom.

For example, if I need $8,000/month to live the life I want to in retirement, I can complete this objective by owning rental properties that cash flow $8,000 per month. Therefore, in retirement I have the cash flow and can access the equity from the property if needed or sell it entirely if I just want the cash.

A major downside I have seen regarding stocks is the market itself. It is a true rollercoaster, except your retirement and livelihood are at stake. How much control do you have when you are on a rollercoaster? Can you make it go left or right or speed up or slow down?

I know most financial advisors just cringed, and if this were a blog post, they would have vehemently commented on the absurdity of such a statement. So let me finish. The stock market does have a place in your retirement plans, but it should not be the sole source. A strong retirement would have the cash flow of rental income and long-term notes and the security and appreciation of investment in the stock market.

Millennial Retirement Model: Financial Freedom

At this point, the term Financial Freedom should be etched in the core of your being. Your new retirement plan requires getting enough passive income to attain the required monthly income necessary to retire. Financial Freedom, again, is when you generate enough income to pay all of your expenses for the rest of your life. Typically, this would be income from real estate, dividends, payments from notes, and other IPAs. The goal is to start young and build as many streams of income as possible.

Financial freedom is not a new concept but few people strive to achieve it. Mr. Money Mustache is a financial blog run by a man who reached financial independence in his 30s. By investing 50 to 75% of his income during his working career in his 20s and early 30s, he reached financial independence before 40 (Moore 2015). Some people have done it by starting and selling a business, others use rental properties, and others use hobby income or part-time income to make it happen. As Allan Moore states, "The most popular way [to get financial independence] is probably the most accessible: save huge percentages of income. [People]…report saving anywhere between 30% and 70% or more of their income. The majority of this group then invests that money in inexpensive, passively-managed index funds" (Moore 2015). Mr. Moore goes on to opine, "They don't need $1 million to $3 million in the bank when they're 63 years old. Instead, they may need to reach an investment goal of $250,000 or $500,000 in assets before they can start withdrawing 3–4%, because, along with other income streams, this is enough to cover their expenses each year for life" (Moore 2015).

This approach seems more manageable and achievable before we are too old to take advantage of the freedom. "Financial independence allows you to experience the kind of freedom that retirement does not. Free from the obligation of working a job because it's necessary to pay bills and allows financially independent people to explore new work, projects, businesses, and opportunities. It enables individuals to try new hobbies or go new places that old age and ill health may eliminate in traditional retirement after a decades-long working career" (Moore 2015).

By buying IPAs, you can develop these streams of passive income that free you from the burden a 9-to-5 job and provide the flexibility to dabble in activities of interest or volunteer just because. Remember, we just need a set monthly income that grows with inflation well into the future.

Diversification

Similar to real estate where the mantra is "location, location, location," financial advisors preach "diversify, diversify, diversify." But what does this really mean? I had a little encounter that went something like this…

"What about diversification? Jordan, you need to diversify if you want to be successful! You have all of your investments tied up in real estate." A financial advisor pointed out.

"Why? I know real estate. I understand it." I pleaded.

"What if the market turns like 2008 and real estate values plummet? You would lose all of your equity. You need to make sure when, and I mean *when* not *if*, real estate values drop again, you have other investments that make money. Diversification."

"So you are saying I need to break even to prevent me from losing everything?" I paused. "Sounds like a bad investment."

I thought about what the advisor said and I understand the foundation for his statement. Nobody wants to lose everything. I have a majority of my investments tied up in real estate. But does that mean that we invest in things that lose money now in order to prevent us from losing more later? I struggled with this concept for several weeks and finally found an article that helped explain it:

It's a classic moment in sports history. With less than 20 seconds left in Game 6 of the 1998 N.B.A. finals and the Chicago Bulls down by one, Michael Jordan goes one-on-one with Bryon Russell of the Utah Jazz. He pushes off (clearly!),

Russell stumbles and the ball hits nothing but net. Game over. Bulls win.

Now let's imagine that something different happened. Jordan misses the shot in Game 6, and Game 7 comes down to the same spot: fewer than 20 seconds left with the Bulls down by one. If you're Phil Jackson, the head coach, do you set up the last play for Jordan, or does the ball go to someone else? Remember, Jordan missed the night before.

Of course the right strategy is to put the ball in Jordan's hands. Just because he missed the shot before doesn't mean it was the wrong strategy to have Jordan shooting the ball in the final seconds. The odds are incredibly high that he will make the shot even though he missed it the night before. I bring this up because it perfectly captures the investing adage that never seems to die: diversification is "broken" (Richards 2013).

Carl Richards wrote an article in *Business Insider* stating that diversification is simply hedging your risk on your investments. Basically, diversification is boring. It works if you give it time to work. He likens it to a baseball analogy saying that diversification is the "investing equivalent of hitting singles and doubles your whole life, and who grows up wanting to do that? We want to hit home runs. Players who try to hit home runs every time (like timing the market) are going down swinging in a blaze of glory or knocking it out of the park. Either way, it's cool, sexy, and exciting — all the things diversification is not" (Richards 2013).

I look at multiple streams of income as diversification. Diversification has merits and can be the balancing factor that allows you to weather any economic storm.

Types of Retirement Accounts

Now that we've got diversification out of the way, we have more questions to answer. What exactly are the different accounts that you can utilize to save money for retirement? What does it look like to contribute to a retirement account? Do you pick the stocks? Do you decide when to sell and when to buy? Maybe. (This is why I stick to real estate…less confusing!)

Retirement accounts have always confused me. So I will provide a little information on different types of accounts and how you go about using them. Again, these sections are informational, and I always recommend talking with an expert about each option.

The 401(k)

The 401(k) is the holy grail of retirement accounts that is available to full-time employed persons at a firm that offers this option. Some firms may have another form of a defined contribution plan like a 403(b) which functions very similarly (Rosenberg 2014).

There are several benefits for utilizing this plan:

- Contributions are made with pre-tax income and lower your year-end income tax bill.
- Your company is likely to automatically enroll you in an investment offered under its 401(k) plan. Most companies allow you to adjust the default investment and contribution percentage.
- Your employer may offer you a matching contribution up to a certain amount (Rosenberg 2014).

Remember this is a deferred tax account; meaning that you don't pay tax today but will have to pay taxes on the money you will withdraw in retirement. According to the IRS, "Starting in 2015, the maximum you can contribute to a 401(k) is $18,000 per person, or $1,500 in pre-tax dollars per month. If you are 50 years old or older, you can contribute an additional $6,000 in 2015 for a total of $24,000 per year (Rosenberg 2014)." These limits apply on an individual basis so couples can save $36,000 per year, which really ramps up your retirement savings.

Roth 401(k)

This product follows similar rules as the 401(k) but allows you to be taxed on your contributions now, and every dollar you withdraw in retirement will be tax-free.

Traditional IRA

According to Charles Schwab, the traditional IRA "is an Individual Retirement Account to which you contribute pre-tax or after-tax dollars, and which allows your money to grow tax-deferred. When you make withdrawals after age 59½, they're treated as current income" (Charles Schwab 2015).

According to Eric Rosenberg, "*Anyone can contribute to a Traditional IRA, but your income level and whether or not you also contribute to a 401(k) will determine if you can also get a tax deduction for the year of your contribution.*

In 2015, you can contribute $5,500 if you are under 50 or $6,500 if you are 50 or older. Your 401(k) contributions lower your pre-tax (or gross) income, so if you are the sole breadwinner and your family's gross income is more than $191,000, maxing out your 401(k) could result in lowering your income enough to allow you to fully participate in an IRA."

He goes on to say that, *"unlike a 401(k), IRA contributions are based on family income, not individual income. If only one spouse is working and has access to a workplace benefit plan, as long as your family's total gross income is lower than $191,000 per year, you can contribute to an IRA for partial or full deduction. (See IRS guidelines for spousal IRAs.)* Traditional IRAs can be a good place to start, as they are the most common. Again, consult a financial expert to determine the best fit for you.

Roth IRA

The beauty of a Roth IRA accounts is that it allows you to pay the taxes up front—and withdraw your money tax free down the road. *According to the IRS, to be eligible to contribute to a Roth, you must have earned at least some taxable income in the calendar year and your eligibility phases out once you start earning between $114,000 and $129,000 for an individual. The limit if you're married and filing jointly is $191,000. If you're a high earner, you can take advantage of a Roth by using a Roth 401(k) or by converting money from a Traditional IRA into a Roth. (Learn more about the Roth IRA rules for a conversion.)*

If you're looking to roll over an old 401(k) and trying to decide between a Traditional and Roth, that decision is likely to come down taxes. Many people roll over a 401(k) into a traditional IRA to avoid a tax bill in the current year (Charles Schwab 2015).

There are some flexible options for how you can use the Roth IRA funds penalty free to help purchase a home, collateral for purchasing rental properties, and simply to help in hard times. Talk to a financial professional to know the differences, as the penalties are high for prohibited withdrawal of the funds.

HSA Account

This is a relatively new option for your investment. It works similar to a traditional IRA but can solely be used for healthcare spending, including doctor visits, prescription medications, dental and eye care, and related costs.

The beauty of the product is that the funds roll over from year to year and can only be used on health spending—tax free. If you do not spend the funds in the account, by the age of 65 you can withdraw and use like any other money (which is taxed similar to a traditional IRA) (Charles Schwab 2015).

According to the IRS, "the maximum contribution for a family is $6,650 and $1,000 higher if a family member is 55 or older. For an individual, that amount is $3,350. However, you can only use these accounts if your health plan is considered a high-deductible plan, or one that has a deductible of $1,300 for individuals and $2,600 for families (Charles Schwab 2015)."

There are more retirement plans out there and sites such as Charles Schwab and Shareholder direct you into plans where you can choose yourself. Sites like Acorn take the guesswork out of investing and are able to help you invest with your "extra" change. But remember, the rule about educating yourself on each investment still applies. Try to understand the difference of an index fund and a mutual fund. We do not have enough time to dive into each of the topics, but there is a lot of information out there about the market and how to make it work for you.

Self-Directed IRAs

I wanted you to understand the basics and benefits for the major retirement vehicles. But the vehicle I like the most is the self-directedt IRA. According to the Entrust Group, "the term 'self-directed' simply means that you, as the individual account owner, have complete control over selecting and directing your individual retirement account investments. A self-directed account will give you access to nontraditional assets, such as real estate, notes, limited partnerships, commercial paper, and many other alternative investments" (Entrust Group 2015). What this means is that you can determine where your tax-deferred dollars go like real estate or businesses or most any investment with some caveats.

According to Fox Business, they explain that "when it comes to self-directed IRAs there are two types: self-managed and self-directed. Self-managed IRAs are offered by big brokerages and online trading firms like E*TRADE and Charles Schwab and let you choose the stocks, bonds, mutual funds, and treasuries to invest in. This type tends to provide you more control of your retirement savings beyond choosing the type of mutual fund. A self-directed IRA involves a custodian holding your money in the account and makes investments in things like real estate, private placements and metals for you based on your directive. Self-directed accounts put more responsibility on you, meaning you have to understand all the rules governing any particular investment and the tax implications. Not to mention you'll have to do your own due diligence when choosing investments" (Fuscaldo 2014).

It is very important that you follow the rules. Basically you can do any dealings with a disqualified person as defined by the IRS. Here is a little more clarification. "Every IRA has a list of persons and entities that are considered disqualified to that IRA. IRS rules prohibit the IRA from dealing with these people and entities. Any transactions that do take place between an IRA and Disqualified persons result in what's called a Prohibited Transaction. *Disqualified persons* to an IRA include the account holder and their spouse as well as their lineal ascendants and descendants (parents, children and their spouses, grandparents, grandchildren and their spouses), and certain fiduciaries (CPAs, Attorneys, Financial Planners, etc.). Retirement plans and entities owned or controlled by disqualified persons are also prohibited from dealing with an IRA. Those disqualified persons to an IRA cannot buy or sell any asset from the plan. Nor can they make personal use of an asset. Disqualified persons cannot live in or rent IRA-owned real estate, nor can they provide "sweat equity" to that property. Other prohibited transactions between a plan and Disqualified Persons according to the IRS include the sale, exchange or lease of assets, lending money or extending credit, and furnishing goods, services or facilities relating to the plan's assets. Your IRA can not acquire life insurance or collectibles as assets" (New Direction IRA 2015).

There are some prohibited assets that include any work of art, any rug or antique, any stamp or collectible coin or any alcoholic beverage. This leaves a lot of room for real estate and business purchases. The Self-Directed IRA are a great vehicle to grow your passive income in a deferred tax vehicle. Something to think about.

Financial Advisor: Necessary or Waste of Money?

This is a big decision of whether or not to hire a financial advisor to assist with your retirement efforts. Whitney and I hired a financial advisor because I was spending too much time spinning my wheels researching different stocks, bonds, mutual funds, and every other type of retirement vehicle. Do you invest in Large Cap or Small Cap? Growth? International or Domestic? The possibilities are endless. My financial advisor was able to help me sort through these and design a savings plan based on my risk levels and profile.

If you are considering a financial advisor, here are some questions to ask from an article in US News (Carlozo 2015):

1. What's your education?
2. How are you compensated?
3. Whose responsibility is it to keep connected?
4. What's the past performance of your model portfolio?
5. Do you own any of the same investment and insurance products that you will recommend to me?
6. Why did you choose this work?
7. What were your returns for your clients in 2008?
8. Are you currently licensed to offer investment advice?
9. Can you tell me about the last client that you lost?
10. What happens to my account if something happens to you?

You can ask as many questions as you need so that you feel comfortable. This is your money and you want to make sure your getting the return that is in the best interest of achieving your vision.

LAZ Lifestyle Moves

- Calculate what you would have if you contributed $100/month until you are 65. Start with your current age and use the calculator at http://www.investor.gov/tools/calculators/compound-interest-calculator.

- Setup a separate retirement account and set up auto-pay to start contributing a consistent amount of money each month. (Recommendation: $100)

Wealth Hack Tools

Learnvest

http://www.learnvest.com
Cost: Variable pricing

This site is packed with information and people to help you invest. You fill out an application online and they connect you with the right path for investing based of your preferences. You are assigned a planner that helps you reach your goals. To expand your knowledge, you will have access to classes and articles along with a member only area to look into your finances.

Betterment

http://www.betterment.com
Cost: Variable pricing

This website and app gives you a visual screenshot of your accounts and overall performance. They take your age and ask you for five investment goals, and then they work to help you invest in a mix of stocks and bonds. Fees range between 0.15 percent (for portfolios of $100,000+) and 0.35 percent of your balance.

Acorns

http://www.acorns.com
Cost: Percentage of investment

Don't know where to start, Acorns lets you set it-and-forget-it. Basically, the app syncs with your account to round up to the nearest dollar and invest that amount. It is invested in six different funds, based on your risk tolerance. It is fun to watch the account grow and it allows you to start adding to it if you want. The app is sleek and easy to use. The app charges $1 a month for accounts under $5,000 and 0.25 percent over $5,000.

Stock Market Simulator

Cost: Free

The Stock Market Simulator app makes stock purchasing like buying a car. You get to test drive the stock in a simulated version of the real US stock market. Basically, you start with $10,000 in virtual (fake) money in a virtual stock market that is 15-20 minutes behind the actual

> market. It might be the best way for your to get your feet wet in the market without the risk.
>
> *Yahoo! Finance*
>
> http://www.yahoo.com/finance
>
> I use this site to keep up on the latest trends in finance and to educate myself on different topics. This app allows users to sync portfolios and quotes across multiple devices, tracking stocks, currencies, commodities and more. This user-friendly interface allows for quick stock checks, company information, and notifications and keeps you in the know so you can make the right decision.

- Contact a financial advisor to see if they are a fit for you.
- Google "Self-Directed IRA" to get familiar with the topic and how you can use it.

Wrap up

A good mix of investments is always important. Whether you decide to open retirement accounts or not, it is important to understand the options out there. The goal of the LAZ Lifestyle retirement plan for Millennials is to develop multiple streams of passive income to allow you the freedom to retire when you want. If you want a retirement account, do your research, talk to a financial advisor to see if that is a good fit, and monitor the return. You need to know what investments are generating the best return for you and your vision.

Advice from Millennials

Name: James
Age: 31
Occupation/Job Title: Lawyer
Annual Income: $100,000+
Family Size: 3
Where do you live? Spokane, WA
Do you currently own or rent your home? Own

What is your educational background? J.D. (Law Degree)

How much do you save for retirement?

$1200 per month into 401(k) w/ reinvested capital gains and dividends monthly; $200 into life insurance product; reinvest dividends and capital gains monthly from separate account.

On a scale of 1 to 5, how comfortable are you with your retirement savings? Why?

1. You can never be too comfortable when it comes to savings. I doubt I'll ever be a 5.

I never know if I am saving enough. Do you think there is validity to financial planning "rules of thumb" such as "saving 10% of your gross income"? Why?

Somewhat. In large part, it depends on what your goals are, how much debt you are in, what your business goals are, etc. I think it is healthy practice to save at least 10 to 20% of everything you earn automatically.

Social Security is a big part of people's retirement plans. Do you plan on having it for retirement? Why or Why not?

No. It's a Ponzi scheme. Because our parents' generation complains about us incessantly as whining, ill-prepped, lazy, self-centered "millennials," when in actuality we are squirreling away as much money as possible (since we graduated college/law school into the 2nd worst recession in American history) and rejecting their beliefs about one right way to do things. It would be nice to get that extra $2,500 per month though when I am 67+ that the government takes from me.

If you had $100,000 right now, how would you invest? Why?

I would pay off outstanding consumer debt and invest in safe, consistent, income-generating real estate.

What single piece of financial advice has made the largest impact in your life?

If you're generating $8 to $10k monthly in perpetuity while gaining equity, isn't that retirement at age 40? Jordan Tampien.

What advice do you have for people saving for retirement?

Get in the habit of saving, do not try to "get rich quick," and understand that consistent, smart, and safe investing over 30 to 40 years will guarantee a healthy return, a safe retirement, and encourage you to be a positive contributor to your community.

12

PROTECT YOUR ASSETS

If a child, a spouse, a life partner, or a parent depends on you and your income, you need life insurance.

Suze Orman

I don't want to tell you how much insurance I carry with Prudential, but all I can say is: when I go, they go too.

Jack Benny

You have spent all of this time buying IPAs, saving money, and growing your net worth only to see it all vanish when a tenant trips on a broken stair and sues you.

We definitely live in a litigious society where people appoint blame to everyone but themselves. If you have deep pockets, you will be a target. Trust me, that's all they drilled into my thick skull in law school.

The buzz these days is about health insurance and how not having it can cost you thousands, but have you thought about the less sexy homeowner's or landlord insurance. These are just as important to your financial health, if you will, and must be included in your plan to grow your wealth.

The LAZ Lifestyle caters to living uncomfortably, but not having insurance is simply irresponsible, not uncomfortable. My Grandma always said, "You need to plan for the worst, but pray for the best." This is what insurance does for you.

In this chapter we will discuss why you need insurance to protect your assets, different types of insurance, and some examples of what happens when you don't have it. A quality insurance agent is a good person to have on your team as you grow your assets.

Why Do I Need Insurance?

I tried doing the math on whether I could just save the amount of money I was paying for insurance and be better off rather than paying for it each month. The numbers looked good, but what I couldn't account for was the timing of when an accident would happen and whether it would be to multiple properties. You never know when disaster is going to strike. It is far better to hedge the risk for a monthly payment.

I remember hearing a story about Matt Leinhart, a quarterback for USC, when he decided to come back to college for his senior season instead of enter the NFL Draft (Friend 2009). He took out an insurance policy worth millions of dollars in case he slipped in his overall draft pick selection. He was picked 10th overall in 2006, so it was not enough of a slip to collect on the insurance. He was hedging his bets and protecting his asset: his throwing arm and skills as a football player. This is exactly what insurance is used for, to protect the "just in case" scenarios and, most importantly, to allow you to sleep at night.

Without insurance, every close call or every reported fire would cause panic and you'd simply be left to hope the injury wasn't too serious or the fire wasn't at one of your properties.

Many people don't know that the number one cause of bankruptcies in the United States is medical debt. This is all too true in my life. Before Whitney and I got married, I'd had one injury that required a doctor. It was one crazy day when I was playing "touch" football with some friends. I dove to catch a pass behind me and hit the elbow of the person covering me...with my face. The deafening thud on contact resonated across the field, but the pain wasn't too bad right away. I got up and then immediately checked out of the game and laid down just as a precaution.

The pain worsened by the minute and my face starting swelling up like when Will Smith's character on *Hitch* had an allergic reaction. I called Whitney and told her to bring ice and hurry. It was in that moment I thanked my lucky stars that Whitney had talked me into adding me to her health insurance policy at work only months earlier, even though I kept insisting "I never get hurt."

After waiting in the emergency room for what seemed like hours, I was admitted and, after x-rays, found that I had broken three bones around my eye. It wasn't life-threatening, but I would need surgery for it to heal properly.

A couple weeks later, I went under the knife, stayed the night in the hospital, and was released the next day with a monster black eye and a prescription of pain meds. We got the bill a week later for $25,000. Our portion was $2,000 and I wasn't sure if we could pay *that* amount, let alone if we would have had to pay the entire bill.

So, back to the original question: Why do you need insurance?

You need to protect yourself against *life*. I guess you could live in a bubble, but it would simply be easier and more enjoyable to make sure you are covered against anything life throws your way. I will explain the different types of insurance available and how they can be used to protect your family, possessions, and yourself.

Different Types of Insurance

In the insurance world, there are several different types of insurance ranging from home insurance to pet insurance. We are going to discuss each in detail. (Well, probably not pet insurance. I'll save that for another book.)

Homeowner's Insurance

For every homeowner with a mortgage, having homeowner's insurance is a mandatory requirement from your lender. It protects their interest in your property, but more importantly, it protects you against damage to your home and your possessions in your home.

For instance, if you are burglarized, the possessions taken will be covered by insurance. If there were a fire, your house and any damaged possessions would be covered. Homeowner's insurance also provides liability coverage against accidents in the home or on the property. For example, if your house catches on fire, the insurance will not only cover bringing your house back to normal condition, but it will cover your personal items that were lost in the fire as well.

You can add other protections like flood, earthquake, tornado, or hurricane protection depending on where your property is located. Homeowner's insurance is a great protection for your primary residence or vacation home, but keep in mind there are better policies for investment properties.

These insurance policies may be more or less expensive depending on whether they will give you a "cash value" or a "replacement value" for your property. A "cash value" provides a fixed cash amount for your property if it is completely destroyed, leaving you responsible for any difference in the cost of replacement. I have found these policies to be less expensive. Then there is "replacement insurance" which will pay for the house to be replaced at current replacement value.

For example, for my home worth $175,000 in Washington, I pay between $1,000–$1,200 per year for my homeowner's insurance and it has a replacement value of $230,000 to build the same structure. I pay a higher premium because of the estimated replacement cost. The dip in the housing market created a situation where it was far cheaper to purchase a home than it was to build one. You are starting to see it level out, but for now replacement insurance premiums will run higher.

I would recommend shopping around for the best rates. I have seen 30% differences in insurance quotes for the same policies. Below is a good estimate for what you could be paying depending on the state you are located. The chart is compared to a national average of $978/year.

Although this cost is necessary, it doesn't mean that you can't save as much as possible. Read the fine print and sit down with your insurance agent to ensure you are getting the right protection at the best deal possible for you.

Landlord Insurance

Once you have switched your primary home to a rental or you purchase a rental property, you need to convert your insurance to a landlord's policy. Your normal insurance provider should be able to handle your first four rental properties as long as they are each under four units. Any residential building or apartment with five or more units, however, is considered commercial property and should be assigned a commercial policy.

Landlord insurance takes the personal possession element off of your policy and provides the same great service at a lower cost. It also has some protections for temporary housing for tenants while units are being repaired as well as loss of rent provisions. Under any covered loss, you're covered for the rental income you would have received from your tenants for as long as it takes to replace or repair your rental unit, or up to 12 months. It is important to talk to your insurance provider to ensure that you are fully covered.

Commercial Policies

As referenced above, commercial policies are required for apartments with five or more units and business loans. As you grow your portfolio, it is important to get a good commercial insurer on your team to assist in initial estimates and make sure your entire portfolio is protected.

Liability Insurance

Have you ever heard of an "umbrella policy"? This is a policy that covers your liability at your properties and businesses in case the insurance in place is not enough to cover a liability lawsuit. This insurance can protect against lawsuits against you from tenants that tripped and fell at the property, partner disputes, or disgruntled customers.

Read through your policy carefully, but know that most landlord or homeowner policies provide about $300,000 in coverage for liability suits against the land or business owner. If there are significant injuries, however, this cost can far exceed the $300,000 coverage. An umbrella policy can cover any overages and is relatively cheap (about $300–450 per year for $1,000,000 in coverage.)

We took out a $1,000,000 policy as an additional precaution (law school has forced me to worry about such things). We work hard to prevent situations that could cause us to be liable, but there are simply no guarantees. I like to call it the "sleep at night" factor. If it helps me sleep at night, it is worth its weight in gold.

Life Insurance

How many of you plan on dying?

Despite its inevitability, few people plan for the day they leave this earth. It's hard to think about, and even more difficult to discuss with relevant family members. But what you don't want is a real estate portfolio with a $1,000,000 tax bill that your family is forced to take care of. With no insurance, your family would have to liquidate the portfolio at fire sale prices to pay the bill, leaving little money left over for them.

Knowing the right type of life insurance that is right for you and your family is important. There are two major types of life insurance: whole and term. Whole life insurance is a form of permanent life insurance with features, such as guaranteed premiums for life, death benefits, and cash value. On top of that, whole life insurance policies have the potential to pay out dividends that are tax free (you don't hear that term very often). A whole life insurance policy makes more sense if you want the following:

- Protection for life with no lapse at the end of a term.
- Fixed premiums that stay the same each year, no matter your age or health.
- Beneficiaries will receive at least the face amount of the policy upon the death of the insured, assuming you do not have outstanding policy loans and that the policy premiums are paid on time.
- Increase the value of the policy on a tax-favored basis.
- Ability to take cash out to use while you are living.

Term life insurance, on the other hand, is often the more affordable life insurance option as it offers protection for a specific number of years. If you are young, many financial planners recommend a term policy rather than a whole life policy, mostly because of the costs. They advise that it is better to buy the cheaper term and invest the difference in mutual funds. Thus, the real beauty of term life insurance is that you can get great coverage at an affordable price.

So you're left to decide: Whole or term life insurance?

This is a hard question and the internet is full of proponents for both sides. The answer is one I learned and used all the time in law school: "it depends."

The reason there is a lot of data about whole life policies is that insurance companies make far more off those policies than for term. Whitney and I have purchased whole life insurance because of its long-term application and potential as collateral, since (in theory) it increases in value. It was spendy upfront and was worth significantly less than we had put into it. In fact, it takes 10 years for the cash value of the policy to become more than what we have contributed. Only time will tell if this move will pay off, but I can already see how I can leverage this account (since it has cash value) to purchase real estate, pay for our future children's college, etc.

At the end of the day, either option is better than nothing, so do your research, talk to your insurance agent (or financial planner), and pick the one you feel most comfortable with.

Renter's Insurance

If you are currently renting, I highly recommend renter's insurance. This covers your personal property if something should happen such as a fire, flood, pests…you name it. Your landlord's policy will *not* cover your belongings, so it is important to protect yourself.

Examples of Lawsuits Against Landlords

Every class I sat through in law school reinforced the notion that you can be sued at any time by anybody, especially if you have money. Insurance and proper management of your assets are your protectors against this, but I just wanted to share a couple horrible (but true) stories to drive the point home.

The following are a couple court cases that illustrate the importance of having your ducks in a row because you never know what will happen at your property.

A Marin County jury has awarded a $1.1 million verdict to a man who sued his landlord after falling down

> **Millennial Insight**
>
> *It was not a matter of if but when we were going to get sued. We decided to use a umbrella policy for all of rental properties. We also agree with the sleep at night factor and wanted to be covered.*
>
> Teresa, 34

the stairs at his Larkspur apartment.

Isaac Torres, 41, and his family moved into the Rice Lane apartment in 2008 after losing his Novato home in the foreclosure wave, according to his lawyer, Anthony Label. On Jan. 1 2010, Torres fell down the back stairs and later developed symptoms of lumbar strain and disk injury.

Torres sued the property owner, Thomas Fleming, alleging that he failed to keep the stairs clear of slippery algae and did not install a handrail, as required by local code. Torres, who worked as a houseman for a wealthy San Francisco family, was forced to quit his job because of the pain, Label said.

Torres and Fleming, a retired general contractor living in Sacramento County, took the case to trial. After a 14-day trial, a jury awarded Torres $1,070,801 for economic losses, including $850,000 for future lost earnings.

"If the defendant had provided the minimum protection of a building code-required handrail, at a cost of less than $100 and an hour of time, this lawsuit would have never been necessary and Isaac Torres would still be working in the job he cherished and held for 10 years," said Label, an attorney with the Veen Firm in San Francisco (Klien 2011).

In another case, a landlord has agreed to pay $350,000 to a tenant who was injured when she fell down the stairs at one of his properties. The woman was headed to work when she slipped on something greasy and fell down several steps, breaking her ankle. The woman had to undergo surgery and participate in months of physical therapy. The damage sustained made it impossible to return to work. The woman's attorney drove home the point that residents of the New York City apartment complex complained to the landlord about construction debris left in the way after a repair (Schlitt 2010).

The first two examples are unheeded negligence by the landlord, but you can also be liable in a situation when the person shouldn't have been on your property, like the following:

In 2002, in Lancaster, Pennsylvania, two teens were severely burned atop a parked railroad car. The teens were out skateboarding as they illegally entered property owned by Amtrak and Norfolk Southern Corp. The teens proceeded to climb on top of a boxcar to get a better view of the city. Unfortunately, Klein made contact with the un-insulated wire suspended above the train and was jolted with 12,500 volts of electricity, causing severe burns over 75 *percent of his body. Birdwell received burns over only 12 percent of his body as he tried to help his friend extinguish the fire engulfing his clothes.*

The trial was not until 2006, but a jury found that despite the fact that the teens were trespassing, they were not responsible. Instead they found Amtrak and Norfolk Southern guilty for failing to post signs warning of the danger from the electrified wires that power locomotives. They were awarded $24.2 million combined for medical costs, pain and suffering, and "loss of life pleasures (Pumphrey 2007)".

After talking with more of my friends who practice law, if there is blame and you have deep pockets, you are likely to get sued. This is where insurance can be a buffer. If the dollar amount is high enough, the insurance company will pay for their attorneys to defend and settle the case.

I am not telling you this to scare you away from owning real estate or a business, but just to reinforce the need for insurance to cover yourself.

Wealth Hack Tools

Encircle

http://www.encircle.com
Available for iPhone, Android, and iPad

Encircle is a revolutionary application that utilizes a unique, streamlined, photo-based interface and allows busy homeowners to efficiently inventory thousands of assets in less than an hour. It allows you to take pictures, make notes, and access all of the data anytime and anywhere for your use.

Dropbox

http://www.dropbox.com
Available for iPhone, Android, and iPad

Dropbox is the cloud at its finest, as it allows users to transport and share large files such as documents, photos, and videos simply by saving content to the Dropbox folder. Changes sync immediately across all devices with Dropbox installed. It's compatible with nearly every computer and smartphone operating system. You can put inventory pictures, notes, and asset details in Dropbox and access them anytime and anywhere. It is easy to setup and very user friendly.

GEICO App

Available for iPhone, Android, and iPad

You have probably seen the commercials. Nobody can forget the GEICO Gecko. But what GEICO has created in their app allows for faster insurance claims and digital access to your insurance information. It is user-friendly and allows you to access digital ID cards, manage activity on your policy, find further information about what is needed to file a claim, and then actually file a claim. It's your go-to app when an accident happens.

Auto Accident Help by Travelers

Available for iPhone, Android, and iPad

Getting into a car accident can be scary, but with the Auto Accident Help app from Travelers, you're not alone. Auto Accident Help reminds you and your family of the important steps to take in the event of an accident. Anyone can use the step-by-step guide to collect information right at the accident scene and create an accident report. It allows you to photograph damage and record an audio description and collect information from drivers, passengers, witnesses, and police. It also produces a detailed accident report with attached photos, voice recordings, and contact information. Travelers customers can start their claim at the touch of a button.

LAZ Lifestyle Moves

- Talk with your current insurance provider to make sure that you are protected.

- Research different types of insurance so you are knowledgeable when approached with them.

- Take pictures of your possessions and property to prove the personal and real property that was lost, damaged, or stolen to the insurance company.

Wrap Up

Insurance is a necessary evil when trying to accumulate assets. The deeper your pockets, the more likely you are to get sued. I mean, what is the point of acquiring IPAs if you don't properly insure them and lose all of it because a tenant tripped at your property. You want to be able to sleep at night.

So talk to your insurance provider or find a new one and get the necessary protection so you don't cringe and worry every time you hear the sirens of a fire engine.

Advice from Millennials

Name: Thomas
Age: 30
Occupation/Job Title: Insurance Agent/Principal
Annual Income: $150,000+
Family Size: 2
Where do you live? Post Falls, ID
Do you currently own or rent your home? Own

How long have you been in the insurance industry? What do you like about it?

I have been in the insurance industry for over 4 years. I enjoy getting to know families and helping them protect the things that matter most to them. We insure their current assets and work to help them realize their hopes and dreams. There is no greater feeling than helping someone replace a financial loss, even though we cannot replace property or lives.

What insurance coverage do you have?

I personally have home, auto, landlord, umbrella, business, disability, accident, health, supplemental and life insurance.

What questions should people ask their insurance agent?

Every individual's insurance needs are as different as they are. In general, an individual should purchase insurance for any potential financial loss they could not recover from on their own. Most individuals have a need to insure their home, vehicles, and life at the least.

How does a consumer know they are getting the best deal?

Getting the best deal from an insurance company is difficult as every company has different underwriting guidelines. As an example, some insurance companies offer better rates for younger drivers than others. As a rule of thumb, keeping your policies together with the same insurance carrier generally offers the best pricing.

How does a consumer qualify for discounts?

Discounts vary at each insurance company. Insurers generally reward consumers with discounts for safe driving history, multiple policies, multi vehicles, good credit rating, excellent insurance history, no prior claims, automatic payments, vehicles with safety options, homes with security systems, newer homes and vehicles, age 25+, married, career and company discounts, new customer discounts, and full payment discounts to name a few.

What effect does credit history have on insurance?

Not all insurance companies rate drivers based off their general credit rating. However, there is a strong correlation between higher credit ratings and safer drivers.

We know about the basics (car, home, life); what optional insurance should people consider buying?

With the rising cost of healthcare, many individuals should look into purchasing long-term care and critical illness policies unless they have financial resources to pay for care resulting from illness. Accident and disability policies are great options for active families and families who rely on their monthly paychecks.

How much liability coverage would you recommend for property owners?

We recommend a minimum liability level of $300,000 for property owners. The more assets an individual has the greater their liability coverage should be.

In your opinion, why would someone buy whole life insurance? Term Life Insurance?

Term life insurance has many advantages. It is generally sold in terms of 10, 20, and 30 years and is less expensive than permanent policies. Term life insurance can be used to cover short and long term debt obligations, such as home and auto loans, college tuition, and retirement goals.

Permanent life insurance lasts forever as long as it is funded correctly. Permanent policies often provide cash value that can be borrowed against or withdrawn from. Permanent policies allow individuals to lock in life insurance rates at the time the individual obtains coverage. For younger people, you can purchase a permanent policy at a very affordable premium and have the same low premium your entire life.

What single piece of financial advice has made the largest impact in your life?

Personal finance is about 80% behavior and 20% head knowledge. Dave Ramsey

Poor people sell their time, rich people buy other people's time. Robert Kiyosaki

What advice do you have for people questioning the need for insurance?

Insurance is a very powerful tool used to help prevent financial loss. Risk is a part of everyday life, and you can either manage it or be caught unprepared. I would recommend insurance for any financial loss you can't afford to pay for with your liquid assets.

13

IT'S ALL ABOUT WHO YOU KNOW

Sometimes, idealistic people are put off by the whole business of networking as something tainted by flattery and the pursuit of selfish advantage. But virtue in obscurity is rewarded only in Heaven. To succeed in this world, you have to be known to people.

Sonia Sotomayor

What people say and feel about you when you've left a room is precisely your job while you are in it.

Rasheed Ogunlaru

When I first started in real estate, I thought through all of the advertising options I could use to get clients. Some recommended ads in the paper, billboards, bus benches, and the list goes on. After looking at several ideas, I thought it would be a good idea to get a billboard. Not just one, in fact, but three.

Knowing my face was going to be plastered all over the city on billboards, I wanted to make sure I looked good. I put on my Sunday best and Whitney took some profile shots that would be blown up for all to see. I remember vividly thinking that this would be a great way to get business: if only people could put a face to the name. The billboards were up for one year and I did not get one new client. Zero. Zilch.

Ironically, though, I doubled my business from my friends who saw it and remembered that I was a realtor, and they began to tell their friends and so on. I quickly learned that people want to trust whom they are working with or buying from. With so many dangers and scams out there, a trusted recommendation from a friend was the greatest lead generator I could have had. I stopped focusing on outside recruitment and simply ensured that I was the realtor that my friends referred.

A friend once told me, "Your network is your net worth!" I didn't understand it at the time, as I had a narrow version of what my net worth was. But he was right. Your network opens up doors that allow you to grow and generate the growth of your net worth. Without the network, finding employment is difficult, investors are scarce, and partnerships are tough to come by.

In his address at the George Mason University graduation in 2009, Steve Case focused on the principle that the people around you matter. He said:

No matter what you do in life, your ability to succeed will be largely dependent on your ability to work with people. Indeed, it has often been said that what you do is less important than who you do it with – that the people you surround yourself with, whether a spouse, or friends, or co-workers, will ultimately be the principal determinant of the course your life will take. So don't just focus on the job descriptions, or the brand name of the organization you're going to join—also focus on who you'll be working for, and with (Case 2009).

I immediately focused on building my network. Starting with friends, then through grassroots efforts (coffee meetings, drinks after work, intentional hanging out), I was able to grow my business each year. Again, you must develop your network if you want to grow your net worth.

How to Get a Network

Networking as defined by Webster's Dictionary is "the exchange of information or services among individuals, groups, or institutions; specifically: the cultivation of productive relationships for employment or business" (Merriam-Webster 2015).

I remember telling my career counselor in college that I didn't want to do sales. I didn't have the mentality and tools needed to be a pushy salesperson. I wasn't much for starting conversations with strangers and I never believed in a product enough to sell it to someone else, especially people I knew. But, it didn't take long for me to realize *we are all in sales.* As an employee, you are constantly displaying your talent and ability to get tasks completed to keep employment or get a promotion. As a realtor, I am always selling myself to earn people's trust to assist them in making the largest purchase of their life. As a small business owner, you are constantly pushing your product to get new clients and hang on to the ones you have. As a job seeker, you have the toughest sale of them all, convincing an employer to choose you over the hundreds of applicants.

No matter how far I tried to get away from sales, I found the inescapable truth that every person, whether they like it or not, is in sales. It is important to understand how to use sales to build your network.

There is a basic marketing principle that suggests it takes seven "touches" before someone will buy what you are selling (Cohn 2013). These touches can take various forms, such as a physical connection, seeing an advertisement (billboard, television, photographs), your logo, emails, phone call, or a referral from a trusted recommendation (Cohn 2013). This can be a combination of different forms, but they must have a consistent message.

Ultimately, to effectively build your network, people must know what you do or are planning to do with a consistent message that reaches them through different touches. For example, when I started in real estate, I used Facebook to tell my friends and family that I was now a licensed and practicing Realtor who could help them buy their next home. Next, I used the billboard that on its surface was not overly effective, but it was another touch for each of my friends. Next, I sent out emails to people I knew were in the process of looking for a home, inviting them to coffee or a drink to see if I could help in any way. By having multiple touches and continuing to do quality work, I was able to start getting referred to others through my friends and family. I wanted to ensure that when they thought of buying or selling their home they thought of me first.

This approach allowed me to broaden my network and develop more and more client relationships. I learned that the goal is not always to go find new customers, but to try and reach your potential customers where they are.

First Impression is Everything

The first place to start with networking is your presentation or how people perceive you. Statistics say that you only have seven seconds to make an impactful first impression when you meet someone. That's not enough time to tell them what charity you give to, where you volunteer, or how many diplomas you have on the wall. It boils down to how you present yourself.

Like Henry Ward Beecher said, "clothes and manners do not make the man; but, when he is made, they greatly improve his appearance."

What is the first thought that crosses your mind when you see a panhandler asking for money at an intersection? Do you think he is the CEO of a major company, a millionaire in disguise, or just a poor beggar? If you are honest with yourself, you are judging that person in one way or another, and a bum is likely the first thing you think of.

I'm not here to justify your judgments on others because we all do it simply because of how that person is presenting himself or herself. They wear the uniform (real or not) of a person in need to trigger a certain response from you that evokes pity or understanding to give them money. You don't know them; you likely have never met them. Yet you give them money. *Presentation is everything.*

If you want people to take you seriously, you have to take yourself seriously—starting with your presentation.

I have a really good example of this. In college, I wanted a new car. I was looking for something brand new. (Again, my financial skills in college were not too stellar.) I went to a dealership wearing a suit and tie. I confidently opened the door and was greeted with a handshake by the salesman and immediately put into a Pontiac Grand Am with less than 1,000 miles on it. They let me test drive it for 24 hours and I could bring it back the next day to write up the deal. I quickly wised up, decided it was not for me, and returned the car, much to their chagrin. Six months later, I actually *needed* a new car and I went into the same dealership, this time wearing cargo shorts and a short sleeve shirt. I was not greeted at the door let alone approached by a salesperson for more than five minutes. Needless to say, I was not given a loan for the car. Nothing had changed except my clothing. My presentation made the difference between getting the loan and not.

Mark Twain said it best: "Clothes make the man. Naked people have little or no influence in society." So make sure you are dressing the part and err on the side of overdressed. If you are trying to borrow $100,000, don't show up to the meeting in distressed jeans and a torn ACDC t-shirt. Take yourself seriously and other people will too.

Different Types of Effective Networking

There are several different ways to develop a network. You can attend meetings, request invitations or connections from current friends on social media, or simply cold call people that you want to connect with. Each is effective in different circumstances, but they all will lead to more connections, if done correctly.

Cold Call Networking

One of the hardest skills for me to develop was cold call networking. What I mean is the situation where you don't know anybody in the room and you must start up a conversation, reminiscent of the first time you meet your significant other's family. The entire time is usually riddled with awkward moments and regrettable one-liners until that beautiful moment when you connect on a common thought or interest. Your posture straightens, the banter gets livelier, and you finally feel like you are connecting. For me, this cold call interaction is a lot of work, but it is a necessary evil to making those new connections to getting the job, finding the investor, or just getting your in-laws to like you.

I still remember my first taste of what it was like to cold call network within a group. It was my first real internship working for a Senator in Olympia, Washington. I was in college but none of my previous "networking" was for professional reasons and, to be honest, I didn't see the value in developing strategic relationships. The internship consisted of answering constituent concerns, researching issues, attending functions, and soaking in the legislative experience. It almost felt like a House of Cards episode… almost.

I couldn't have been there more than two weeks when the first event transpired. The other interns and I were scheduled to attend a luncheon provided by a statewide group of ranchers. There would be 120 or more concerned constituents wanting to discuss pending legislation with our Senator.

I was actually excited to see the Senator talk with the people and really try to learn the skill of working a large group. I grabbed my blazer from the coat rack and headed to the door for the short walk to the luncheon. I was ready, but we were missing a key component: the Senator.

"Isn't the Senator coming?" I asked my supervisor, confused how we could do this without her.

"No, we are going to talk to them and report back," my supervisor said.

Puzzled, I asked, "What are we going to talk about?"

"The issues." He responded, calmly opening the door and waving for me to follow.

Nervously, I marched forward. On the outside I looked calm and collected but inside my heart was racing and I think I even started sweating.

What was I going to say? I didn't know anyone there nor did I really want to. But it was part of my job so I trudged forward.

We entered a large room with buffet tables stacked against the walls, a large podium in the front of the room, and multiple round tables each filled with 10–12 people staring at us as we entered. You could have heard a pin drop.

Pointing, my supervisor said, "You take those tables over there and I will take these." He paused, probably seeing my inner turmoil. "Just be yourself," he said, as he quickly left my side.

I walked over to the first table wondering what to say when they asked where the Senator was. I slowly took off my jacket and swung it around my chair. "The Senator could not make it today, but I am her aid and would love to report back to her with your questions and concerns."

I had practiced my lines the whole walk over but I still stuttered a little when they came out. I waited for what seemed like an eternity and a lady started in, "We represent the cattle ranchers…" I didn't even care what she said next. My grandparents and uncle owned cattle in Moses Lake and I had worked on the farm as a kid, helping in every aspect of the operation. I had found our common ground.

We began to talk back and forth about the concerns regarding current legislation, which I had been researching and was very knowledgeable about. They left feeling heard and appreciated for the long trip over to Olympia. I left having learned the valuable lesson of being more prepared going in so that I can better understand and communicate with groups.

Along similar lines, I have attended many Young Professional meetings and different functions where I knew one or two people. My normal course of action was to pull into the parking lot, contemplate at least five reasons why I shouldn't be there, and then have an awkward, drawn-out argument with myself.

I always ended up going inside, but I never could understand why it was so difficult to meet new people and really connect enough to take the next step in the relationship, whether it was as a client or business partner. Honestly, it seemed like too much work. It wasn't that the people weren't friendly at the networking function, but it felt very surface level and nothing ever developed into a trusting, lasting relationship.

Cold calling can be an effective way to meet more people. I recommend starting with relevant groups such as the local Real Estate Investors group or the local business/entrepreneur group. This can be an easy in and a way to jump-start your networking into different crowds.

Warm Call Networking

The next form of networking is what I like to call warm calling. Warm calling is networking where you have some connection to the person you are planning to talk to. For some reason, it is always easier to lead in with "Jon told me I should talk to you about real estate." This is warm lead networking, where you both have a mutual friend that connects you. You don't know the person, but through your friend are able to connect. Facebook, LinkedIn, and every major social media outlet harnesses the power of warm calling, and you should too.

Warm calling leverages friends and family to meet more people, which can be a positive or negative thing, depending on how you go about it. I recommend inviting the person you are trying to connect with to lunch or coffee or a drink after work. Pay for their drink or meal and spend the first visit listening and hearing their needs. There was a reason your friend thought you two should connect. By starting off in a listening capacity and truly hearing what the other person wants, you stand a better chance of them returning the favor later on or at least recommending that his friends should now meet with you.

Social Media Networking

The next form of networking involves all forms of social media through trusted recommendations. Have you ever heard the saying, "It's not *what* you know, it's *who* you know"? This can be frustrating when you look at that 8.5 x 11 framed diploma, hung with a slight tilt, on your wall. How could you have worked so hard for that degree when it actually boils down to who you know?

In today's world, the internet can be your best tool for connecting with people of similar interests (Horrigan 2002). Facebook. Twitter. Yelp. Urbanspoon. TripAdvisor. These are all websites that capitalize on reviews and recommendations from friends. When you want to travel somewhere, you ask a friend if they have been there and what they recommend. We are becoming a "Trusted Recommendation" society.

The reality is that Facebook (and these other sites) is focused on relationship building in one capacity or another (Waters et al. 2009). Ellison et al. (2007) found that that "connections formed through Facebook supported relationships and connectivity in the offline world." This relationship is referred to as "social capital," and helps to build individual and community capacity (Coleman 1988). With Facebook, people can build relationships and establish networks (Mains et al. 2013) that can lead to increasing their social capital (Ellison et al. 2007).

Whitney and I don't travel anywhere without first posting on Facebook to see if there are any recommendations. Without fail, we will get dozens of comments on places to check out and where to stay. Of course, we always try these places first. This is the power of a trusted recommendation. We are basing the decision to try or not try a place on the person that is recommending it.

People just want to have a connection to the person, place or business that they are looking at using. A study by Farrow and Yuan found in a survey of 3,085 university alumni that active Facebook communication led to better communication and emotional connectivity for survey participants

(Farrow and Yuan 2011). When you post those funny cat pictures or your quirky status update, you are connecting with the end viewer. So you can use social media to connect and expand your network. Reach out to your "friends" on social media and try to convert it from an online relationship to actually meeting via the phone, email, or in person. This is where you can actually talk with them and let them know what you are up to. The reality is that people are hesitant to refer to friends just in case the referral doesn't work out. So make sure if you are set to meet that you are punctual, genuine, and simply just willing to listen. It is amazing what kind of impact those three things can have.

Develop a Trusting Relationship Right Away

How, then, do you build a trusting relationship? I have a few ideas. Let's walk through how to build trusting relationships and networks that can change your life. Obviously, trust isn't earned immediately in a conversation over coffee or at the local watering hole after work; it's built over time. But it never hurts to get off on the right foot.

These are four key lessons that I have continued to use in relationships, interviews, and basically any new interaction to establish a common ground and truly hear the needs of the other person:

1. **Listen.** Too often we are nervous going into new interactions and our immediate trigger response is to talk and talk. This never allows the other person to connect with you. But by listening, you can find out how the other person best communicates, what they are interested in, and really craft the conversation to connect with the other person. Perhaps more importantly, people feel valued when someone listens to them...and the opposite is also true. You want the other person to feel like an active participant in the relationship, as they will be more receptive (Mincemoyer and Thomson 1998).

> *The mark of a good conversationalist is not that you can talk a lot. The mark is that you can get others to talk a lot. Thus, good schmoozers are good listeners, not good talkers.*
>
> Guy Kawasaki

This is a good challenge: try talking as little as you can in the

251

conversation and simply answer with questions whenever possible, such as "Why did you pursue that degree? What things are you interested in?" This method has proven true time and time again. The best advice I received for interviews was that a good interview meant the interviewer talked more than I did.

2. **Find a common ground.** Immediately upon meeting someone or going into an interview, I try to find something common to talk about besides the weather. If they are wearing a Gonzaga Bulldogs sweatshirt, I know I can talk about the basketball team or going to school there. If they have pictures of vacations abroad, I know I can ask how the trip was (everyone likes talking about his or her vacations).

   Like the story about my experience as an intern, once I found out the group was interested in cattle farming, I had a common ground topic that I could discuss with them, and I made the transition from stranger to "friend" quickly and easily. Like Dale Carnegie stated, "You can make more friends in two months by becoming interested in other people than you can in two years by trying to get other people interested in you."

3. **Do your research.** This one doesn't necessarily apply to the Young Professionals meeting over drinks or the blind dates you constantly get set up on, but rather to interviews or groups where you know their interests in advance. If it's an interview, know the company in and out by combing their website, read the "About Us" section, take the time to show you care because that could be the difference in getting the job and not getting the job. If you are going to an investment club or gathering of like-minded folks, understand what they are about and use that as your lead-in. If worse comes to worst, you can always play the weather card, but treat it more like the Twix commercial where it simply buys you time to ask or talk about something a little more relevant and substantial.

4. **Create an "elevator pitch" for yourself.** An elevator pitch is a statement that explains who you are and what you are in about 30 seconds or less (the amount of time you would have with a potential contact or investor in an elevator). It is important to be concise yet informative. You need to be clear and impressionable without sounding confusing or talking at a world record speed.

The elevator pitch can allow you to articulate your vision so others can see it, fund it, and be a part of achieving it.

Maintain and Grow Your Networks

Now that you have conquered the difficult task of developing a network, you must now maintain it. What does this entail? It is far more than well-timed comments on Facebook posts or a couple Snapchats to a friend.

You have done the hard part, but you must learn to engage and maintain these networks (Doyle and Briggeman 2014). The Extension network developed the Social Media Marketing Map (SMMM) to help with engaging audiences and marketing yourself and events via social media (Christensen et al. 2015). The SMMM tool can be used to organize your social media networks for events or even target potential client or relationship efforts (Christensen et al. 2015). It is a simple chart of your social media outlets and a timeline of when you need to complete a task. This structure gives you a snapshot of your social media efforts to grow your network.

The key to developing social media relationships is to listen to the end user. You should not "treat social media as another broadcasting platform like direct mail, email, outdoor media, TV, and radio commercials. Individuals have a voice, and they can now respond in real time to whatever is presented to them. One "listens" in social networks by engaging in online conversation and providing opportunities for individuals to respond back by replying, retweeting, commenting, sharing, and asking questions (Figure 5). This type of communication allows your audience to feel [you] want to hear what they have to say (Christensen et al. 2015)."

It is no easy task to build your network, so take the time to preserve it once you do. If you haven't talked to someone in a while, drop him or her a line just to say "Hi." It does take time, but it's worth every second invested. You never know how or when people's lives might change and, believe me, they can go from a friend to an investor or client very quickly.

The SMMM tool can help you organize your social media efforts, but here are some other tips to help maintain your network:

1. **Stay relevant.** You want stay on people's radar and make sure that they know what you do. Pictures, posts, or whatever can keep you connected with your clients.

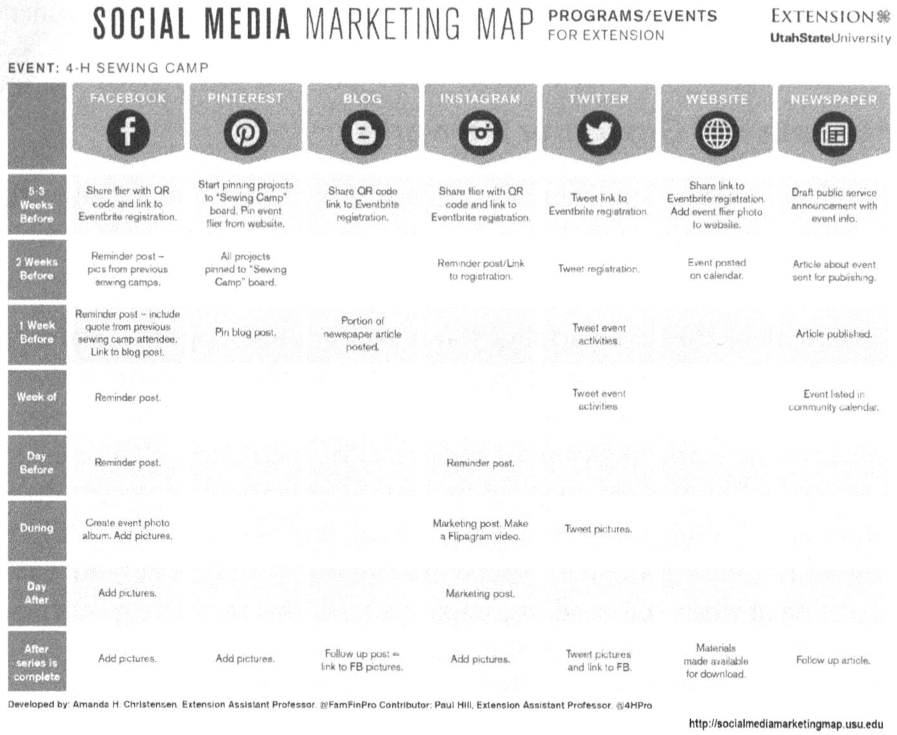

SOCIAL MEDIA MARKETING MAP PROGRAMS/EVENTS FOR EXTENSION

EXTENSION UtahStateUniversity

EVENT: 4-H SEWING CAMP

	FACEBOOK	PINTEREST	BLOG	INSTAGRAM	TWITTER	WEBSITE	NEWSPAPER
5-3 Weeks Before	Share flier with QR code and link to Eventbrite registration.	Start pinning projects to "Sewing Camp" board. Pin event flier from website.	Share QR code link to Eventbrite registration.	Share flier with QR code and link to Eventbrite registration.	Tweet link to Eventbrite registration.	Share link to Eventbrite registration. Add event flier photo to website.	Draft public service announcement with event info.
2 Weeks Before	Reminder post – pics from previous sewing camps.	All projects pinned to "Sewing Camp" board.		Reminder post/Link to registration.	Tweet registration.	Event posted on calendar.	Article about event sent for publishing.
1 Week Before	Reminder post – include quote from previous sewing camp attendee. Link to blog post.	Pin blog post.	Portion of newspaper article posted.		Tweet event activities.		Article published.
Week of	Reminder post.				Tweet event activities		Event listed in community calendar.
Day Before	Reminder post.			Reminder post.			
During	Create event photo album. Add pictures.			Marketing post. Make a Flipagram video.	Tweet pictures.		
Day After	Add pictures.			Marketing post.			
After series is complete	Add pictures.	Add pictures.	Follow up post = link to FB pictures.	Add pictures.	Tweet pictures and link to FB.	Materials made available for download.	Follow up article.

Developed by: Amanda H. Christensen, Extension Assistant Professor, @FamFinPro Contributor: Paul Hill, Extension Assistant Professor, @4HPro

http://socialmediamarketingmap.usu.edu

Figure 5. Social Media Marketing Map.

2. **Stay in touch.** I have a stack of Thank You cards on my desk to send to clients or vendors that we work with. This handwritten note makes the receiver know that I was thinking of them and genuinely grateful for the relationship. Send an email or letter, or simply a Facebook message, but make sure you do something. There is no point in building a network if you can't keep it going.
3. **Do what you say you are going to do.** This seems like a no brainer, but follow through is a major pitfall for most people. Now you have the client but make sure you keep the client by providing quality work in a timely manner. Show up on time, communicate with the client, and provide the best service possible. This tip alone will put you ahead of most people out there.

You Are Who You Hang Out With

A recent study revealed that your income is within 20% of the incomes of the five people you hang out with the most (Groth 2012). I initially thought this was because those people gave you the money to keep within that range, but what actually happens is that your conversations at the local watering holes and events you attend change. You are no longer talking about what to do this weekend but what your stocks did over the week.

Working in a non-profit arena, we often used the following analogy when we talked about poverty: *Did you know that in a bucket of crabs, if one tries to climb out of the bucket, the other crabs actually pull that crab back in (Loper 2013)? No matter how hard they try, their external circumstances and friends prevent them from growing and obtaining things outside the realm of their friends.*

We have all experienced this. In college, I hung out with friends that drank a lot, so I inevitably drank a lot or was at least in situations where drinking was involved. Then I realized the importance of getting good grades, so I hung out with a more studious crowd and my grades got better. I didn't magically get smarter; my spare time with friends was spent studying instead of drinking. Eventually, your friend group ends up reflecting the things you enjoy doing.

As you've probably noticed, Mark Twain is one of my favorite writers and he so cleverly opined, "Keep away from people who try to belittle your ambitions. Small people always do that, but the really great make you feel that you, too, can become great."

Really examine your group of friends and look at whether they are helping or hurting your ability to meet your objectives and, ultimately, your vision.

Above All, Value Relationships

Life is busy. There are so many things to do and important tasks to attend to that we often forget to recognize the valuable relationships all around us.

It is important to take the time to recognize the importance of relationships in your life. You can have all of the success in the world, but without true relationships in your life, it is meaningless. Trust me, it's not as much fun to lie on a beach by yourself.

I was recently talking with my dad about some adventures we had growing up. We couldn't remember the details of what we did and where we were, but we both remember *who was there*. So take a moment now and think of the important relationships in your life and make a point to drop them a note or a text and just say thank you.

LAZ Lifestyle Moves

- Send an email to two friends each day for one week just to say hi and see what they have been up to.

- Invite one friend per week to coffee, lunch, or a drink for one month. (Try to avoid dinners for these meetings.)

- Update your About Me section of your Facebook profile. If you don't have a Facebook account, create one now and start reaching out to friends.

- If you don't have one already, create a Facebook and LinkedIn account and starting connecting to people you may already know.

Wrap Up

No matter how hard you work, it will likely come down to who you know. I know this isn't fair, but neither is life. Work hard now to start developing your network, maintaining relationships and looking for ways to let people know what you are about. Try to implement the "7 touches" rule, and look for creative ways to reach out to people so that you are the trusted recommendation they make. You don't have to be as good as Kevin Spacey in the hit series House of Cards, you just need to be genuine and do what you say you are going to do. Remember, your network generates your net worth.

Advice from Millennials

Name: Mick
Age: 37
Occupation/Job Title: Self-Employed—Restaurant Business
Annual Income: $170K
Family Size: Married no kids
Where do you live? Spokane, WA
Do you own your home or rent? Own

One a scale of 1 to 10, how comfortable are you with your finances?

Why?

5. Having partnerships and not always being on the same page as my partners means I am not in complete control of my finances.

"It's not what you know, it's who you know." Do you agree with this? Why or why not?

I disagree. It has to be a blend of "what" and "who." If you know everybody in the world but don't know how to do anything you will have a lot of friends but you will not able to monetize your connections. On the flip side, if you invent a world-changing widget but do not know anybody that can help you, it would be very difficult to capitalize on your widget.

What are some ways that you have built up your network?

Being in the restaurant industry, it is my job to network. Everywhere I go, whoever I may meet, I invite them to come check out one of my places. Furthermore, if I was invited to a wedding, a dinner, a party, a fundraiser, a function, a BBQ, a (insert whatever function you want), I went. I don't have the time anymore to attend everything, but it certainly helped in the beginning. I of course try and maximize social media now as well.

Do you have any tricks or tips for making networking easier?

Be genuinely interested in people and what they do. Ask a lot of questions. Get to know somebody the best you can in the shortest amount of time. When you are doing this see if you have ANYTHING that you can offer to somebody before you ask for anything. If you can do somebody a favor, they will be apt to go the extra mile for you and open doors for you that they might not have otherwise opened.

What is a difficult networking situation you've dealt with?

The first thing that comes to mind is "motivation." My life is networking and I get burnt out on it. Sometimes I have to give myself a pretty good pep talk when I am not in the mood to turn on the charm and meet some new people.

Do you use social media to promote?

YES. Heck yes. As often as possible.

Do you consider your Facebook friends and Twitter followers to be part of your "network"?

I consider my Social Media "friends" to be a network all on their own. I have 3,600 Facebook friends and I probably would not recognize half of them if I walked by them on the street.

How have you seen your network impact your financial life?

Trick question for me. I owe EVERY aspect of my financial life to my network. From finding great employees, to getting and keeping customers, to finding investors for my projects…it is all based on my network.

What single piece of advice has made the largest impact in your life?

"Take your 5 best friends, average their income, and usually that will be pretty close to your income." When I simply bartended and hung out with bartenders, my income was on the high end of what bartenders make. Once I branched out and started hanging out with and learning from people who made more money than I did, doors began to open around every corner.

What advice do you have for trying to build a network?

Challenge yourself. Challenge yourself to attend as may functions as possible. Challenge yourself to volunteer and donate your time to great causes. Challenge yourself to step outside of your current, comfortable relationships and make new connections.

14
THE BALANCED LIFE

Life should not be a journey to the grave with the intention of arriving safely in a pretty and well-preserved body, but rather to skid in broadside in a cloud of smoke, thoroughly used up, totally worn out, and loudly proclaiming 'Wow! What a Ride!'

Hunter S. Thompson

'Do it now!' can affect every phase of your life. It can help you do the things you should do but don't feel like doing. It can keep you from procrastinating when an unpleasant duty faces you. But it can also help you do those things that you want to do. It helps you seize those precious moments that, if lost, may never be retrieved.

Napoleon Hill

Life is busy. Life is complicated. You go and go and only every once in a while stop to wonder why you are running so fast. My grandfather recently passed away from pancreatic cancer. He was 75 years old. He lived a full life. But it wasn't until I was sitting at the memorial service staring out across the sea of people that were there for him that I realized what we are here for. They shared their experiences and his impact on their life. He had affected so many lives. I know this is the last chapter and I don't want to take away from any momentum built, but I definitely saved the best for last.

We have talked about all of the ways to grow your potential and purchase IPAs to be financially free, but if we stop there you can never truly live the LAZ Lifestyle. The Lifestyle requires that you understand why you are doing all of this and forces you throughout the journey to reflect and ensure that you live a balanced life full of travel, relationships, experiences, and helping others.

Focusing too much on one task can lead to burnout, no matter your passion, as you get stretched too thin in the various commitments you have in your life (Barnett and Hyde 2001). In a University Extension article, Ensle warns "avoiding burnout by balancing job and family is a necessity (Ensle 2005)." Your work can take over, so it is imperative to find this balance in your life.

Below is a story that is cited in several books but it helped me put it all in perspective and really drive home the reason for a vision and enjoying the journey, not just the destination:

An American investment banker was at the pier of a small coastal Mexican village when a small boat with just one fisherman docked. Inside the small boat were several large yellow fin tuna. The American complimented the Mexican on the quality of his fish and asked how long it took to catch them.

The Mexican replied, "only a little while. The American then asked why didn't he stay out longer and catch more fish? The Mexican said he had enough to support his family's immediate needs. The American then asked, "but what do you do with the rest of your time?"

The Mexican fisherman said, "I sleep late, fish a little, play with my children, take siestas with my wife, Maria, stroll into the village each evening where I sip wine, and play guitar with my amigos. I have a full and busy life."

The American scoffed, "I am a Harvard MBA and could help you. You should spend more time fishing and with the proceeds, buy a bigger boat. With the proceeds from the bigger boat, you could buy several boats, eventually you would have a fleet of fishing boats. Instead of selling your catch to a middleman you would sell directly to the processor, eventually opening your own cannery. You would control the product, processing, and distribution. You would need to leave this small coastal fishing village and move to Mexico City, then LA and eventually New York City, where you will run your expanding enterprise."

The Mexican fisherman asked, "But, how long will this all take?"

To which the American replied, "15–20 years."

"But what then?" asked the Mexican.

The American laughed and said, "That's the best part. When the time is right you would announce an IPO and sell your company stock to the public and become very rich, you would make millions!"

"Millions—then what?"

The American said, "Then you would retire. Move to a small coastal fishing village where you would sleep late, fish a little, play with your kids, take siestas with your wife, stroll to the village in the evenings where you could sip wine and play your guitar with your amigos" (Carver 2015).

Enough said. Next, I want to talk with you about how to live a balanced life.

Live in the Present

Take risks, travel, seek out opportunities, give back. Rather than treat your financial makeover as a crash diet that works for a short time then falters from overindulgence two weeks later, treat yourself to your favorite restaurant, go to the movies, buy the latte, or take a long overdue vacation. Pause during the day and stare out a window, simply appreciating the beauty of nature or man-made buildings around you. Make a phone call to a person you haven't talked to in a while, just because. Send a text to your parents or grandparents and tell them thanks.

Every day that you wake up, you are presented with an opportunity. What are you going to make of it?

Michael Landon Jr. helps put it in perspective, "Somebody should tell us, right at the start of our lives, that we are dying. Then we might live life to the limit, every minute of every day. Do it! I say. Whatever you want to do, do it now! There are only so many tomorrows."

Too many times, I find myself planning so far in the future that I fail to live in the present. I fail to recognize what an amazing life I have with family and friends. The goal for any person pursuing the LAZ Lifestyle is to not be the richest man in the graveyard. You can't take any of it with you when you die. Treasure relationships and experiences. You can still plan for the future but live like there is no tomorrow.

Abraham Lincoln said, "In the end, it's not the years in your life that count. It's the life in your years." Make them count.

If in Doubt, Travel!

Traveling can give you the greatest experiences of your life. Whitney and I love to travel. We can't wait to plan and go on our next adventure. But more than just the experience, traveling has taught me so many lessons about life.

I was in my second year of law school and Whitney shouted from her chair across the room as she stared at her laptop, "This is what I want to do!"

I continued typing, looked up from my computer, and haphazardly said, "Yeah, what is that?"

She turned her computer to show me a picture taken by one of her friends of the majestic seaside city of Vernazza, one of the cities built into the side of a hill in Cinque Terre, Italy.

I paused for a minute, assuming I misunderstood her previous statement and thinking to myself, "How can you just *do* that? Travel is not a job and definitely doesn't pay bills."

Instead of voicing my thoughts, I casually nodded and replied, "Yeah, that would be fun."

I thought about her comment for the next two days, wondering why we couldn't travel to foreign lands or even live abroad. Why that couldn't be us in the pictures. After realizing this and admitting I was tired of living vicariously through others, I looked into a study abroad program in London for law school where we could go live for six months. I got accepted and we stuffed two suitcases full of most of our belongings and boarded the plane for the unknown.

I attended school during the week and we traveled on the weekends. The experience opened my eyes to new ways of thinking and living. Richard Burton put it ever so creatively by stating, "One of the gladdest moments of human life, methinks, is the departure upon a distant journey into unknown lands. Shaking off with one mighty effort the fetters of habit, the leaden weight of routine, the cloak of many cares and the slavery of home, man feels once more happy."

Travel can have an impact on every part of your life. Even with my job at Washington State University, colleagues are writing, "it is time for Extension agents to get out, explore the world, and enhance program delivery using their international Extension experience (Harder et al. 2010)." They understand that travel allows us to increase what we know about a different culture or generate new ideas (Rogers 1993) and gives insight in the public's understanding of global issues (Ludwig and McGirr 2003). This can have a powerful impact on your perspective.

Traveling provided the opportunity to look at life in a whole new way. From London's underground transportation to the canals of Venice to the halls of the Louvre, inspiration and new ways of doing things were all around us. As Ralph Cranshaw put it, "Travel has a way of stretching the mind. The stretch comes not from travel's immediate rewards, the inevitable myriad new sights, smells, and sounds, but with experiencing firsthand how others do differently what we believed to be the right and only way."

It was in London that our first business was developed. She started Flat 4 Photography, named after the flat where we lived in London. She got her first wedding and has not looked back since. As of January 1, 2013, she realized her dream of working only at Flat 4 Photography, turning her hobby into a full-time career.

Mary Ritter Beard said it so well, "Travel is more than the seeing of sights; it is a change that goes on, deep and permanent, in the ideas of living."

I do understand not everyone can leave their jobs and move to London for six months, but even taking a day for a road trip, giving yourself a chance to really identify what it is that truly makes you happy, can spark inspiration and new ideas.

Travel can be a time to start treasuring what you *do* have. "To my mind, the greatest reward and luxury of travel is to be able to experience everyday things as if for the first time, to be in a position in which almost nothing is so familiar it is taken for granted" (Bryson and Wilson 2000).

Even now when I travel, I am constantly looking for opportunities. If I go into a bar that I like, I note why I like it and whether it would work in Spokane; or if I like a particular building or design, I look for ways to use it in my own businesses. When Whitney and I travelled to Iceland, I was blown away by the modern architecture and interior design in most buildings we entered. I have now used those designs in the flip houses and rentals that we own, garnering a quick sale and top dollar for rents. Had I not been exposed to different design ideas, this would not be possible.

The next time you travel, think of it as an opportunity to gather new ideas and enhance the way you live. Keep your mind open and let your thoughts wander. You never know what you will think of. It is a chance to think outside the box and see things in a different light.

Lessons Learned from Traveling

Traveling is an important part of our life, whether it is a 2-hour road trip or a European vacation. Travel allows us to get outside of our current situation, get inspired by new ideas we don't see every day, and plan for the future. It allows us to experience different cultures and find our inspiration again. These are just some of the lessons I have learned from traveling:

Keep your mind open. Traveling exposes you to different cultures, experiences, people, and lifestyles. Take this opportunity to think outside the box and embrace the food and culture. Truly immerse yourself in each place you go and each thing you experience. Drive slower, use public transportation, eat at hole-in-the-wall restaurants. Remember, it is not about the destination; it's the journey that counts.

We were fortunate to live in London where we frequented local markets, plays, street performances, parks, and little out-of-the-way shops that the average tourist would never see. You get to see how people live differently than you, yet it still works. We have incorporated so many of these things into our life simply because we kept an open mind.

When in Rome. In our daily life, we get into such routines and habits that it makes the spontaneous and bizarre impossible to achieve. Maybe it doesn't fit our schedule or is never the right time to try something new. But when you travel, try not to use "no" as an answer and do as the locals do. Try it, test it, taste it, smell it, live it. You will not be disappointed.

One problem, multiple solutions. You learn quickly that there are many ways to solve a problem. Just as 5 + 4 = 9, so does 6 + 3. You quickly realize that the U.S. is not the only place dealing with poverty, unemployment, high inflation, government problems, transportation, mounting debt. By looking at how other countries deal with these issues, we can take lessons to improve things we do in the U.S. You can see how foreign businesses operate to bring change to your business.

Travel now. There is value in delayed gratification, but you are only this age one time in your life. When we lived in London, my parents and grandparents came to visit us and it was clear that age played a role in the sites we were able to see during their stay. Don't delay your traveling until you retire or have enough money to do it. It was the experiences we had with no money, staying at hostels and living out of backpacks as we roamed around Scotland and Ireland that I remember the most.

Avoid analysis paralysis. How often do you think about something so much that you never actually act? For Whitney and I, when we want to make a trip happen, we buy the plane ticket and the rest gets worked out some way or another. We plan the trip, are more motivated to save, and have always saved enough for each trip. Could we have saved more and stayed in nicer hotels? Sure. But by committing to flights, we get resourceful about how to make the rest of the trip happen. So think a little less and do a little more.

Giving Back

Next to travelling, giving back ranks among the top priorities in my life. *Give*: verb, freely transfer the possession of (something) to (someone); hand over to. Giving is taking something you own or possess and giving it to another (Merriam-Webster 2016b). Such a simple definition, but so overly difficult and complex in practice.

> ## Millennial Insight
>
> *I'm the most happy and feel the best about my work when I know I've given back to others with a heart full of love. There is no better feeling!!*
>
> Natalie, 33

I remember sitting around the tree on Christmas morning, my brothers and sisters shaking and evaluating presents to see what they got. My guesses were rarely accurate, but it was the anticipation that made the event so memorable. I remember opening the gifts and being excited for the new Tonka trucks and noticing the satisfied, happy facial expressions on both of my parents' faces. My parents were truly happy to buy us gifts rather than get their own.

In fact, studies indicate that giving actually makes us, the givers, feel happy. A 2008 study by Harvard Business School professor Michael Norton and colleagues found that giving money to someone else lifted participants' happiness more than spending it on themselves (Suttie and Marsh 2010).

Similarly, in a 2006 study by the National Institute of Health, they concluded that when people give to charities it activates regions of the brain associated with pleasure, social connection, and trust, creating a "warm glow" effect. Scientists also believe that altruistic behavior releases endorphins in the brain, producing the positive feeling known as the "helper's high" (Suttie and Marsh 2010).

Giving not only makes us happier, but studies also show it improves health, social connections, and simple gratitude (Suttie and Marsh 2010). There is proven power in giving, yet why is it still so hard to part with that hard-earned cash?

No matter what my income is, I never seem to have "enough money" to give. Funny how that works. I keep promising to give once I get a raise or the next commission hits my bank account, but I always seem to find a valid justification of why I should invest it instead.

"I will give more next time." It's my classic excuse.

I started doing an exercise that has helped immensely and I want you to try it. Take out a piece of paper and draw two, vertical lines so that you have three columns. Next, on the left hand column, write down all of the things that you need in order to live (or general necessities). I am thinking shelter, food, car, phone, etc. (I guess a phone would be arguable, but you get my point.) Now in the middle column, write *yes* or *no* if you have that item. What I found was that I already had everything I needed to live and then some. Then, in the third column, next to each item listed, write the names of people you know that don't have these items or are in jeopardy of losing them.

This exercise helped me realize that assistance isn't just needed in Africa and third world countries, but friends I knew didn't even have some of these basic items. The exercise did two things: it reassured me that I had what I needed to survive and identified people close to me who could use some help to jumpstart my giving.

Importance of Giving Back

Do you ever find yourself saying, "I'll give when we have X amount of money"? But then you hit X, and you create a new number you need to reach.

Being raised in a religious family, it is surprising that I never understood tithing and giving. It seemed too ritualistic to be effective and I never really saw it do any good. I was too young to understand where it was going and who it was helping. I didn't understand just giving to give. It releases the hold of money on you and your life.

What I came to realize was that I was clinging to the money and justifying my actions by telling myself that I was working hard for my money, so why would I give it to someone who wasn't or who was just sitting at home? I thought of every reason why I shouldn't give, so inevitably I didn't.

"He is probably going to buy booze or drugs with it."

"They don't really need the money."

"They already get welfare, why do they need my money too?"

"They are just taking advantage of the system."

But what I slowly began to understand was that I had to start giving without knowing or being skeptical about the outcome. Sure, they could buy drugs, but what if they *don't*? They might take advantage of the system, but what if they aren't?

Ann Wilson from WealthChef shares this outlook on giving:

If you do give, do you do it in a big way, in a loving and trusting way, and without strings attached and expectations of some sort of trade? I used to resist giving, too. If I gave at all, it was a tiny amount. It took me a long time to realize that my not giving, or not giving freely, was sending messages to my mind such as "There isn't enough," "I won't get any more," "I might need this for an emergency," "I feel safer with this in my pocket," and so it goes. All fear-based thoughts. All self-fulfilling prophecies (Wilson 2014).

You start convincing yourself that what you have is not enough, so you need more to create an illusion of safety. A bigger house, a nicer car, more money in your savings account. You begin to cling to your possessions and they start to characterize who you are. This is the point where you are no longer in control of your money; it controls you.

Giving of your money, time, energy, or whatever, triggers in your mind that you *do* have enough. I know you are saying, "I just don't have enough (fill in the blank here)," but until you make giving a priority, you can never truly be fulfilled in the LAZ Lifestyle.

Money is like a drug that can consume you if you let it.

In the same article above, Ann Wilson goes on to summarize her transformation with giving.

When I first started giving money, I felt uncomfortable. I was leaving my comfort zone and pushing all my security boundaries. I was stretching limiting beliefs about there being enough until they finally snapped and dissolved. At that point, I started to receive money in a significantly bigger way. Some might argue that I can give because I'm now wealthy, but that would be overlooking the fact that I got wealthy by giving in the first place (Wilson 2014).

So what is your excuse? Too many people justify why they can't give. The more reasons you come up with, the more you need to give.

The truth is that you never know the impact of giving and how you can change a life! There are stories of such heroism and sacrifice that you read in books and movies, but everyday heroes are often overlooked. I look at the life of a parent, constantly giving up their time, dreams, and ambitions; but when you ask any parent, they wouldn't trade it for the world.

You don't have to overcomplicate giving to others; it is simply giving of yourself, your money, and your possessions for another. And, in truth, even though you are giving to another, you are the one most benefited from it.

How Much and Where Should I Be Giving

These are two questions that I get asked a lot and, to be honest, there really is no right answer. How much and where to give is truly up to you – the important part is that you do it.

So let's start with the first question, "How much should I give?" I would recommend starting with 10% of your net income. If you can give more that is awesome, but it is good to have a baseline to start with. If 10% of your income is too much, then find a number that works for your budget or think of giving back with your time instead of your money. Both are valuable and both can impact the lives of others.

Next, let's talk about where you should be giving.

How many people know someone who has adopted a child from another country? How many people know somebody who adopted locally? Both children were impacted and had their lives changed.

Basically, there is no wrong way to give. Whether you give to the panhandler on the street, sponsor a child in a third world country, or donate your time to your church or a struggling family member or friend, it doesn't matter.

HELP! I Still Don't Know Where to Give?

Where you give is far less important than the fact that you give. Many people use organizations that support particular interests or passions, others use churches, and others just give to family, friends, and neighbors. But if you are struggling to decide where and who to give to, refer to the Tools section for some apps and websites that can help you get started.

Wealth Hack Tools

TripAdvisor

http://www.tripadvisor.com
Cost: FREE

We used this app extensively when traveling. There are millions of traveler reviews, photos, and maps available. TripAdvisor makes it easy to find the lowest airfare, best hotels, great restaurants, and fun things to do wherever you go. And booking options for hotels, restaurants and flights are just a tap away. Some of the amazing features of the TripAdvisor mobile app are:

- Browse reviews, opinions, videos and photos by travelers

- Find the best hotels, including Travelers' Choice award winners
- Explore restaurants and reserve tables online
- Discover cool things to do in any destination
- Compare airfares and find great deals
- Use Near Me Now to discover places near your location
- Get answers to your specific travel questions in the forums
- Download maps, reviews, and your saves for over 300 cities worldwide onto your phone for free; avoid using expensive data roaming plans while you travel

Kayak

http://www.kayak.com
Cost: FREE

This is becoming one the more popular search and booking sites on the web. It has great prices and is easy to navigate. A unique feature that is has it the ability to see a map of the world and the prices that it would cost to travel to various locations. It allows you to dream and plan, knowing what it will cost you to get to your most exotic destinations.

Tripit

http://www.tripit.com
Cost: FREE

Does your email ever get clogged with all of the reservation and confirmation emails? Do you ever lose an important email with your flight times? TripIt allows you to simply forward emails along to plans at tripit.com, which will then magically generate a digital itinerary that you can refer to on your mobile device. Some of the key features, per the Apple site:

- Forward hotel, airline, car rental, and restaurant confirmation emails to plans@tripit.com to create an instant itinerary (If you use Gmail or Google Apps, it happens automatically)
- Access itineraries anytime, on any device (even offline)
- Get directions, maps and weather for each destination
- Sync trip plans with Calendar, Outlook, or Google Calendar
- Add or edit plans manually—from the app or on tripit.com
- Share some (or all) of your trip plans via email or social media

Viber

http://www.viber.com
Cost: FREE

As a competitor with Skype, Viber allows everyone in the world to connect for free using the internet. Users text, call, and send photo and video messages worldwide over WiFi or 3G - for free. Viber Out can be used to make calls to non-Viber landlines and mobile numbers at low rates. Viber is available for many smartphones and platforms. Some key features for Viber are:

- Free text, calling, photo messages and location-sharing with Viber users*
- No registration, alias or invitations required
- Instantly integrates with your own contact list
- Best-quality mobile calls using 3G or Wi-Fi

Google Translate

http://www.google.com
Cost: FREE

Ever travel and have no idea what the locals are saying? Google Translate helps solve this issue. It allows you to speak in English (or another language) and it will translate what you said into the language of your choice. Some of the key features are:

- Translate 80 languages
- Listen to your translations spoken aloud
- Directly translate speech and handwriting
- View dictionary results for single words or phrases

Airbnb

http://www.airbnb.com
Cost: FREE (Have to pay for the place though)

This app is catered for budget-friendly travelers as it lists affordable accommodation around the globe – ranging "from a private apartment to a private island."

In addition to searching for places to stay, you can also offer your own room for rent, if you'd like to make a little extra money. So far there are 150,000 places listed in 190 countries. This affordable option allows you to meet locals and stay in far less touristy areas of places you travel.

HomeAway and VRBO

http://www.vrbo.com
Cost: FREE (Again, have to pay for the room)

Similar to Airbnb, the HomeAway app allows you to browse more than 1 million vacation rental property listings all over the world. It provides listing descriptions, pricing, photos of the property, and everything you will need to know to find a place to lay your head. We used this app on our most recent trip to Eastern Europe and it was awesome. We found unique places and an experience of living like a local if only for a few days.

Givelocity

http://www.givelocity.com
Cost: FREE

Givelocity helps take the guesswork out of giving. With Givelocity, they have harnessed the crowdfunding model and applied it to giving! You are able to pool your money with other people that care about the same things you do and vote on which causes receive your collective support. It definitely is the new wave of raising funds for charities.

iCare

Cost: FREE

"iCare is a free, fun, and convenient way to discover your cause and spark real-world change right from your phone!" That verbiage is straight from their website and it has a model that allows you to start your own fundraising campaign right from your phone and generate interest and contributions from friends and connections. You can also find volunteer opportunities and donate to over 6,000 nonprofits from the app.

Charity Miles

http://www.charitymiles.org
Cost: FREE

This is for you exercise junkies out there. Charity Miles is a free app that empowers you to earn money and raise awareness for charities by walking, running, or biking. All you do is choose a charity and hit the streets! As you walk, run or bike, the app will measure your distance and you will earn money for your charity: 10¢ per mile for bikers; 25¢ per mile for walkers and runners, all up to their initial $1,000,000 corporate sponsorship pool. Find out more on their website.

> **Volunteer Match**
>
> http://www.volunteermatch.org
>
> Volunteer match helps you find places to volunteer in your community. It is similar to a job finder and allows you to sift through opportunities until you find the perfect fit for you. See what's closest to where you live, work, or go to school. Read reviews from real volunteers. Share your activities with your friends and family. They have served over 5,000,000 volunteers and are growing quickly.

LAZ Lifestyle Moves

- Plan a short road trip with a friend, significant other, or family member. Find something new you can experience within a 2-hour drive.

- Try a local restaurant that you have never tried or order something off a menu that you may never try.

- Volunteer at a local organization or event of interest to you for at least two hours a week for one month.

- Start giving any amount to a local charity of your choice.

Wrap Up

You can have all of the money in the world, but if you don't live a balanced life, it is all for naught. Remember, to live life for the journey, not just the destination. Travel to distant lands or simply around your town looking for new experiences with a different lens. Try that restaurant you have always wanted to try and even see how fun the "touristy" things are. Lastly, give with no strings attached. You now have the recipe to generate significant amounts of income but do not let it control you. Find ways to give back and make your community a better place.

Advice from Millennials

Name: Nicole
Age: 29
Job Title: Content Strategist
Annual Income: appx. $50k

Family Size: 1 (single)
Where do you live? Spokane, WA
Do you currently own or rent your home? I rent a studio.

What is the one job/cause/activity that could get you out of bed happily for the rest of your life? Are you doing it now?

Job, cause, and activity are all very different in my mind. If I could write books for a living, I would be fulfilled in my career. I am not doing this now. And adventure is my "happy" activity—near or far, luxury or backpacking—I'll take it however I can get it. I do this as much as my other obligations and current energy level will allow.

What inspires you?

Nature. There's nothing like standing beside the ocean or in a forest of massive trees to clear your head and make you feel like you can conquer the world.

Why do you travel? Is it worth it?

I travel because I love it. New sites, new sounds, new flavors. I believe travel is the way to truly live. Without it, you're closing yourself off to new opportunities and missing some of the greatest experiences of your life. Travel is always worth it. Even the "bad" experiences can teach you something valuable.

Where is the best place you have been? Worst?

I find both of these questions extremely difficult to answer. I have to rack my brain to think of a terrible place I've visited... I would say that Soweto Slum in Nairobi, Kenya is the worst place I've been, but the experience I had there was quite the opposite. It was just heart wrenching to witness people living in such dire conditions, yet extremely uplifting to encounter their joyous spirits in spite of their circumstances.

And the best place? It's hard to pick just one... like trying to decide between French toast and waffles. Even if I change the qualifier to "unique", it's a struggle. Eeny, meeny, miny, moe! I'm going with Guanajuato, Mexico. I spent three weeks there in college, and I still reflect on that trip as three of the best weeks of my life.

Name a place that changed the way you look at life.

Absolutely without a doubt, Kenya. I met my sponsor child one day and dined with Nairobi's richest the next. It challenged the way I view philanthropy—internationally and locally. The problems we face in America, although on a different scale, are the same problems seen around the globe. Kenya's wealthy don't care that there isn't running water in remote areas of the country, just like some Americans don't care that there's a hunger problem in our country. While I still send a check to my sweet Velma girl every month, I doubt that I would visit Africa for philanthropic purposes again. I would rather volunteer at my local soup kitchen to benefit my neighbor and strengthen my own community.

Have you learned any valuable lessons from traveling?

Several, but I think the most obvious is that of the human experience. We are all the same; seeking happiness and trying to make the best of the time we have here spinning around the sun. We are all as fragile and resilient as the next, and the most important thing will always be love.

When do you stop calculating the risk and just do it?

I am admittedly not a risk taker. I analyze and analyze, and then analyze again, what many would call this "spinning your wheels." Most of the time it just comes down to me reprimanding myself for thinking too hard on something that really doesn't deserve that amount of consideration.

How do you fund your travels?

Save, save, save.

"You only live once!" What does this mean to you?

Besides being the worst acronym in all of history (YOLO), it means that life is short and doors close just as fast as they open. If you don't act, there's a good chance you'll never see what was in that room because some opportunities don't present themselves more than once. Take the plunge!

What financial advice made the largest impact in your life?

Cut out the crap. There are certain purchases we make daily, weekly, or monthly that really don't have any benefit on our long-term well-being or happiness. Trading in your daily coffee is worth the trade-off of whatever experience results from the money you save. I recently gave up energy drinks, which doesn't seem like a huge expense at $2 almost every day, but the annual cost of my "addiction" was over $500. Turns out, that's a lot of nights in an affordable Thai hotel room.

What advice do you have for people looking to travel?

Just go. Quit making excuses of why you can't, and start coming up with reasons why you can and make it happen. Travel is just like anything else and requires sacrifice, but it's worth it every time.

A FINAL WORD

So you made it through the book in one piece. We covered a lot of information in a relatively short amount of time. I hope it was entertaining and educational. But I don't want you to stop here; I want you to keep going. I want you to take action and start making changes in your life. This book provides a template for changing your mentality and learning the value of investing in IPAs so you don't have to wait to start living your life. Check out the website www.lazlifestyle.com for articles and more insight on how to get started and connect with me.

Millennials do not want to wait 40 years to start living. You need to find ways to increase your earning potential through education and experience so you too can live the LAZ Lifestyle. Go forth and conquer!

ABOUT THE AUTHOR

Jordan is a serial entrepreneur with a thirst for learning. He is an assistant professor at Washington State University working in economic development. He is a licensed realtor and attorney in Washington. He owns rental properties, a restaurant, photo booth business, marketing company, and real estate company. He is driven to constantly learn more and help people follow their passion and realize their dreams. He loves to travel, play golf, spend time with friends and family, and is always looking for the next experience.

REFERENCES

Abasov, F. 2014. Network Relations In The Hierarchical Structure Of Society. Journal of American Science 10(1): 11–14. http://www.jofamericanscience.org.

Anders, A. 2014. How Financial Planning Can Save Your (Startup's) Life. Inc. Magazine. http://www.inc.com/aaron-aders/how-financial-planning-can-save-your-startup-s-life.html

Bach, D. 2004. The Automatic Millionaire: A Powerful One Step Plan to Live and Finish Rich. Broadway Books.

Ballmer, S. 2011. University of Southern California Graduation Ceremony.

Bank of America. 2016. Dealing with Credit Card Fraud or Identity Theft. Bank of America Official Website. https://www.bankofamerica.com/credit-cards/education/dealing-with-credit-card-fraud.go

Bankrate. 2013. June 2013 Financial Security Index Charts. Bankrate. http://www.bankrate.com/finance/consumer-index/financial-security-charts-0613.aspx

Barnett, R.C., and J.S. Hyde. 2001. Women, Men, Work, and Family: An Expansionist Theory. American Psychologist 56: 781–796.

Bennett, J. 2006. Spend Cycle. Newsweek. http://www.msnbc.com/id/14251360/site/nesweek/print/1/displaymode/1098/

Berardino, M. 2012. Mike Tyson Explains One of His Most Famous Quotes. Sun Sentinel. http://articles.sun-sentinel.com/2012-11-09/sports/sfl-mike-tyson-explains-one-of-his-most-famous-quotes-20121109_1_mike-tyson-undisputed-truth-famous-quotes

Beverly, S.G., and E.K. Burkhalter. 2005. Improving the Financial Literacy and Practices of Youths. Children and Schools 27: 121–124.

Boone, A. 2013. The 2% Rule: Fact, Fiction or Feasible? Biggerpockets http://www.irs.gov/taxtopics/tc409.html

Bortz, D. 2012. Do You Need Help From a Credit Counselor? US News Money. http://money.usnews.com/money/personal-finance/articles/2012/10/24/do-you-need-help-from-a-credit-counselor

Brinkley, D. 2003. The 40-Hour Revolution. Time Magazine. http://content.time.com/time/specials/packages/article/0,28804,1977881_1977883_1977922,00.html

Brunvard, J.H. 1989. Curses! Broiled Again! New York: W. W. Norton. 191–192.

Bryson, B. and Wilson, J. (2000). The Best American Travel Writing 2000. Mariner Books.

Business Model Innovation Matters. 2012. Understanding Banking Business Model. Bmimatters.com http://bmimatters.com

Carlozo, L. 2015. 20 Questions to Ask Before Hiring a Financial Advisor. US News Money. http://money.usnews.com/money/personal-finance/mutual-funds/articles/2015/04/08/20-questions-to-ask-before-hiring-a-financial-advisor

Carver, C. 2015. The Story of the Mexican Fisherman. Bemorewithless. com. http://bemorewithless.com/the-story-of-the-mexican-fisherman/

Case, S. 2009. George Mason University Graduation Address.

Charles Schwab. 2015. Retirement and Planning. Charles Schwab Official Website. http://www.schwab.com/public/schwab/investing/retirement_and_planning/understanding_iras/traditional_ira

Chen, H., and R. Volpe. 1998. An Analysis of Personal Financial Literacy Among College Students. Financial Services Review 7: 107–128.

Christensen, A., P. Hill, and S. Horrocks. 2015. The Social Media Marketing Map (Part 1): A Tool to Empower the Digital Leaders of Extension. Journal of Extension 53(4). http://www.joe.org/joe/2015august/tt3.php

Cohn, M. 2013. Seven Touches: A Basic Marketing Principle in Action. SocialMediaToday.com. http://www.socialmediatoday.com/content/seven-touches-basic-marketing-principle-action

Coleman, G., C. Byrd-Bredbenner, S. Baker, and E. Bowen. 2011. Best Practices for Extension Curricula Review. Journal of Extension 49(2). http://www.joe.org/joe/2011april/tt1.php

Coleman, J.S. 1988. Social Capital in the Creation of Human Capital. American Journal of Sociology 94: S95–S120.

Conger, R.D., G.H. Elder, F.O. Lorenz, K.J. Conger, R.L. Simons, L.B. Whitbeck, and J.N. Melby. 1990. Linking Economic Hardship to Marital Quality and Instability. Journal of Marriage and the Family 52: 643–656.

Corcoran, B. 2015. Sales Rule No. 1: Everybody Wants What Everybody Wants.

Dailyworth. 2012. Thank Steven Covey for the "Abundance Mentality". Daily Worth https://www.dailyworth.com/posts/1370-thank-stephen-covey-for-the-abundance-mentality

Danesi, M. 2009. The Original "Thinking Outside the Box" Puzzle! Psychology Today. https://www.psychologytoday.com/blog/brain-workout/200903/the-original-thinking-outside-the-box-puzzle

Decker, D.J. 1990. Analyzing Program "Failure". Journal of Extension 28(3). http://www.joe.org/joe/1990fall/a7.php.

Dell, M. 2008. Michael Dell Biography – Academy of Achievement. Academy of Achievement. http://www.achievement.org/autodoc/page/del0int-6

Dent, H. 2009. The Great Depression Ahead: How to Prosper in the Crash Following the Greatest Boom in History. Free Press Publishing.

Detweiler, G. and M. Reed. 2015. Debt Collection Answers: How to Use Debt Collection Laws to Protect Your Rights. Press One Publishing.

Dolak, K. 2011. Woman Leaves $13M Fortune to Pet Cat. ABC News http://abcnews.go.com/blogs/headlines/2011/12/woman-leaves-13m-fortune-to-pet-cat/

Doyle, M., and B. Briggeman. 2014. To Like or Not to Like: Social Media as a Marketing Tool. Journal of Extension 52(3). http://www.joe.org/joe/2014june/iw1.php

Eker, H.T. 2005. Secrets of a Millionaire Mind: Mastering the Inner Game of Wealth. HarperCollins Publisher.

Ellis, B. 2014. Identity Fraud Hits New Victim Every Two Seconds. CNN Money http://money.cnn.com/2014/02/06/pf/identity-fraud/

Ellison, N., C. Steinfield, and C. Lampe. 2007. The Benefits of Facebook "Friends": Social Capital and College Students' Use of Online Social Network Sites. Journal of Computer-Mediated Communication 12(4): 1143–1168.

Ensle, K.M. 2005. Burnout: How Does Extension Balance Job and Family? Journal of Extension 43(3). http://www.joe.org/joe/2005june/a5.shtml

FDCPA (Fair Debt Collection Practices Act). 1978. 15 U.S.C. § 1692(a)

Farrow, H., and Y.C. Yuan. 2011. Building Stronger Ties with Alumni Through Facebook to Increase Volunteerism and Charitable Giving. Journal of Computer-Mediated Communication 16(3): 445–464.

Ferriss, T. 2007. The 4-Hour Workweek: Escape 9–5, Live Anywhere, and Join the New Rich. Crown Publishing Group.

Friend, T. 2009. Finishing School. ESPN. http://sports.espn.go.com/espnmag/story?id=3740097

Fuscaldo, D. 2014. Better Know Your Stuff. Fox Business News. http://www.foxbusiness.com/personal-finance/2014/01/31/interested-in-self-directed-ira-better-know-your-stuff/

Galinsky, E., and D. Friedman. 1993. The Changing Workforce: Highlights of the National Study. New York: Families and Work Institute.

Gauba, V. 2015. Nearly a Third of All Savers Have Less Than $1000 for Retirement. CNBC. http://www.cnbc.com/id/102606784

Girard, L. 2014. How to Find Your Passion in 5 Creativity Exercises. Entrepreneur Magazine. http://www.entrepreneur.com/article/219709

Green, R.K. and M.J. White. 1997. Measuring the Benefits of Homeowning: Effects on Children. Journal of Urban Economics 41: 441–461.

Gross, D. 2013. Amazon's Drone Delivery: How Would It Work? CNN News. http://www.cnn.com/2013/12/02/tech/innovation/amazon-drones-questions/

Groth, A. 2012. You're The Average Of The Five People You Spend the Most Time With. BusinessInsider.com. http://www.businessinsider.com/jim-rohn-youre-the-average-of-the-five-people-you-spend-the-most-time-with-2012-7

Guillot, C. 2015. $100,000 Income: No Big Deal Anymore. Bankrate. http://www.bankrate.com/finance/personal-finance/100-000-income-no-big-deal-anymore-1.aspx

Hall, B. 2015. A Case Against Frugality: Why Pinching Pennies is Not the Best Path to Wealth. Bigger Pockets. http://www.biggerpockets.com/renewsblog/2015/04/05/case-frugalitypinching-pennies-path-wealth/

Hardekopf, B. 2010. Credit Card Tips for Holiday Shopping. Forbes. http://www.forbes.com/sites/moneybuilder/2010/11/12/credit-card-tips-for-holiday-shopping/

Harder, A., A. Lamm, and P. Vergot III. 2010. Explore Your World: Professional Development in an International Context. Journal of Extension 48(2). http://www.joe.org/joe/2010april/a3.php

Haughey, D. 2015. SMART Goals. Project SMART.co.uk. http://www.projectsmart.co.uk/smart-goals.php

Hendricks, D. 2014. 5 Sage Words of Advice from Millionaires. Inc. Magazine. http://www.inc.com/drew-hendricks/5-sage-words-of-advice-from-millionaires.html

Hiemstra, G. 1999. The End of Retirement is Near. The Futurist. http://www.futurist.com/articles-archive/the-end-of-retirement-is-near/

History.com. 2009. Ford Factory Workers Get 40-Hour Workweek. http://www.history.com/this-day-in-history/ford-factory-workers-get-40-hour-week

Horrigan, J.B. 2002. Online Communities: Networks that Nurture Long-Distance Relationships and Local Ties. Pew Internet and American Life Project. http://www.pewinternet.org/Reports/2001/Online-Communities.aspx

Houglum, L.E. 2011. Leadership for a Change. National Ruby Award Lecture. Epsilon Sigma Phi Luncheon at Galaxy II Conference. Salt Lake City, UT. http://espnational.com/index.php?option=com_content&view=article&id=184:houglum-2003&catid=88:ruby-lectures&Itemid=130&el_mcal_month=2&el_mcal_year=2011

Ingraham, C. 2014. America's Top Fears: Public Speaking, Heights, and Bugs. The Washington Post. http://www.washingtonpost.com/blogs/wonkblog/wp/2014/10/30/clowns-are-twice-as-scary-to-democrats-as-they-are-to-republicans/

Institute for College Access and Success. 2012. Average Student Debt Climbs to $26,600 for Class of 2011. The Project on Student Debt. http://www.ticas.org/files/pub/Release_SDR12_101812.pdf

Investor.gov. 2013. Investor Bulletin: Accredited Investors. US Securities and Exchange Commission. http://www.investor.gov/news-alerts/investor-bulletins/investor-bulletin-accredited-investors

IRS. 2013. http://www.irs.gov/publications/p527/ch02.html

IRS. 2016. http://www.irs.gov/taxtopics/tc409.html

Jobs, S. 2005. Stanford University Graduation Ceremony.

Johnson, A. 2013. 76% of Americans Are Living Paycheck-to Paycheck. CNN News http://money.cnn.com/2013/06/24/pf/emergency-savings/

Jones, L., and M. Jost. 1993. Beyond Business as Usual. Journal of Extension 31(2). http://www.joe.org/joe/1993summer/a6.php

Jorgensen, B.L., and J. Savla. 2010. Financial Literacy of Young Adults: The Importance of Parental Socialization. Family Relations 59: 465–478.

Kahneman, D., and A. Deaton. 2010. High Income Improves Evaluation of Life but Not Emotional Well-Being. Proceedings of the National Academy of Sciences of the United States of America 107(38): 16489–16493.

Kiyosaki, R. 2000. Rich Dad, Poor Dad. Business Plus.

Klien, G. 2011. Larkspur Tenant Wins $1.1 million in Negligence Suit Against Landlord. Marin Independent Journal http://www.marinij.com/general-news/20111104/larkspur-tenant-wins-11-million-in-negligence-suit-against-landlord

L'Abate, L. 1975. Pathogenic Role Rigidity in Fathers: Some Observations. Journal of Marriage and Family Counseling 1: 69–79.

Land, G. and B. Jarman. 1998. Breakpoint and Beyond: Mastering the Future Today. Leadership 2000 Inc.

Lawton, K. 2013. Nearly Half of US Households Have Almost No Savings to Cover Emergencies or Save for the Future. CFED. http://cfed.org/newsroom/pr/nearly_half_of_us_households_have_almost_no_savings_to_cover_emergencies_or_save_for_the_future/

Leo, J. 2012. Is $250,000 a Year Rich? Let's Break It Down. CNBC News. http://www.cnbc.com/id/49807529

Leuci, M.S. 2012. The Nature of Organizational Learning in a State Extension Organization. Journal of Extension 50(3). http://www.joe.org/joe/2012june/a1.php.

Liu, W., and J. Aaker. 2008. The Happiness of Giving: The Time-Ask Effect. Journal of Consumer Research 35(3): 543–557.

Locke, E.A., and G.P. Latham. 2002. Building a Practically Useful Theory of Goal Setting and Task Motivation. American Psychologist 57(9): 707–717.

Loper, N. 2013. The Bucket of Crabs Theory. SideHustleNation.com. http://www.sidehustlenation.com/the-bucket-of-crabs-theory/

Ludwig, B.G., and M.J. McGirr. 2003. Globalizing Extension – A National Initiative for US Land Grant Universities. Proceedings of the Association for International Agricultural and Extension Education: 19: 401–411.

Mains, M., B. Jenkins-Howard, and L. Stephenson. 2013. Effective Use of Facebook for Extension Professionals. Journal of Extension 51(5). http://www.joe.org/joe/2013october/tt6.php

Mandell, L. 2008. Financial Literacy of High School Students. In J.J. Xiao, ed. The Handbook of Consumer Finance Research 351–361. New York, NY: Springer.

McCormick, M. 2009. The Effectiveness of Youth Financial Education: A Review of the Literature. Journal of Financial Counseling and Planning 20(1). http://www.afcpe.org/publications/journalarticles.php?volume=383&article=354

Merriam-Webster Dictionary. 2016a. Security. http://www.merriam-webster.com/dictionary/security

Merriam-Webster Dictionary. 2016b. Give. http://www.merriam-webster.com/dictionary/give

Merriam-Webster Dictionary. 2015. Networking. http://www.merriam-webster.com/dictionary/networking

Mincemoyer, C.C., and J.S. Thomson. 1998. Establishing Effective Mentoring Relationships for Individuals and Organizational Success. Journal of Extension 36(2). http://www.joe.org/joe/1998april/a2.php

Mind Tools. 2014. SWOT Analysis. http://www.mindtools.com/pages/article/newTMC_05.htm#

Moore, A. 2015. Forget About Retirement Planning for Millennials. Time.com. http://time.com/money/3686209/retirement-planning-millennials/

Morton-Ross, R. 2014. The Elephant Rope Mindset Story. Inspire Orb Blog. http://blog.inspireorb.com/the-elephant-rope-mindset-story/

Moss, W. 2015. Doubling Your Money: The Rule of 72. USA Today. http://www.usatoday.com/story/money/personalfinance/2015/04/25/adviceiq-doubling-your-money/26339307/

National Chamber Foundation. 2012. The Millennial Generation: Research Review. US Chamber of Commerce. http://emerging.uschamber.com/MillennialsReport

Nisen, M. 2013. 12 Successful Entrepreneurs Share the Best Advice They Ever Got. Business Insider. http://www.businessinsider.com/entrepreneurs-best-advice-2013-12?op=1

Petronio, S. 2002. Boundaries of Privacy: Dialectics of Disclosure. Albany, NY: State University of New York Press.

Polgar, S., and D. Goldstein. 2015. Rich as A King: How the Wisdom of Chess Can Make You a Grandmaster of Investing. Grandmaster 117

Pumphrey, C. 2007. 10 Outrageous Lawsuits. http://money.howstuffworks.com/8-outrageous-lawsuits.htm

Ramsey, D. 2009. Get Out of Debt with the Debt Snowball Plan. Daveramsey.com. http://www.daveramsey.com/article/get-out-of-debt-with-the-debt-snowball-plan/

Rawlinson, G.E. 1976. The Significance of Letter Position in Word Recognition. Unpublished PhD Thesis. Psychology Department, University of Nottingham, Nottingham UK.

Richards, C. 2012. A Financial Plan for Misbehaving Lottery Winners. New York Times. http://bucks.blogs.nytimes.com/2012/12/03/a-financial-plan-for-misbehaving-lottery-winners/?_r=0

Richards, C. 2013. Diversification Isn't Broken, It Just Takes a While. Business Insider. http://www.nytimes.com/2013/08/12/your-money/asset-allocation/diversification-isnt-broken-it-just-takes-a-while.html?_r=0

Robin, V., and J. Dominguez. 2008. Your Money or Your Life: 9 Steps to Transforming Your Relationship with Money and Achieving Financial Independence. Penguin Books 57–61.

Rogers, B. 1993. Gaining International Experience through Job Exchanges. Journal of Extension 31(1). http://www.joe.org/joe/1993spring/intl2.php

Rosenberg, E. 2014. How to Save for Retirement: 5 Essential Savings Accounts to Consider. Betterment.com. https://www.betterment.com/resources/retirement/401ks-and-iras/how-to-save-for-retirement/

Rosenberg, T. 2013. Escaping the Cycle of Poverty. New York Times. http://opinionator.blogs.nytimes.com/2013/09/25/escaping-the-cycle-of-scarcity/

Roth, J.D. 2013. Pay Yourself First. Get Rich Slowly Blog. http://www.getrichslowly.org/blog/2009/10/19/pay-yourself-first/

Rowling, J.K. 2008. Harvard University Graduation Ceremony Address.

Schlitt, C.L. 2010. $350,000 Settlement for Bronx Woman Hurt in Slip and Fall on a Stairway. The Schlitt Law Firm. https://www.schlittlaw.com/2010/10/350000-settlement-bronxslip-and-fall-on-stairway/

Schmidt, R. 2013. Understanding the Cash on Cash Return in Commercial Real Estate. Property Metrics. http://www.propertymetrics.com/blog/2013/11/14/cash-on-cash-return/

SEC (Securities and Exchange Commission). 1933. Securities Act of 1933. https://www.sec.gov/about/laws/sa33.pdf

Siebold, S. 2014. How Rich People Think. Simple Truths.

SBA (Small Business Administration). 2014. Loan Program Quick Reference Guide. Small Business Administration. https://www.sba.gov/sites/default/files/files/Loan_Chart_Baltimore_October_2014a.pdf

Smaragdis, G. 2014. FINRA Foundation Study Finds Millennials Struggle Financially. FINRA Foundation. https://www.finra.org/Newsroom/NewsReleases/2014/P456463

Suttie, J., and J. Marsh. 2010. 5 Ways Giving Is Good for You. Greater Good. http://greatergood.berkeley.edu/article/item/5_ways_giving_is_good_for_you

Taube, A. 2014. Billionaires Carlos Slim and Richard Branson Want A 3-Day Workweek- Here's Why It Isn't Practical. http://www.businessinsider.com/slims-3-day-workweek-is-not-practical-2014-7

The Entrust Group. 2016. Self Directed IRA Basics. http://www.theentrustgroup.com/self-directed-ira-basics/what-is-a-self-directed-ira

Turner, B. 2013. The 50% Rule: How to Quickly Analyze a Multifamily Investment Property. Biggerpockets. http://www.biggerpockets.com/renewsblog/2013/06/14/50-percent-rule/

US Census Bureau. 2006. Facts for Features: Oldest Baby Boomers Turn 60! Washington, DC.

New Direction. 2016. Self Directed IRA Rules. New Direction IRA Inc. Website. https://newdirectionira.com/self-directed-ira-rules.php

Vilorio, D. 2014. Self Employment: What to Know to Be Your Own Boss. Bureau of Labor Statistics. http://www.bls.gov/careeroutlook/2014/article/self-employment-what-to-know-to-be-your-own-boss.htm

Walsh, T. 2005. Timeless Toys: Classic Toys and the Playmakers Who Created Them. Andrews McMeel Publishing.

Waters, R.D., E. Burnett, A. Lamm, and J. Lucas. 2009. Engaging Stakeholders through Social Networking: How Nonprofit Organizations Are Using Facebook. Public Relations Review 35(2): 102–106.

Wessel, R. 2014. The Best Way To Crack Your To-Do Lists. BBC Capital. http://www.bbc.com/capital/story/20140731-the-secret-to-getting-it-all-done

Westbrook, L., and C. Lifer. 1976. But I Don't Have Time! Journal of Extension 76(5). http://www.joe.org/joe/1976september/76-5-a1.pdf

Wilson, A. 2014. The Power of Giving – The Secret of an Abundant Life. The Wealth Chef. http://thewealthchef.com/wealthy-mindset/the-power-of-giving-the-secret-of-an-abundant-life/

Wintle, W.D. 2008. Think Big. Inspiration Peak. http://www.inspirationpeak.com/cgi-bin/poetry.cgi?record=37

Yoskovitz, B. 2011. Someone Else is Already Working on Your Idea. Instigator Blog. http://www.instigatorblog.com/someone-else-is-already-working-on-your-idea/2011/01/10/

Ziglar, Z. 2016. Official Ziglar Quotes. Zig Ziglar Offical Website. http://www.ziglar.com/quotes/money-isnt-everything-it-ranks-right

College of Agricultural, Human, and Natural Resource Sciences

Issued by Washington State University Extension and the U.S. Department of Agriculture in furtherance of the Acts of May 8 and June 30, 1914. Extension programs and policies are consistent with federal and state laws and regulations on nondiscrimination regarding race, sex, religion, age, color, creed, and national or ethnic origin; physical, mental, or sensory disability; marital status or sexual orientation; and status as a Vietnam-era or disabled veteran. Evidence of noncompliance may be reported through your local WSU Extension office. Trade names have been used to simplify information; no endorsement is intended. Published August 2016. EC006.

www.ingramcontent.com/pod-product-compliance
Lightning Source LLC
Chambersburg PA
CBHW070923210326
41520CB00021B/6778